The Kids' Diary of 365
AMAZING DAYS

Written and Illustrated by Randy Harelson and _____.
(your name)

Workman Publishing, New York

Library of Congress Cataloging in Publication Data

Harelson, Randy.
   The kids' diary of 365 amazing days.

   The author statement is followed by the word "and"
with a space for inclusion of the book's owner.
   SUMMARY: Presents a daily calendar of occasions,
historical events, and miscellaneous celebrations, each
accompanied by suggested activities.
   1. Amusements — Juvenile literature. 2. Calendars —
Juvenile literature. [1. Amusements. 2. Calendars]
I. Title.
GV1472.H36   793   78-73727
ISBN 0-89480-071-X

Cover Illustrations: Randy Harelson

Workman Publishing
1 West 39 Street
New York, New York 10018

Manufactured in the United States of America
First Printing September 1979
10 9 8 7 6 5 4 3 2 1

To the freedom and happiness of children everywhere

Acknowledgments

Many thanks to all the people who provided information and helped with research, especially: the librarians of the Providence and Barrington, Rhode Island Public Libraries; David Macaulay; Tom Dolle; Laurie MacDonald; Fred M. Meyer of the International Wizard of Oz Club; Don Rouser of the Chamber of Commerce, Sun Prairie, Wisconsin; J. Paris-France and Robert M. Gibson of the Smilepower Institute; Margaret MacDonough of the International Friendship League; Laura T. Schneider of the National Gallery of Art; Bets Vondrasek of Walt Whitman House; Glenn Smedley of the American Numismatic Association; Anthony Slide of the National Film Information Service; the Academy of Motion Picture Arts and Sciences; Mrs. Hemmick of the Popcorn Festival, Van Buren, Indiana; Becky Evans of the Sierra Club; Gustav Detjen, Jr. of the Franklin D. Roosevelt Philatelic Society; Reg Slater of the Chamber of Commerce, Hinckley, Ohio; Jayne Gordon of Orchard House; Patricia Ann Sexton of the Good Bears of the World; Judson W. Compton of the National Office of the Boy Scouts of America; Lloyd D. Hardesty of Turtles International; Les Waas of the Procrastinators Club of America; Marian Jose of the Red Cross; William D. Chase, author of *Chases' Calendar of Annual Events*; the Information Center on Children's Cultures; and the U.N. Office of Public Information.

Thanks also to Vicki Bartolini and Maureen Lee and their class of super kids who helped in so many ways. Also to Don Brigham, Evelyn Silva, Ron Koback, and all the people of the Attleboro, Massachusetts Public Schools who showed so much support for the project.

Thanks to Bill and Bette Baker for their invaluable assistance, Tom Payne for his photography, and Suzanne Rafer, Jim Harrison, Gail MacColl, Paul Hanson, Charles Kreloff, Peter Workman, and all the folks at Workman Publishing who worked so hard at making *Amazing Days* come true.

Finally, lots of thank yous, hugs and kisses to: Connie, Clint, Margo, Karen and Richard, Vicki, O'Bie, Trudy Bee, Becca, John, Bunny, Lisa, Ron, Dowell, Debbie, Scott and Helen, Mr. and Mrs. Bryan, Gil, Kay, Jimi, Michele, Susan, Eddie, Cathy, Joan, Dan and Tracy, Albert, Betty, Bev, Dean, Kelly and Erin, Anthony, Patty and Camille, Josie, Margaret, Aunt Elmira, Cousin Ruth, Frank, Stevie and Minnie; and to Mom and Dad who encourage all my interests; and Richard who helped (and put up with) every stage of this book's development.

This Book Is Amazing!

Amazing Days is your treasure trove of fun for every day of the year. It's bursting with games, pleasures, puzzles, jokes, codes, crafts, recipes, special facts, and space for writing all the important and private personal things that go on in your life.

Amazing Days makes every day a celebration. Read each day's entry early to find out what special things the day holds in store. Often you'll want to share traditions, riddles, poems, tricks, and treats with your friends and family. There's always something to do!

Amazing Days is a diary. Write down anything you want to remember: ideas, feelings, what you did and what you plan to do, funny jokes, firsts and favorites. If you want to keep it secret, write in code (see February 10 and March 25).

Amazing Days is a calendar. Ask your friends to sign their autographs on their birthday pages, then check out the sticker page at the back. You'll find ones for special birthdays (including your own, of course!), moving holidays — like Easter, Chanukah, and Mother's Day — plus special stickers to fit all your moods, the seasons, and even the different kinds of weather.

Amazing Days is a scrapbook. Add to it. Draw in it. Paste in snapshots, favorite cards, ticket stubs, stamps, and stickers. Press leaves and flowers in its pages. At the end of 365 days you will have a sort of time capsule full of memories of an amazing year.

Happy Everyday!
Randy

January 1
New Year's Day

Today is the first day of a brand-new year! It's time to turn over a new leaf, hang up a new calendar, and set the tone for the next 12 months, because according to an old American superstition, the way you act and feel all day will be the way you'll act and feel all year.

Be sure to:

KISS at least one person and make sure at least one person kisses you before you go to sleep—can you imagine what the year will be like if you don't?

EAT some black-eyed peas and green cabbage. According to Southern tradition the peas will bring you LUCK and the cabbage will bring you money.

Happy New Year!

Invite friends over for punch and cookies. Visitors bring good luck on January 1. Spread the luck around by visiting a friend or two.

Write your New Year's resolutions in the diary space below.

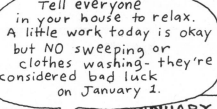

Tell everyone in your house to relax. A little work today is okay but NO sweeping or clothes washing—they're considered bad luck on January 1.

Dear Diary:

January 2
Sci Fi Celebration

Flying saucers, creatures from outer space, journeys to unknown planets, all make up the world of science fiction, sometimes shortened to sci fi. Whether it's comic strip characters like Flash Gordon, Wonder Woman, and Superman, or a movie like *Star Wars*, sci fi stories are some of America's favorites.

You don't have to be an adult to write science fiction. In fact, one of science fiction's most popular authors, Isaac Asimov, who celebrates his birthday today, started writing science fiction when he was 11 years old. Since then he's written book after book—not only science fiction, but science fact as well.

Make a flying saucer.

① **Decorate** the back of a paper plate as if it came from another planet.

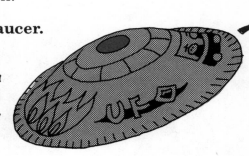

② **CUT** a piece of stiff paper about an inch larger than the plate all around.

③ **PUT** the plate, decorated side up, in the center of the stiff paper circle and **STAPLE** it four or five places around the edge.

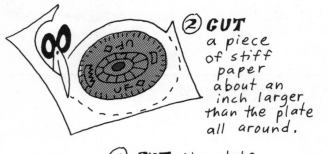

④ **SAIL IT THROUGH THE AIR** TO A FRIEND OR BY YOURSELF OUTSIDE.

Make up a story about your flying saucer. Where does it come from and why has it come? Write it down and you're a science fiction writer too!

Dear Diary:

January 3
Wax Paper Drinking Straws Patented

Without straws how would you drink milk at school? Everybody would walk around after lunch with white mustachios looking perfectly ridiculous. And how would poor souls with the mumps ever drink their juice? And how could you enjoy an ice cream soda if the ice cream kept hitting you in the lip? Drinking straws are wonderful things.

Today almost all straws are made of plastic, but the first straws (made of wax paper) were patented in 1888 on this day—an event most deserving of a celebration!

DRINKING-STRAW JEWELRY:

You can use any kind of straws as long as they can be cut with scissors.

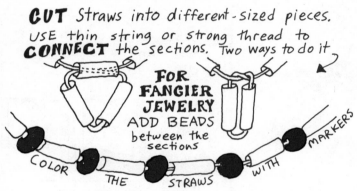

CUT Straws into different-sized pieces. **USE** thin string or strong thread to **CONNECT** the sections. Two ways to do it

FOR FANGIER JEWELRY ADD BEADS between the sections

COLOR THE STRAWS WITH MARKERS

Dear Diary:

You can make fantastic sculptures in this way too. The trick is to use triangles of straws for your building unit.

January 4
Louis Braille's Birthday

Thanks to Louis Braille, whose birthday we celebrate today, blind people can read.

Born in 1809 in France, Louis was blinded by a bad accident when he was three years old. When he was older he wanted to develop an alphabet that people could read with only their fingertips so that he, and other blind people, would be able to read books and learn things more easily. But it wasn't until Louis met an army captain who told him about "night writing," a dot-dash code punched in cardboard, that he had the idea for how to make his alphabet.

Millions of blind people are now able to read books printed in "Braille" by feeling coded dots embossed (raised) on paper.

The Braille Alphabet

In real Braille you can FEEL the dots.

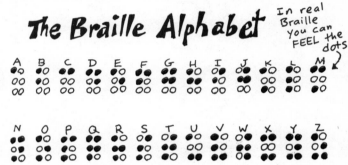

Write a code message in Braille.

Each cell is one letter. Skip one between words.

January 5
George Washington Carver Day

Dr. George Washington Carver did not invent the peanut, but through scientific experiments he developed over 300 different things that could be made from peanuts—including cheese, coffee, ink, plastics, soap, and medicines. Through Dr. Carver's work the peanut became one of America's most important crops.

Dr. Carver, a black American born of slave parents during the Civil War, also developed products made from soybeans and sweet potatoes. Can you believe he made postage stamp glue from sweet potatoes! Anyway, have yourself a big peanut butter sandwich treat today.

Grow a sweet potato vine.

① **GET** a sweet potato with "whiskers."

whiskers →

② **PUT** the skinny end down in a jar of water.

③ **PUT** it in a dark place until it grows roots - about 2 weeks. **CHECK DAILY** to make sure the jar is filled with water. **REFILL** with fresh water when necessary.

Don't forget to give your "sweet patootie" a name...

④ When your potato has roots and a stem, **PUT** it in a sunny window.

⑤ When the roots look long enough, **REPLANT** your potato in a pot of soil or into your garden (in the spring).

Dear Diary:

January 6
Three Kings Day

Surprise—it's still Christmas! You've heard of the 12 days of Christmas? Well, this is the twelfth day, and it is called Three Kings Day. Legend has it that the three kings brought their gifts of gold, frankincense, and myrrh to the Baby Jesus on January 6.

For hundreds of years families have celebrated this day (also called Epiphany) with a "king's cake." This cake has a bean or toy crown baked into it and when the cake is served the person who gets it in his or her piece of cake becomes "king" of the party.

Make a king's crown.

① **MEASURE** the king's head with a tape measure or string.

② **FIND** a piece of fairly stiff paper about an inch longer than the king's head measured. Several pieces can be taped together.

③ **FOLD** it accordion-style with about three inches between the folds.

④ **CUT** a roof-shape with a fancy shape on top.

⑤ **UNFOLD** the paper. **GLUE** or **TAPE** the two ends together to make it a crown.

⑥ **DECORATE** with paint, crayons, ribbons, colored paper, buttons, beads, glitter, foil, or whatever makes it **FIT FOR A KING!**

Dear Diary

January 7
Jupiter's Moons First Seen

Imagine how exciting it would be to see something in the sky that no one had ever seen before!

From the time Galileo was a child (over 400 years ago in Italy) he loved to watch the stars and planets. He built one of the first telescopes in 1609, and on this date in 1610 he first saw through his telescope the planet Jupiter's major satellites, its moons. This was very important because at that time people believed that all heavenly bodies revolved around the earth. Through his telescope, Galileo could clearly see three moons revolving around Jupiter! Now we know that this big planet has 13 moons, but Galileo's discovery made people think about the universe in a new way.

Dear Diary:

MAKE A JUPITER PIZZA
A SUPER SUPPER TO CELEBRATE GALILEO'S DISCOVERY (Ask an adult to help with this.)

① This pizza looks just like the giant planet Jupiter with its thirteen moons. START with a pizza crust, homemade or frozen, even Syrian bread will do nicely.

② SPREAD it all over with tomato sauce. A sprinkle of basil and oregano add Italian flavor.

③ Now put the 13 moons around "Jupiter's surface." The caps of fresh mushrooms look just like moons. Green or black olives make good moons too. Or use onion rings or bell pepper circles.

REMEMBER
13 MOONS IN ALL! (when Galileo first looked he saw only 3.)

④ Sprinkle grated mozzarella and Parmesan cheese all over.

⑤ Bake according to your pizza crust instructions - at least 15 minutes at 350°.

ADULT HELPER

⑥ Tomorrow you can tell your friends: LAST NIGHT I DINED ON JUPITER.

January 8
Elvis's Birthday

Almost everyone in the world knows who the great Elvis Presley is from his countless hit records and over 30 movies. Born in 1935, Elvis is the most popular singer in rock 'n' roll history.

Have a rock 'n' roll party. Get a few friends and some Elvis records together and dance the day away. Make it a fifties-style party—boys should wear their hair slicked back with a big pompadour in the front and girls should pull their hair back into ponytails if possible. And, don't forget the bobby sox.

How many Elvis hits can you name?

All the vowels are missing from these Elvis songs. Can you fill them in to complete the titles?

"BL _ _ S _ _ D _ SH _ _ S"
"H _ _ _ ND D_G"
"D_N'T B_ CR _ _ L"
"H _ _RTBR _ _ K H_T_L"
"J _ _LH _ _S _ R _CK"
"_LL SH _ _K _P"
"R _ T_RN T_ S_ND_R"
"L _V_ M _ T_ND_R"

Dear Diary:

Answers appear at the back of the book.

January 9
First Balloon Flight in America, 1793

Up, up, and away for the daring French *aeronaut* J. P. F. Blanchard who took the first balloon ride in the United States on this date in 1793. He carried an American flag and was accompanied by a little black dog on his 45-minute flight. (He went up 5,812 feet.)

George and Martha Washington, Betsy Ross, and Thomas Jefferson were on hand to watch the lift-off in Philadelphia.

Decorate Monsieur Blanchard's balloon with your own initials, symbols, or pictures →

Dear Diary:

January 10
10-Day Check

When someone buys a new car he or she takes it back to the car dealer for a 10-day check. It's a good idea to check out a new *year* also—just to make sure you don't want to trade it in on another one.

- ☐ Look in the mirror to make sure you're still you.
- ☐ Find the date January 10, this year, printed in the newspaper to make sure the year is progressing normally. Cut it out and glue it on this page.
- ☐ Measure your height to make sure you're not shrinking.
  How tall?_____feet_____inches
  or_____centimeters
- ☐ Watch the sun set to make sure the earth is still turning.
- ☐ What time did the sun disappear?_____ (Don't look right at the sun.)
- ☐ Ask your parents their names to make sure you're living with the right family. They may sign their names below.

If these things check out, the new year is probably okay. But one more thing: Look back at the resolutions you made on January 1. How are you doing? If you want to change any, now's the time!

Dear Diary:

Amazing Daily

January 11   *All The News That's Fit To Tickle*

NEAT NUMBERS NOTED

Numerologists and other people interested in numbers point out that today's date, January 11, can also be written 1/11 and then it reads the same forwards, and backwards. They are predicting an amazing phenomenon for the year 2011 when the date will be 1/11/11. Number-noters point out that this number only occurs once every 100 years.

Big Birthdays Celebrated

Eleven-year-olds born on January 11 are celebrating their "big birthdays" today. Big birthdays are a tradition observed by some cajuns in southern Louisiana. A cajun interviewed said, "Here's the idea: Everybody has a big birthday. Yours comes on the eleventh, six on the sixth, thirty-one on the thirty-first. You only get one big birthday, so live it up. Have a once in a lifetime celebration.

Puerto Rico Celebrates Hostos' Birthday

Eugenio Maria de Hostos was born on this date in 1839. He is remembered by the Puerto Rican people as a great hero who fought for freedom and independence from Spanish rule. Hostos's birthday is a government holiday in Puerto Rico. Everyone has the day off from work or school.

Today's Puzzle

The figure 1 is hidden in this picture 11 times. How many can you find?

Dear Diary:

January 12
Charles Perrault's Birthday

Who is Charles Perrault???
Even though you probably don't know his name, you probably do know many of the stories he wrote. Born in 1628, this Frenchman is most famous for his *Tales of Mother Goose*, which include:

SLEEPING BEAUTY

Puss in Boots

THE RIDICULOUS WISHES

CINDERELLA

Little Tom Thumb

Bluebeard

DONKEY-SKIN

Little Red Riding Hood

PATIENT GRISELDA

All these titles and the author's name are in this word-search puzzle. Can you find them?

They may be read

```
P A G H Y Z H G L M N I J K N A P D C
C U F I X A B F K J O P M L D O Q O E
I B S J W V C E D I H Q R L T S R N F
N C E S L E E P I N G B E A U T Y K B
D D L K I U D B C E F S S Z V Y X E Z
E M S R T N E A Z Y I U T Y W V W Y A
R N B L U E B E A R D V W X X U T S R
E O P Q H G F O G X W H G F Y H I K Q
L L I T T L E T O M T H U M B G J I P
L N O P I Q N T U T V U V E Z F E N O
A M L K J E R S Q R S T W D C A D K N
T H E R I D I C U L O U S W I S H E S
L I T T L E R E D R I D I N G H O O D
I J A K O P D C B A Z Y X A B B C L M
N P M L C H A R L E S P E R R A U L T
```

Hint: You'll have to be very patient to find "Patient Griselda," who is hiding uphill.)

Dear Diary:

January 13

Stephen Foster Memorial Day

Did you know that some of the songs you sing were written over 100 years ago?

When Stephen Foster was writing his songs, there were no such things as record players or radios. If folks wanted music, they had to make it themselves. They'd get together and sing the "hit songs" of the day, and Stephen Foster's became so popular that people all over America knew them by heart. His songs are still so popular that each year the president proclaims January 13, the day Foster died in 1864, Stephen Foster Memorial Day.

A Foster Challenge.

Can you figure out what the lyrics to "Oh! Susannah" mean?

I come from Alabama with a banjo on my
*   knee,*
I'm go'n' to Lou-siana, my true love for to see.
It rained all night the day I left
The weather it was dry,
The sun so hot I froze to death,
Susannah, don't you cry.
Oh! Susannah, oh don't you cry for me.
I've come from Alabama with a banjo on my
*   knee.*

January 14

Albert Schweitzer's Birthday

Dr. Albert Schweitzer's life (1875-1965) was quite an adventure. He devoted most of it working as a medical missionary in Gabon, Africa, where he brought modern medicine to people who needed it badly. With the help of contributions from around the world, he was able to build and expand his hospital in Africa.

Dr. Schweitzer believed in never hurting or killing any living thing and in his book *The Animal World of Albert Schweitzer* he tells many stories of the leopards, gorillas, elephants, snakes, and other animals that make Africa the wild and dangerous place it sometimes is. In 1952, in recognition of his work, Dr. Schweitzer won a very important award—the Nobel Peace Prize.

Make a set of AFRICAN ANIMALS!
USE shirt cardboard or fairly stiff paper.

DRAW your animals so their feet touch the flat edge of the cardboard.

Make tabs to fold back so your animals will stand up.

make trees, clumps of tall grass, and whatever you think will add to your JUNGLE SCENE!

Dear Diary:

Dear Diary:

FOSTER'S HIT PARADE:
Swanee River
My Old Kentucky Home
Doo Dah! Doo Dah!
Jeannie with the Light Brown Hair

January 15
Martin Luther King Day

"I have a dream" ... Martin Luther King, Jr. was a black American civil rights leader, born on January 15, 1929. He believed in nonviolence and spent his life working for justice and equality for *all* Americans.

In 1963 he spoke to 200,000 people gathered in Washington, D.C., to demand fair laws. Millions watching on TV heard him say these famous words:

> *So I say to you, my friends, that even though we must face the difficulties of today and tomorrow, I still have a dream. It is a dream deeply rooted in the American dream that one day, this nation will rise up and live out the true meaning of its creed—"we hold these truths to be self-evident, that all men are created equal."*
>
> *I have a dream that one day on the red hills of Georgia, sons of former slaves and sons of former slave owners will be able to sit down together at the table of brotherhood.*
>
> *And when we allow freedom to ring ... we will be able to speed up that day when all of God's children— black men and white men, Jews and Gentiles, Catholics and Protestants—will be able to join hands and sing in the words of the old Negro spiritual. "Free at last, free at last; thank God Almighty, we are free at last."*

In 1964 Reverend King won the Nobel Peace Prize (as did Dr. Schweitzer in 1952). He will always be honored as a great leader who worked for a better world.

Why not write your ideas for a better world in today's diary space?

January 16
National Nothing Day

It's National Nothing Day—unless it's your birthday in which case it's National Nothing-But-the-Best Day!!!

You can become a member of the National Nothing Foundation by *not* sending any dues to anybody and by *not* celebrating January 16. (Well, *everybody* needs a day off now and then.)

Dear Diary:

Dear Diary:

January 17
Ben Franklin's Birthday

Benjamin Franklin was "energy conscious" 200 years before the expression was invented. He did important research on electricity, invented the lightning rod (which kept lightning's energy from burning down buildings), and invented a free-standing, wood-burning stove that many people today are using during our "energy crisis" because it gives off more heat than a fireplace.

Ben Franklin was also a fireman, printer, writer, statesman, diplomat, and America's first postmaster. Wow! How could one person do so many things?! Well, for one thing, he had 84 years (1706-1790) in which to do it all!

BE ENERGY CONSCIOUS.

Don't forget to turn off lights not in use!

Dear Diary:

GO ON A *Treasure hunt* TO FIND EVERYTHING IN YOUR HOME THAT RUNS ON ELECTRICITY

Make a LIST in your diary space.

HOW IS YOUR HOME HEATED ?
☐ Oil
☐ Gas   ☐ Electricity
☐ Wood   ☐ Solar

Does the sun shine in and heat up some rooms?

Does your family's cooking stove run on gas, electricity, or is it wood-burning?

When you've found out these things you are energy-conscious. Sign your name on the certificate below.

ENERGY-CONSCIOUS

January 18
Pooh Day

Have you met Winnie-the-Pooh? Christopher Robin? Piglet and Eeyore and Tigger? Well, today is their extra special day because A. A. Milne, who wrote *Winnie-the-Pooh* and *The House at Pooh Corner*, was born on January 18, 1882.

Have a friend over for
AN AFTERNOON SMACKERAL
(That's Pooh's name for a snack.)

MAKE A HOT DRINK

Tea with honey and lemon **OR** heated-up apple cider or cranberry juice spiced with cinnamon and cloves makes a wonderful Pooh-type drink.

Serve GRAHAM CRACKERS or buttered toast with honey. **HONEY** (Pooh's favorite) is definitely the food of the day!

Ask your sisters, brothers, and your folks to join in the smackeral— POOH DAY FUN is for everyone

ADULT HELPER

Dear Diary:

January 19
Poe Night

Once upon a midnight dreary, while I pondered, weak and weary,
Over many a quaint and curious volume of forgotten lore—
While I nodded, nearly napping, suddenly there came a tapping,
As of some one gently rapping, rapping at my chamber door.

Those lines set the creepy mood for Edgar Allan Poe's famous poem, "The Raven." Poe's poems and stories are mysteriously scary to read. On this, his birthday (1809), why not have an off-season Halloween!

Turn the lights down low...
light a candle or two, and read one of Poe's stories with your friends or family.
("The Black Cat" is a scary one.)

Dear Diary:

Happy Birthnight to you

Eat a big lunch tomorrow...

January 20
St. Agnes' Eve

Would you like to dream of the person you might marry? According to an old legend, girls and boys may be granted this favor by St. Agnes this one night of the year.

To have a "St. Agnes dream" the old custom requires you to go to bed with only bread for supper (now you know why you should eat a big lunch today) although if everyone at the table can hear your stomach grumbling you can stretch it to a sandwich, to sleep alone, and tell no one of your purpose. You mustn't look behind you when you climb into bed. Just before you go to sleep say:

Agnes sweet and Agnes fair,
Hither, hither, now repair;
Bonny Agnes, let me see
The lad (lass) who is to marry me.

All this fuss for a dream! (But you never know—it might work.) Tomorrow morning as soon as you wake up, write in the space below *everything* you can remember from your dreams. By the way, John Keats, a famous poet wrote a poem called "The Eve of St. Agnes" which is based on this legend.

January 21
Aquarius Begins

People born between January 21 and February 19 are born under the sign of Aquarius, the water bearer. According to astrologers they are friendly and usually popular, self-confident but quiet. They like to be alone and are hard to get to know. They have to watch out for their own laziness, their worst fault. They like to help others, but they sometimes like to shock people by the way they act! List all the people you know born under the sign of Aquarius. Which ones seem to fit the description?

Dear Diary:

Winter getting you down? Tired of taking half an hour putting on coats, scarves, sweaters, caps, mittens, earmuffs, six pairs of socks, *and* boots before you can go outside? Tired of oatmeal for breakfast *every* morning? Granted, some things about winter get boring. Kick the winter blues—get out of your rut.

Make today different!

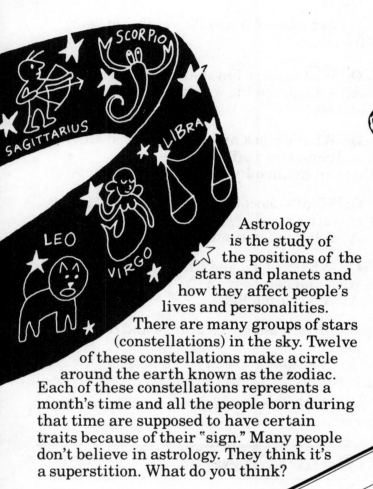

Astrology is the study of the positions of the stars and planets and how they affect people's lives and personalities. There are many groups of stars (constellations) in the sky. Twelve of these constellations make a circle around the earth known as the zodiac. Each of these constellations represents a month's time and all the people born during that time are supposed to have certain traits because of their "sign." Many people don't believe in astrology. They think it's a superstition. What do you think?

① GIVE the oatmeal to your cat and have peanuts and raisins for breakfast – or grilled cheese and a milk shake – ANYTHING but oatmeal!

② Comb your hair a completely new way.

③ WEAR your scarf like a turban and your socks on your hands.

④ Give your room a whole new look. Rearrange the furniture.

⑤ Try writing by holding a pencil with your foot.

⑥ PUT on your bathing suit and take a bath. PRETEND you're at the beach. DRY OFF with a beach towel.

Dear Diary:

It's hard to get out of a rut!

January 23
Welcome Back, Sun!

What if the sun went down in November and didn't come back up again till today?! That's one long night—almost *two months* long! Well, in the far north that's exactly what happens. Imagine the celebration people in Hammerfest, Norway, are having today to welcome back the sun, which they haven't seen since last year!

To make up for all this night, in midsummer Norwegians (and everybody else around the world who lives way up north above the Arctic circle) will have almost two months of *daylight* when the sun never sets. This is why northern Norway is called The Land of the Midnight Sun.

Have you noticed the daylight hours getting longer where you live? Watch the sun set tonight. What time did it disappear? Compare this time with the time you wrote down on January 10. With days getting longer, warmer weather can't be *too* far away.

Give this sun a face!

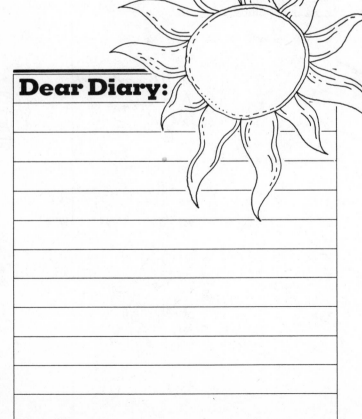

Dear Diary:

January 24
Eskimo Pie® Patented, 1922

What's the original chocolate on the outside, vanilla ice cream on the inside, on a stick treat?

—An Eskimo Pie.

Try out these Eskimo Pie riddles on your friends:

Q: What's more fun than an Eskimo Pie?
A: An Eskimo Pie with tickets to the movies.

Q: What's black and white and red all over and comes on a stick?
A: An Eskimo Pie dipped in ketchup.

Q: What's chocolate and vanilla and comes on a stick?
A: A hot fudge sundae playing "pogo."

Q: What's black and white, comes on a stick and begins with "*N*"?
A: A Neskimo Pie.

Q: What's black and orange and comes on a stick?
A: An Eskimo Pie in its Halloween costume.

Make up some of your own Eskimo Pie riddles.

Dear Diary:

January 25
Robert Burns Day

Make supper a Scottish celebration tonight! People around the world celebrate the birthday of Scotland's favorite poet, Robert Burns (1759-1796) with a "Burns supper." Any menu will do, but you might want to include Scottish food: scones, Dunlop cheese (the national cheese), or shortbread for dessert. After supper read several of Burns's poems aloud. "To a Mousie" and "A Red, Red Rose" are favorites. After dessert, join hands and sing "Auld Lang Syne" (even though it isn't New Year's Eve), Burns's most famous song. This is the traditional ending of the festivities.

Make shortbread for dessert.

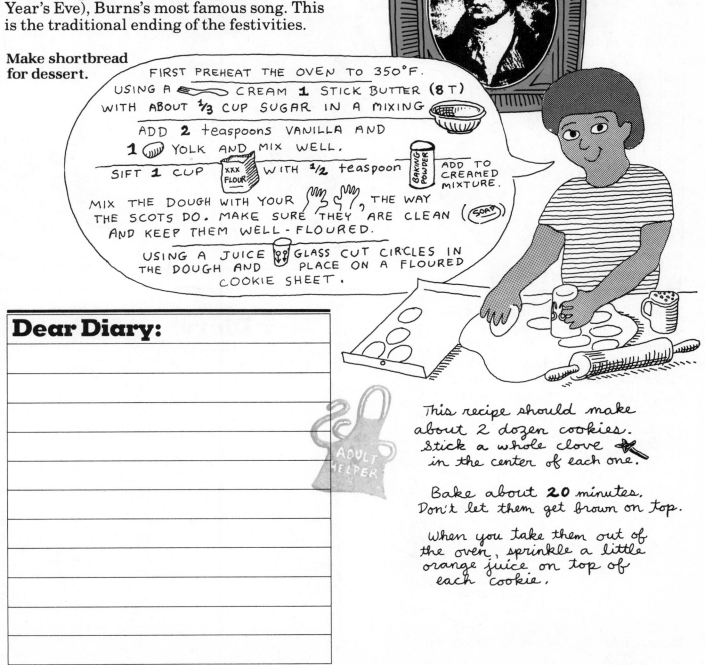

FIRST PREHEAT THE OVEN TO 350°F.
USING A [fork] CREAM **1** STICK BUTTER (8 T) WITH ABOUT 1/3 CUP SUGAR IN A MIXING [bowl]
ADD **2** teaspoons VANILLA AND **1** [egg] YOLK AND MIX WELL.
SIFT **1** CUP [XXX FLOUR] WITH 1/2 teaspoon [BAKING POWDER] ADD TO CREAMED MIXTURE.
MIX THE DOUGH WITH YOUR [hands], THE WAY THE SCOTS DO. MAKE SURE THEY ARE CLEAN ([SOAP]) AND KEEP THEM WELL-FLOURED.
USING A JUICE [glass] GLASS CUT CIRCLES IN THE DOUGH AND PLACE ON A FLOURED COOKIE SHEET.

This recipe should make about 2 dozen cookies. Stick a whole clove in the center of each one.

Bake about **20** minutes. Don't let them get brown on top.

When you take them out of the oven, sprinkle a little orange juice on top of each cookie.

Dear Diary:

January 26
India's Republic Day

Fireworks blasting! Flags flying! It looks like the Fourth of July! But it's India!? Today is Republic Day—the date in 1950 when India became a republic. Buildings all over India are decorated with banners and flags.

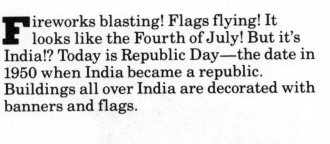

FIND YOUR WAY TO INDIA
Starting from the west coast of the U.S., sail your pencil point through the ocean maze to find India. Then, join in the celebration.

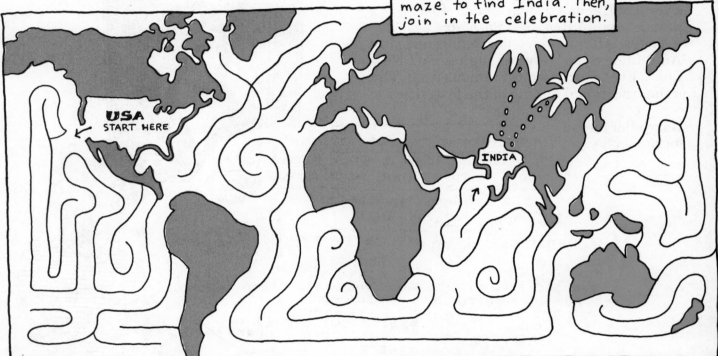

This is what India's flag looks like:
Color the top stripe saffron (deep yellow-orange).
Leave the middle stripe white.
Color the wheel blue.
Color the bottom stripe green.

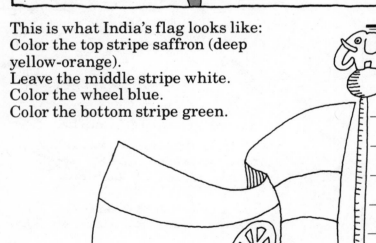

If you'd like to find out more about India write to: Embassy of India, 2107 Massachusetts Ave., N.W., Washington, D.C. 20008.

ear Diary:

January 27
A Most Brillig Day

Can you find the way to read this strange poem by Lewis Carroll, born January 27, 1832? It is from *Through the Looking-Glass and What Alice Found There* the successful follow-up to Carroll's first book, *Alice's Adventures in Wonderland*. By the way, Lewis Carroll is a pseudonym (a phony name). The author's real name was Charles Lutwidge Dodgson, and this is one of the most famous of all nonsense poems in the English language.

This illustration is by Sir John Tenniel.

Jabberwocky

'Twas brillig, and the slithy toves
Did gyre and gimble in the wabe:
All mimsy were the borogoves,
And the mome raths outgrabe.

"Beware the Jabberwock, my son!
The jaws that bite, the claws that catch!
Beware the Jubjub bird, and shun
The frumious Bandersnatch!"

He took his vorpal sword in hand:
Long time the manxome foe he sought—
So rested he by the Tumtum tree,
And stood awhile in thought.

And as in uffish thought he stood,
The Jabberwock, with eyes of flame,
Came whiffling through the tulgey wood,
And burbled as it came!

One, two! One, two! And through and through
The vorpal blade went snicker-snack!
He left it dead, and with its head
He went galumphing back.

"And hast thou slain the Jabberwock?
Come to my arms, my beamish boy!
O frabjous day! Callooh! Callay!"
He chortled in his joy.

'Twas brillig, and the slithy toves
Did gyre and gimble in the wabe:
All mimsy were the borogoves,
And the mome raths outgrabe.

Dear Diary:

January 28
Festival of the Arts

Today's a day to celebrate your talents! Paint a picture, sing, play an instrument, dance, write, make something—whatever you enjoy.

Of all the arts, which is your favorite? Music, literature, painting, sculpture, dance, theater, movies? Below are the names of five artists all of whom were born on January 28. The names of a painter, a sculptor, a musician, a writer, and an arts critic. Figure out who's who by the way their names are written.

Write your name in special artistic ways.

Jackson Pollock BORN 1912

Colette born 1873

Susan Sontag born 1933

ARTHUR Rubinstein born 1886

CLAES OLDENBURG BORN 1929

Dear Diary:

January 29
Eve of the Purple Cow

Don't wait until tomorrow—drink a toast to the purple cow tonight! The perfect beverage for the occasion is called (guess what) a Purple Cow. Here's how to make it:

1 In a tall, skinny glass put several scoops of ICE CREAM OR YOGURT— vanilla or any flavor you like

2 Pour grape juice into the glass. Careful not to fill it up too high.

3 Add a straw AND CLINK GLASSES with all the other PURPLE COW drinkers. Propose a toast: "Here's to all the purple cows I never saw..."

January 30
Purple Cow Day

I never saw a purple cow,
I never hope to see one,
But I can tell you, anyhow,
I'd rather see than be one!

This popular verse (see how many people you can find who know it by heart) was written by Gelette Burgess (1866-1951) whose birthday is today.

← Color this cow, please.

Make up other silly verses.

I never saw a_____,
    I never hope to see one,
But I can tell you, _____,
    I'd rather see than be one!

    You could fill in the first line with "hairless moose" and the other one with "silly goose." See how it's done? Now you do it. Write your other rhymes below.

Dear Diary:

Dear Diary:

January 31
Anna Pavlova's Birthday

MAKE THIS HOLE FIT YOUR FIRST TWO FINGERS

The greatest ballerina in history—that's the way Anna Pavlova (1885-1931) is remembered. There are only a few people alive today who saw her dance, but dancers everywhere know her from her photographs and the dances she made famous (like "The Dying Swan"). Pavlova had an unusual pet at her home in London—a swan named Jack!

Perform a finger ballet.

① Make a little dancing puppet like the one above out of stiff paper. (For a female puppet add tissue paper for the tutu if you wish.)

② YOUR POINTER AND MIDDLE FINGERS BECOME THE DANCER'S LEGS. Paint the ends of your fingers to make his or her slippers →

③ Turn on some classical music (TCHAIKOVSKY IS PERFECT) and let your dancer dance away.

④ Practice before a mirror – long beautiful leaps and quick little jumps.

February 1
National Freedom Day

The first of February has been proclaimed National Freedom Day by the president.

Hidden in the word-search puzzle below are the names of eight people who fought for freedom in different ways and for different groups of people: Martin Luther King (January 15), Susan B. Anthony (February 15), Helen Keller (June 27), A. S. Neill (October 17), Isadora Duncan (May 27), Walt Whitman (May 31), Mohandas Gandhi (October 2), and Scott Nearing (August 6).

```
M E X Y Z A B C D E F G H S J K
O A N O P Q R S T L V W X U Z A
H C R D E F G H L J K L M S O P
A R S T U V W I Y Z A B C A E F
N H I J I L E N O P Q R S N U S
D X Y Z A N C D E F G H I B K C
A N O P S R L T U V W X Y A A O
S D E A G H I U K L M N O N Q T
G T U V W X Y Z T B C D E T G T
A J K L M N O P Q H S T U H W E
N Z A B C D E F G H J K O M C A
D P Q R S T U V W X Y R A N C R
H E L E N K E L L E R P K Y S I
I S A D O R A D U N C A N I J N
L M N O P Q R S T U V W X Y N G
B W A L T W H I T M A N V O P G
```

Dear Diary:

Dear Diary:

Answers appear at the back of the book.

February 2
Groundhog Day

Yes, there really are groundhogs, but the "official" one lives in Sun Prairie, Wisconsin, and is named Jimmy. (There is some heavy competition from a groundhog in Punxsutawney, Pennsylvania.) Every February 2 around 7:00 A.M. he comes out of his hole to tell the world whether we'll have an early or late spring. If he sees his shadow and runs back to his hole there will be six more weeks of winter; if he stays out and hams it up for the TV cameras, spring's almost here. Since folks in Sun Prairie started keeping track, Jimmy's been right 16 out of 19 times!

Starting early in the morning people from all over the country start calling Sun Prairie to find out if Jimmy saw his shadow. You can usually find out by watching the national news on TV or by reading the newspaper, but if these don't work get an adult to dial the Sun Prairie Chamber of Commerce, (608) 837-4547. The folks there will tell you Jimmy's forecast. (Remember, long distance calls cost extra. Don't stay on long.)

Also, if February 2 is your birthday or that of any of your friends you can get a Groundhog Birth Certificate by sending the birthday-person's name, address, place and year of birth, along with four 15-cent stamps to: Chamber of Commerce, 243 E. Main St., Sun Prairie, Wisconsin 53590.

Jimmy the Groundhog may be afraid of his own shadow, but *you're* not. Make shadow pictures today. Here are a few to try:

Dog Deer Rabbit Eagle Alligator Cow

Dear Diary:

February 3
Bean Throwing Night

Throw a bean for good luck. Well, that's what some kids are doing in Japan, since it's Setsubun or Bean Throwing Night in that country. On February 3, each person eats one bean for every year of his/her life plus one for luck in the coming year. In olden days people scattered beans through their houses to drive out evil spirits (uncooked ones that is; if not, squish . . . yuk!). Nowadays folks gather in shrines where famous people throw beans at the crowd for good luck.

GROW a BEAN GARDEN in a jar!

① Fill a wide-mouth jar ½-inch deep with beans.

NO SOIL NEEDED

USE MUNG BEANS. (You can get them at many grocery stores or any health food shop.)

② RINSE beans well and soak overnight in warm water.

POUR OFF H₂O next A.M.

KEEP US MOIST

③ RINSE beans 2 or 3 times a day but don't let them _sit_ in water.

④ In 3 or 4 days when the sprouts are about this long they're ready to eat. YEP, the _whole_ thing...

Put them in a salad or on a peanut butter and banana sandwich. YUM!

February 4
Lucky Lindy's Day

Happy Birthday, Lucky Lindy—that's the nickname the world gave Charles Lindbergh in 1927 when he became the first person to fly nonstop across the Atlantic Ocean in his plane, *The Spirit of St. Louis*. He became the real-life superhero of the 1920's. Who would have believed then that a little over 40 years later people would fly to the moon?

Help Lucky Lindy make it from New York to Paris.

This maze will probably take you less than the 33½ hours it took Lindbergh to complete his flight.

CANADA

PARIS (FINISH)

START

NEW YORK

ATLANTIC OCEAN

NX211

Dear Diary:

February 5

Start Your Valentines Today

Only nine days till Valentine's Day! Time to start making those extra-special greetings you'll give to your favorite people. Homemade valentines are best of all, and they're fun to make! Start today. Get together scissors, glue, colored paper, old magazines you can cut up, markers, crayons, doilies, and anything else that strikes your fancy. Don't be too serious. Funny valentines are just as good as pretty ones. Sign them "Guess Who" and drive your friends nuts!

Make up your own ideas ➔ _and make_ a list of the friends you're sending valentines.

February 6
Mardi Gras

Mardi Gras means "Fat Tuesday" in French and is the last big day of fun and feasting before the 40 days of Lent begin. Mardi Gras is celebrated in France with crepes—thin pancakes filled with sweet foods like applesauce or cooked fruit and sprinkled with powdered sugar. With a menu like that *any* Tuesday would be fat!

In New Orleans, Louisiana, it's celebrated with a whole day of parades and an evening of masked balls. Nobody has to go to school and lots of kids and grown-ups go in costume to watch the colorful parades. Masked revelers on the floats throw "doubloons" and strings of beads to the crowds who shout, "Throw me somethin', Mister!" It's all like one big party.

Make a string of MARDI GRAS BEADS

① **HUNT** for things like these to string together →

② **CUT** a strong piece of thread or fishing line long enough to fit over your head.

③ **STRING** the things you collected and **TIE** the two ends together in a knot.

February 7
Beatles Begin First U.S. Tour, 1964

Beatlemania! That's what began when four young English musicians first sang "I Want To Hold Your Hand" in America. Suddenly *everybody* had a "Beatle haircut." It's hard to believe now when you look at early pictures of the Beatles that their hair was shockingly *long* in 1964. John, Paul, George, and Ringo went on to make great music and change styles in clothes and hair for the rest of the sixties. Nowadays, people wear their hair long, short, and in between, and nobody much cares.

Have a Beatle bash!

Borrow some Beatles albums, have some friends over, and *groove out!* Wear your hair down over your eyes. If your hair's short, make a Beatle wig.

① **FIND** an old nylon stocking or a stocking cap.

② **SEW** cloth fringe or crepe paper fringe to the cap

③ **START** at the bottom, and spiral up to the TOP.

Dear Diary:

Dear Diary:

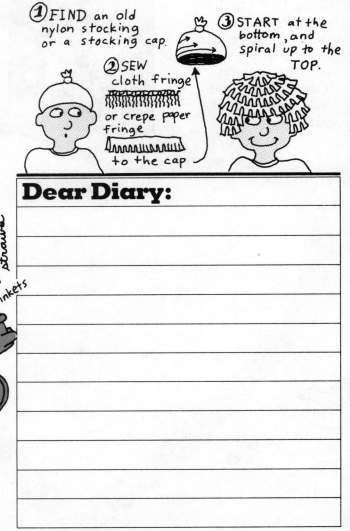

Shells

drinking straws

trinkets

Beads

Buttons

Bells

Doubloon

REX

February 8
Boy Scout Day

How many Scouts do you know? Since Scouting began in 1907 thousands of boys have enjoyed the fun *and* work of Cub Scouts, Boy Scouts, and Explorers. There are lot of things to learn by being a Scout. Each time a Boy Scout perfects a certain skill he wins a merit badge. Here are some badges; can you guess which badge fits each skill named below?

Cooking, Weather, Indian Lore, Astronomy, Radio, Lifesaving, Cycling, Lifesaving, Hiking.

Dear Diary:

February 9
"Weather" We Like It Or Not

On this day in 1870 the U.S. Weather Service was established. The people who work for the weather service have all kinds of special equipment to keep track of changes in weather activity. They pass their forecast predictions to the media—radio, television, and newspapers—and they, in turn, pass the information on to us. Even though their predictions aren't always right, if we remember to listen to or read the weather forecast then we have a better chance of knowing whether or not to carry an umbrella, wear galoshes or plan on getting a sunburn.

Make a WIND CHIME.
1. FIND a handsome tree branch (not too large)
2. COLLECT small metal objects - anything that makes a nice tinkling sound when it bumps something else.
3. CUT lengths of strong thread and TIE one end of each to an object and the other end to the branch. Hang the objects close enough for them to touch each other. BALANCE IT CAREFULLY!
4. HANG your wind chime from the ceiling near a window or outdoors from the porch roof.

Dear Diary:

February 10
Nose Encounters

CELEBRATE your NOSE!

Make a nose bow by cutting a bow shape out of paper or tie a real bow with a piece of ribbon. Use a loop of tape to attach it to your nose.

NOSE HIEROGLYPHICS

Write in your diary using this nose code.

A	B	C	D	E	F	G	H	I	J	K

L	M	N	O	P	Q	R	S	T

IT'S HARD TO FIND A NOSEGAY OF WILDFLOWERS IN WINTER... BUT

U	V	W	X	Y	Z

IT'S EASY TO GO THROUGH THE KITCHEN SPICE CABINET SMELLING ALL THE GOODIES.

CLOVES · CINNAMON · CURRY · NUTMEG · BASIL

Note: Jimmy Durante, a wonderful comedian famous for his big nose, was born on February 10, 1893.

February 11
National Inventors' Day

The Wizard of Menlo Park was the nickname for Thomas Edison (1847-1931). When he was only 10 years old he set up a real laboratory in his father's basement. Later on in his life, he invented the light bulb, the phonograph, the movie projector, and the mimeograph—that funny machine that prints all the purple papers your teacher gives you to do. No wonder National Inventors' Day is celebrated on his birthday!

Design a wonderful machine to do something amazing.

Dear Diary:

February 12
Honest Abe Day

Not only was Abraham Lincoln, sixteenth president of the U.S.A., born on February 12, 1809, but on this date 71 years earlier the first puppet show in America was presented in New York.

Make an Honest Abe rod puppet.

1. **CUT** Abe's tall, thin figure (minus his right arm) out of cardboard.
2. **CUT** out the right arm.
3. **COLOR** or paint your puppet.
4. **ATTACH** a stick ★ (ice cream, long lollipop, dowel or twig) to the back of the puppet using tape. Leave enough of the stick below Abe's feet to hold onto.
5. **ATTACH** the right arm of the puppet to the shoulder using a paper fastener. Use a long stick attached to the wrist to move the arm up and down.

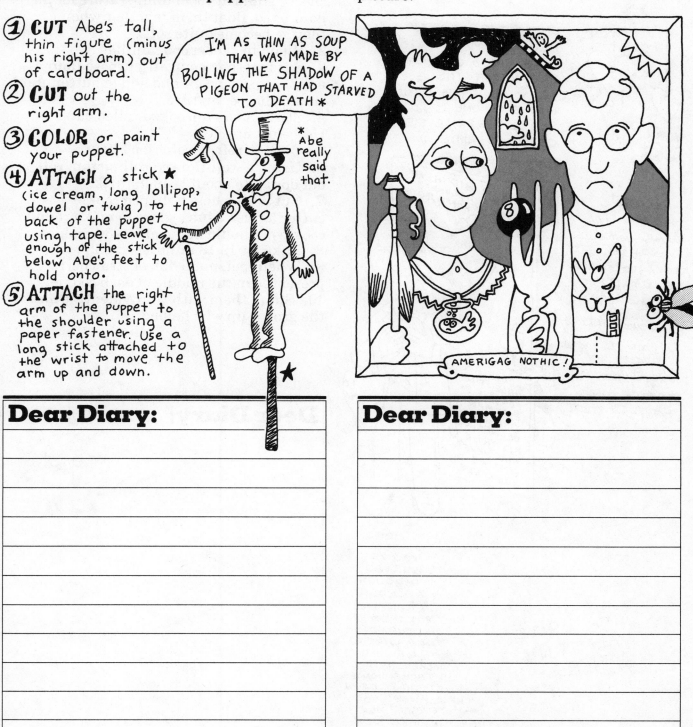

I'M AS THIN AS SOUP THAT WAS MADE BY BOILING THE SHADOW OF A PIGEON THAT HAD STARVED TO DEATH *

* Abe really said that.

February 13
Weird-Work-of-Wood Day

Grant Wood is *not* a kind of tree! He's the artist who painted *American Gothic* in 1930 and his birthday is today.

Here's a silly version of his famous painting called *Amerigag Nothic*. See how many weird things you can find in the picture.

AMERIGAG NOTHIC!

Dear Diary:

Dear Diary:

February 14
Valentine's Day

Time to give the hearts you made.
Time to get some too.
And figure out who sent the ones
That only say, "Guess who."

Decorate for Valentine's Day.

CUT OUT COLORED HEARTS AND HANG THEM ON STRINGS OVER THE BREAKFAST TABLE. (IF YOU GET THIS DONE WHILE NO ONE IS LOOKING YOU'LL SURPRISE THE REST OF YOUR FAMILY.)

Decorate yourself! Wear white sneakers with red shoelaces or anything red and white or pink and white Wear a paper valentine pinned over your heart.

CUT A BIG HEART TO DECORATE THE FRONT DOOR.

LEAVE A VALENTINE FOR THE POSTMAN. → IMAGINE DELIVERING ALL THOSE ♥s AND NEVER GETTING ONE YOURSELF.

PASTE A FAVORITE VALENTINE HERE.

TONIGHT WHEN YOU'VE SORTED THROUGH ALL YOUR VALENTINES PUT THEM UP IN YOUR ROOM ON A WINDOW OR WALL OR WHEREVER TAPE OR TACKS WON'T HURT. DON'T THROW THEM AWAY! YOU CAN USE THEM NEXT YEAR TO MAKE NEW VALENTINES SO SAVE THEM IN A SPECIAL PLACE.

Make St. Valentine's cookies.

These are delicious. They taste like old-fashioned biscuits with jam. Ask a grown-up to help.

1. Let 1 cup butter and 6 ounces cream cheese stand at room temperature for an hour or so. Beat them together when they've become quite soft.
2. Blend in 1 teaspoon vanilla.
3. Sift together 1 cup all-purpose flour and ½ teaspoon salt and add to butter and cream cheese mixture.
4. Stir in 1 cup uncooked rolled oats. Use your muscles!
5. Chill in refrigerator for 1 hour.
6. Using a well-floured rolling pin, roll out dough to about ¼-inch thick.
7. Cut with a heart-shaped cookie cutter (or use a juice glass to make round cookies). Should make about 30 cookies.
8. Bake for 16-18 minutes at 350°.
9. When cool, put a dab of strawberry preserves in the middle of each cookie.
10. Share them with your valentine *and* the grown-up who helped.

Dear Diary:

ADULT HELPER

February 15
Susan B. Anthony Day

There was a time when women in the U.S. did not have the right to vote. Susan B. Anthony (1820-1906) knew this was wrong and worked hard for change. She made speeches and wrote letters and talked to *everyone* she could and even voted illegally. Susan was called a suffragette. (The word "suffrage" means "the right to vote.")

Susan died before women were granted the vote in 1920, but she made a famous prediction. Solve this puzzle to find out what she said.

Another word for "the vote" is

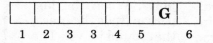
1 2 3 3 4 5   6

There are books about Susan B. Anthony

in the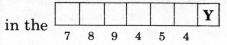
7 8 9 4 5 4

Another word
for "verse" or "rhyme" is ☐ ☐ ☐ ☐
10 11 6 12

Susan said: ___ ___ ___ ___ ___ ___
3   5   8   7   2   4   6

___ ___ ___ ___ ___ ___ ___ ___ ___ ___ ___
8 1   8 12 10 11 1 1 8 9 7 6

Dear Diary:

February 16
Dummy Day

Charlie McCarthy was a dummy! Well, it's true. He was the wooden dummy of the most popular ventriloquist ever, the late Edgar Bergen, whose birthday is today.

Bergen started "throwing his voice" when he was 11 and created Charlie when he was in high school. He went on to delight audiences around the world with his very believable puppet partner (who got more fan mail than Bergen did).

Try your voice at ventriloquism.

MAKE YOUR HAND INTO A DUMMY. USE LIPSTICK TO MAKE A MOUTH. PAINT EYES ON WITH EYEBROW PENCIL OR EYE SHADOW.

Practice making your "dummy's mouth" move as you talk so it looks like your hand is talking.

IN FRONT OF A MIRROR, SMILE WITH YOUR TEETH A LITTLE APART, AND TRY TALKING WITHOUT MOVING YOUR LIPS.

Don't try to say M or P - instead say N or H, ("important" becomes "inhortant"). Just leave out B altogether (for "bird" say "ird"). Well, it's just a start! Ventriloquism takes years to perfect.

Dear Diary:

Amazing Daily

February 17, 1876　　　　　*All The News That's Fit To Tickle*

FIRST SARDINE CANNED IN EASTPORT, MAINE

Sardines Declare Day of Mourning

Atlantic Ocean fish are wearing black today and flying all fish flags at half mast in honor of the canned sardines they are calling the Sans Sardinas (sardine saints).

Fishwatchers Note High Tide

Fishwatchers report the tide is $1/16$-inch higher than usual today. Some believe the phenomenon is due to the many teeny sardine tears shed over the recently canned fish. Mr. Terence Trout, interviewed in Carp County said, "Why couldn't they pick on something their own size."

New Expression Coined

"Packed like sardines" is what people are saying about the fate of Sans Sardinas.

Today's Puzzle

Below is an empty sardine can. Leave it empty if you are a fish-lover or see how many sardines you can draw inside it.

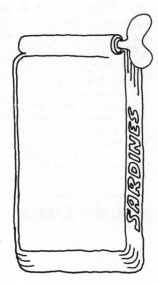

New Game Named After Sardines

The sardine saints are being remembered by children through the playing of a new game called Sardines. According to Suzy Sardi, one of the players interviewed, the game is a variation of Hide-and-Seek and can be played in or outdoors. One person is chosen to be *It* and hides while the rest of the players (any number) count to 100. Then they begin to hunt for *It*.

When somebody finds *It*, that person hides in the same place without saying anything. Somebody else finds them and hides there also. Finally, all the players are packed like sardines in the hiding place. When the last person finds the place, that round is over. The player that found *It* first becomes the new *It* and hides in a new spot.

Ms. Sardi said, "You just want to crack up when you're all squooshed together hiding, but if you laugh everybody will find you. Sardines is really fun."

Dear Diary:

Cannery at Eastport

February 18
Anniversary of the Flying Cow

Elm Farm Ollie proved to the world that cows really can fly . . . with a little help, that is. Although she didn't jump over the moon, she really was the first cow in an airplane (on February 18, 1930). She was a shining example of bovine bravery. She was even milked during the flight and the milk was put into paper containers and parachuted over St. Louis, Missouri. When asked by reporters for her comment, she modestly replied, "Moo."

How do you think Ollie's great-grandmother jumped over the moon? Was she really in a rocket ship or slung by a giant slingshot? Draw what you think happened.

Dear Diary:

February 19
Pisces Begins

People born between February 19 and March 21 are born under the sign of Pisces, the fishes. According to astrologers, they are imaginative, intelligent, and very talented. Because they can do many things well, they often drift from one project to another. If you have a good friend born under Pisces, you're lucky. They are devoted friends, sensitive to the feelings of others. They usually like history, the arts, and everything about nature—especially fish!

List all the people you know born under the sign of Pisces. Which ones seem to fit the description?

Make FISHY BIRTHDAY CARDS for your Pisces friends.

1. Fold a piece of colored typing or colored paper in half (TOP MEETS BOTTOM)

2. Draw a fish shape then cut it out.

3. Make sure you leave a hinge of uncut paper at the top so the front and back stay hooked together.

4. write a silly message on the front: YOU LOOK LIKE A MILLION BUCKS

But on the inside turn the compliment around: ALL GREEN AND CRUMPLED UP! HAPPY BIRTHDAY

Dear Diary:

February 20
Brotherhood Week Celebration

Buffy Sainte-Marie, an American Indian singer whose birthday is today, wrote a terrific song for Brotherhood Week. It's called *The Seeds of Brotherhood*.

It's time to open your eyes,
    take a look outside, and all around
    to North and South, and up and down.
The weather is right, the time is here,
    there'll never be a better year;
    for brotherhood to take its root,
    to bloom its blossom and sprout its shoot.
Open, open up your eyes,
    it's time to find a place to hoe,
    to find a place to plant your row,
    where the seeds of love can grow and grow,
    your heart's the perfect spot you know;
    it's time to clean your garden plot
    of sticks and stones and other old rot.
Time to plant a brand new world,
    where promises keep and paths unfurl,
    to young and old,
    to boy and girl,
    to rich and poor,
    to woman and man,
    to black and white,
    and gold and tan,
    to big and little,
    and fast and slow,
    oh, see how brotherhood
    can GROW.
Let the sun shine in your face
    to everyone of every race.

Note: Brotherhood Week always includes Washington's Birthday.

Dear Diary:

February 21
Millay Day Eve

Edna St. Vincent Millay, (1892-1950, whose birthday is tomorrow), became famous when she was only 20 years old. She had written a beautiful poem that touched the hearts of many people and contained these lines:

> *I know not how such things can be;*
> *I only know there came to me*
> *A fragrance such as never clings*
> *To aught save happy living things;*
> *A sound as of some joyous elf*
> *Singing sweet songs to please himself,*
> *And, through and over everything,*
> *A sense of glad awakening.*

When she was older, Millay wrote this poem:

> *Look, Edwin! Do you see that boy*
> *Talking to the other boy?*
> *No, over there by those two men–*
> *Wait, don't look now–now look again.*
> *No, not the one in navy-blue;*
> *That's the one he's talking to.*
> *Sure you see him? Striped pants?*
> *Well, he was born in Paris, France.*

Why not memorize the second poem and say it to a friend at school as if you're just talking, but instead of "Edwin" say your friend's name, "Look, Lucy . . ."

Dear Diary:

February 22
George Washington's Birthday

George Washington: the first president of America; "Father of Our Country"; folk hero; namesake of the capital of the U.S., one state, over 20 towns, and 32 counties. If you want to see his picture look on a one dollar bill, a quarter, or one of many postage stamps.

Here are some hints about other famous presidents. Which ones do you know?

3rd president:
T_____   J_____
(His picture's on the nickel.)

16th president:
A_____   L_____
(His nickname is Honest Abe.)

25th president:
T_____   R_____
(The teddy bear was named for this president.)

27th president:
W_____   W_____
(W. W. was president through WWI.)

34th president: J____   F. K_____
(He was the youngest of all presidents.)

38th president: J_____   C_____
(He's the only president ever to work for peanuts.)

Dear Diary:

Answers appear at the back of the book.

February 23
Take a Bath Day

Speaking of presidents, you can be sure *all* the presidents since Millard Fillmore have been very happy that he had the good sense to install the first bathtub in the White House back on February 23, 1851.

Bathtubs are great! They're just like little indoor heated pools, and in February *that's* something to celebrate!

Have a ball in the bath.

GET TOGETHER ALL YOUR TOY BOATS AND HAVE A REGATTA — A SAILBOAT RACE. TRY FLOATING OTHER SMALL TOYS THAT WON'T GET RUINED IN THE WATER.

MAKE LOTS OF BUBBLES IN YOUR TUB. USE BUBBLE BATH POWDER OR LIQUID OR HOLD A BAR OF SOAP UNDER THE FAUCET AND RUN THE WATER FAST... BUBBLE BATHS ARE SO MUCH FUN!

Drop food coloring in the water and watch the swirls the color makes. Just a few drops.

ADD SOME GERANIUM LEAVES OR ROSE PETALS TO YOUR BATH WATER. MMMM... SMELLS GREAT!

Dear Diary:

February 24
A Day to Picture the Sea

The American painter Winslow Homer (1836-1910) loved to paint the sea. He painted waves and rocks, fog, rain, wind and storms, sharks, shipwrecks and rescues, and the fisherfolk who worked on and by the ocean. In his painting Homer showed the power of the sea and the beauty and bravery of the people who faced it daily.

Make a picture that shows above *and* below the surface of the sea. (That silly shape that looks like an anthill is an island.)

Dear Diary:

February 25
Bank Your Money

Did you know that you can open a savings account all by yourself? Since one of the first savings banks in North America was opened on February 25, 1819, this is as good a time as any to think about having your own account. All you need is some of your own money—even a few dollars is enough—that you'd rather save than spend. Next time your folks go to the bank, see if you can go with them. Bring your money along and open your account. You'll get a savings passbook from your bank with your name on it, and the amount of money you deposited. If you don't understand how the savings bank is able to add *interest* to the money in your account, ask someone at the bank to explain it to you.

Make a Piggy Bank
(TO SAVE YOUR MONEY TILL YOU TAKE IT TO THE BANK)

FIND AN EMPTY PLASTIC BLEACH CONTAINER (RINSED WELL) OR A ROUND OATMEAL BOX.

CUT A SLIT WITH ONE END OF THE SCISSORS.

MAKE LEGS FROM SPOOLS, CORKS, OR CARDBOARD TUBES. ATTACH WITH WHITE GLUE.

Draw a face with a marker.

Dear Diary:

February 26
Wild West Quest

What do you think of when you hear the words "Wild West?" Cowboys and Indians, buffalo, stagecoaches, and covered wagons? These things really were a part of the early American West, but it was Buffalo Bill (1846-1917, birthday today) who brought them to the rest of the world as *entertainment*. His Wild West Show featured fancy shooting by stars like Annie Oakley, real Indians—especially Chief Sitting Bull—and melodramas such as "The Capture of the Deadwood Stagecoach."

The show was so popular that people believed the West was really like that, and some people *still* have that idea. Of course, history buffs know that the West wasn't a very glamorous place. By the way, Buffalo Bill's real name was William Frederick Cody.

FIND YOUR WAY through the wilds of this western cactus maze...

(START)

Dear Diary:

February 27
February Fun Day

Make today from beginning to end. FUN

① PRETEND it's your birthday and put a candle in the middle of your morning toast. Make a wish and blow the candle out. Won't your mother wonder!

② WEAR your funniest, favorite clothes.

③ BEFORE you go to school, wrap up a favorite toy like a present. When you get home pretend it's a gift from the Queen of England that arrived by special delivery.

④ Tell jokes to everyone! How about this one:

Q. MAGGIE MOREFUN HAD A BABY; WHO WAS MORE FUN THEN?

A. THE BABY, BECAUSE THE BABY WAS A <u>LITTLE</u> MOREFUN.

Write down your favorite joke.

Dear Diary:

(FINISH)

February 28
Nijinsky's Birthday

Dancers are some of the finest athletes in the world. They exercise constantly, always working to make their movements more beautiful and expressive.

Waslaw Nijinsky was probably the greatest male dancer in the history of ballet. He was so strong that he could leap across a whole stage in a single bound. He was born in Russia in 1890 and trained there. Later he danced throughout the world with the finest ballerinas of the day (including Pavlova).

Celebrate with exercise.

① STAND in front of a full-length mirror so you can see your whole body. (Dancers almost always work this way.)

② Begin by moving every part of your body - one part at a time.

③ BEND OVER and try to touch your toes without bending your knees. Just bend as far as possible - don't strain.

④ Now STRETCH yourself up. Try to touch the ceiling standing on your tip-toes.

Dear Diary:

February 29
Leap Year Day

If your birthday is today you only get a birthday every four years. It's true! February 29 only comes in leap years, which is one out of four. Usually February has only 28 days.

Here's a list of leap years so you'll know whether today's a real day *this* year:

To celebrate Leap Year Day *make up* a tradition—something you'll only do every four years (like eat lima beans).

Dear Diary:

March 1
In Like a Lion . . .

Today is not only the first day of blustery March but also the Feast of St. David, patron of Wales. (St. David is as important to the Welsh as St. Patrick is to the Irish.) So a perfect celebration to welcome this month "in like a lion" is Welsh Lion for lunch or supper.

You may have had Welsh Rabbit (or Rarebit), a popular cheese dish, before; Welsh Lion is different mainly because you make it look like the king of beasts.

Welsh Lion.
This recipe makes two or three lions.

Get everything you need out and READY before you start cooking, and ask an adult for assistance. Get together the

Lion's Features
and put them on a plate.
FOR EACH LION:

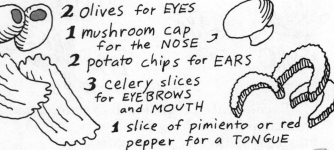

2 Olives for EYES
1 mushroom cap for the NOSE
2 potato chips for EARS
3 celery slices for EYEBROWS and MOUTH
1 slice of pimiento or red pepper for a TONGUE

① GRATE about 2½ cups of sharp cheese. Cheddar's fine. Put ½ cup of it on the "features plate"

② MELT remaining 2 cups grated cheese in a double boiler (over lightly boiling water.)

③ MIX together ½ cup cream with a dash of salt and pepper and ¼ tsp. dry mustard and ¼ tsp. Worcestershire sauce. Slowly STIR this mixture into cheese.

④ MAKE 1 slice of toast for each lion. Place each in the center of a plate.

⑤ When the sauce is smooth and hot POUR over toast

⑥ Quickly ARRANGE lion's features using the extra grated cheese to make the mane. (Now let's hope March will go out like a lamb.)

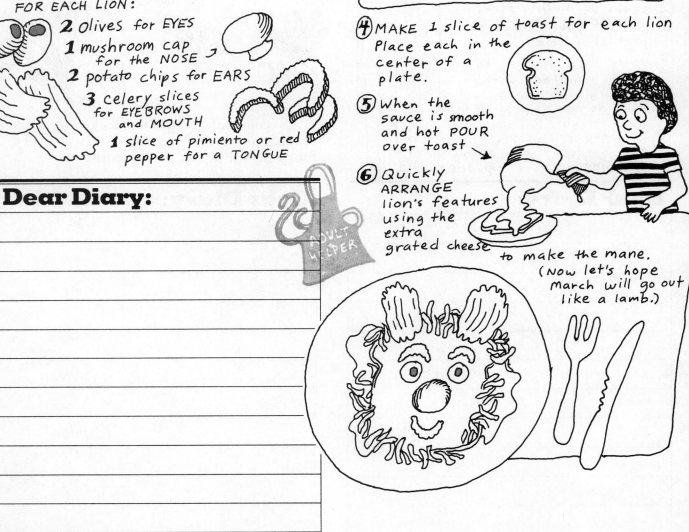

Dear Diary:

March 2
Pyramid Day

One of the three famous pyramids near Giza in Egypt was opened by archaeologists on March 2, 1818. These huge structures were built more than 4,000 years ago and even though they have been studied by experts for many, many years, they remain mysterious. Why were thousands of people made to work so hard building such elaborate tombs? Was the burial chamber the main reason for each building? And, how did they build such complicated structures in the first place?

The Great Pyramid, one of the seven wonders of the ancient world, is 450 feet high (almost as tall as a 50-story building).

CLIMB THE GREAT PYRAMID
Start at the bottom of this maze and work your way up.

March 3
Dolls' Day

Almost everybody has enjoyed playing with small figures of people and animals at some time. In Japan doll-making is a fine art and certain dolls are family treasures passed from generation to generation. Every March 3 in Japanese homes these special dolls are set up in beautiful displays on red cloth-covered steps decorated with peach blossoms (which are blooming now in Japan). On the top step are two dolls that represent the emperor and empress of Old Japan. On other steps are people of the court, tiny pets, furniture, and musical instruments. Families and friends visit each other all day to admire the dolls and share tea and rice cakes. The day is called Hina Matsuri, the doll festival.

You can celebrate Dolls' Day by creating a display of your own dolls, toys, and favorite things. Fix up one part of your room (your desk or bed or windowsill) as a display. If there are any flowers blooming outside bring some in to brighten up the show. Invite your family and friends in for a surprise. Tell them about Hina Matsuri.

Dear Diary:

Dear Diary:

March 4
Play Cards Day

Q: What can you cut without knife, razor, or scissors?
A: A deck of cards.

Play concentration.
This is a game for two or more people.
1. Shuffle the cards and lay them all out face down on a large table or on the floor, in rows and columns. Don't let them touch each other.
2. The first player turns up any two cards. If he's very lucky and they're a pair (two aces, two 2's, two 3's, etc.) he keeps them and gets another turn. If they're not a pair, he puts them back in the same place face down, and the next player gets a turn.
3. At each turn a player gets to turn over two cards trying to match pairs. The object is to remember which cards are where so you can make pairs.
4. When all the cards have been won, everybody counts the cards he has and the one with the most cards wins.

By the way Charles H. Goren, a well-known bridge player (bridge is another card game) and U.S. national bridge champion more than 30 times, was born on this date in 1901.

March 5
Illustration Celebration

One of America's first great illustrators (an artist who makes pictures for books or magazines) was Howard Pyle, born March 5, 1853, in Wilmington, Delaware. He not only drew and painted but he wrote books too: *Otto of the Silver Hand, Pepper and Salt, The Wonder Clock,* and *The Garden Behind the Moon.*

This picture is from his book *The Merry Adventures of Robin Hood,* published in 1883.

Look back to January 9 and 23, and February 11, 18, and 24. When you drew those pictures you became a book illustrator. Now write your name on the title page where its says "Written and Illustrated by Randy Harelson and _____."
(writing in your diary space certainly makes you co-author too!)

Dear Diary:

Dear Diary:

← Draw what you had for lunch today.

March 6
Michelangelo's Birthday

Michelangelo (his full name was Michelangelo Buonarotti, but he was—and still is—called by just his first name), born about 500 years ago in Italy, carved his first sculpture when he was in his teens. It was the figure of a person. When he was only 24 he completed his *Pietá*, a sculpture of Mary and Jesus, which made him famous all over Italy. He created many other masterpieces, including his mural on the ceiling of the Sistine Chapel in the Vatican which took four full years to finish. He was one of the greatest artists who ever lived.

Michelangelo thought the human body was the most beautiful thing in the world, and he drew, painted, and sculpted human images until he died at almost 90 years of age.

Make a clay figure

You'll be using inexpensive modeling clay for this project.

① Get a friend to **MODEL** for you. He or she will have to sit on the floor for 10 or 15 minutes so make sure the position is comfy.

② Start out by **LOOKING** carefully at your subject.

MICHELANGELO

③ Begin the **SCULPTING** by forming the body, then arms, legs and head.

WORK the clay on a piece of cardboard so your furniture stays clean. You can **KEEP** your sculpture on the cardboard when you're finished.

④ Now **TRADE PLACES** with your friend; **YOU** be the model.

Dear Diary:

March 7
Do Plants Have Ears? Day

Talk to plants. They listen. At least they listened to Luther Burbank, the famous plant breeder who produced more than 800 new kinds of plants (including the white potato). Burbank, born March 7, 1849, selected the best individual plants and cross-pollinated different varieties to develop stronger, faster-growing plants that produced more and better-tasting fruits and vegetables. Whenever he wanted a plant to develop in an unusual way, he would talk to it, explaining what he wanted. Living and working at his nursery near Santa Rosa, California, Burbank produced over 100 new kinds of plums and prunes, the giant white Shasta daisy, a spineless cactus, and a white blackberry.

Talk to plants.

Do you have a houseplant of your own? If you don't, ask someone who does for a cutting. Spider plants, Swedish ivy, and Wandering Jew are all easy plants to root in water. Use a glass, fill it close to the top with water, and add your cutting. When new roots grow (two to three weeks), you can transplant it in soil.

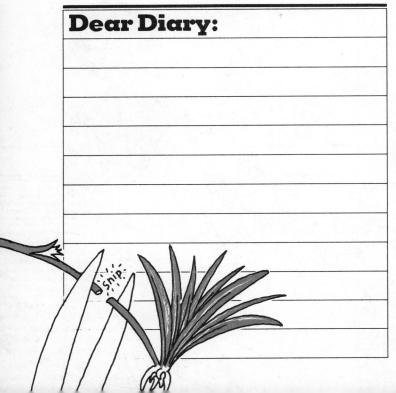

Dear Diary:

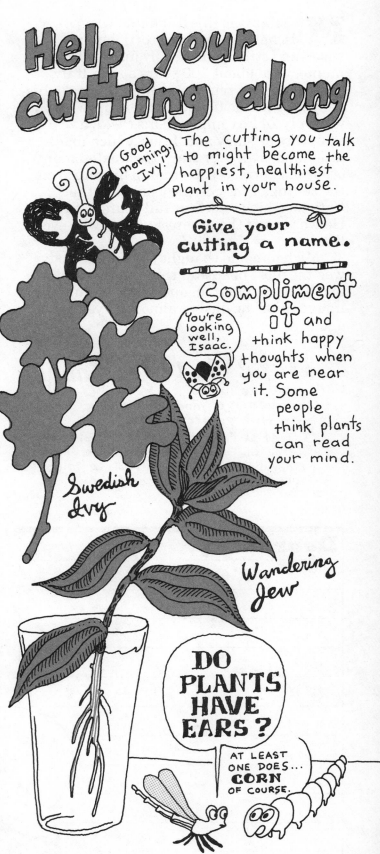

Help your cutting along

Good morning, Ivy!

The cutting you talk to might become the happiest, healthiest plant in your house.

Give your cutting a name.

You're looking well, Isaac.

Compliment it and think happy thoughts when you are near it. Some people think plants can read your mind.

Swedish Ivy

Wandering Jew

DO PLANTS HAVE EARS?

AT LEAST ONE DOES... CORN OF COURSE.

March 8
International Women's Day

International Women's Day is a day to honor all women. In the U.S.S.R., where the holiday began, women don't have to work today and they often get little gifts from men they work with. In China, women are entertained by children's concerts and plays and athletics.

In America, Women's Day is finally being celebrated. Maybe the best way for you to honor the women in your life is simply to let them know you think they're doing a good job at whatever work they've chosen.

Make an international paper doll.

② **DRAW** and cut out changeable costumes for her-clothes of different countries and occupations...

① **CHANGE** this figure to look like a woman you love - your mother, grandmother, teacher, friend, ANYONE. **REDRAW** the woman on stiff paper and cut her out.

③ **PUT** the costumes on the paper doll and imagine the real woman living in faraway countries and working at unusual jobs.

Dear Diary:

March 9
False Teeth Patented, 1822

Have you ever seen a picture of George Washington smiling with his teeth showing? Probably not. Washington had false teeth and didn't like to show them. His dentist, Dr. John Greenwood, introduced porcelain teeth about 1785, but the first patent for false teeth was granted to Charles Graham of New York City some 37 years later.

Make a set of funny teeth.

Make several sets of cardboard teeth—buck teeth, vampire fangs, a set with some teeth missing. (White thin cardboard will work best.)

Put them in your pocket and wait till you can slip them on without anyone noticing. Then just smile. Talk about catching people off guard—what a laugh!

March 10
Harriet Tubman Day

Born about 1820, Harriet Tubman was the great black American woman who led more than 300 slaves to freedom before the Civil War and worked for women's suffrage till her death in 1913.

More than 50 years after her death, on March 10, 1971, the U.S. Senate approved the vote for 18-year-olds. For the first time people all over America who were under 21 could become voting members of society. Now, will 16-year-olds ever get the right to vote? And six-year-olds? What do you think?

Make political buttons.

CUT circles from colored paper or cardboard. Write your message clearly with crayon or marker. Tape a safety pin on the back ... (Look for the VOTES FOR KIDS sticker on the sticker page.)

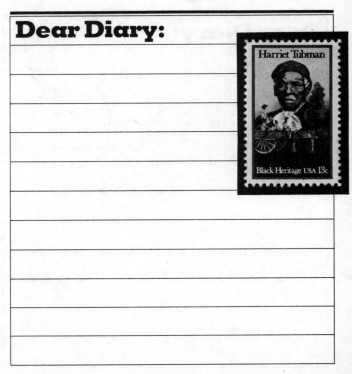

WE WANT THE VOTE

KID SUFFRAGE

VOTES for KIDS

ONE ME, ONE VOTE

Dear Diary:

Dear Diary:

Harriet Tubman
Black Heritage USA 13c

March 11
Knock-Knock Day

Knock knock. *Who's there?*
  Marge. *Marge who?*
Marge eleventh is a great day for knock-knock jokes.

Try these on your friends. They all start with:
Knock knock. *Who's there?*
  Won-Won *Won-Won who?*
Won-Won! There's a gowilla after you!

  Ahab. *Ahab who?*
Ahab a cold. By dose is stobbed ub.

  Who. *Who Who?*
Do you hear an owl? (Look around as you ask this.)

  Atch. *Atch who?*
God bless you! (or the German equivalent . . . gesundheit.)

  Amos. *Amos who?*
Amosquito. (Then pinch the person you're telling the joke to.)

  Shelby. *Shelby who?*
"Shelby comin' round the mountain when she comes . . ." (Sing it.)

Write your favorite knock-knock jokes in your diary. Try making some up too.

Dear Diary:

March 12
Girl Scout Day

Have you noticed lots of your friends in their Brownie or Girl Scout uniforms at school? If they seem to be wearing them more than usual it's because this is Girl Scout Week. Juliette Gordon Low, who brought Girl Scouting from England to the U.S., held the first troop meeting on March 12, 1912.

Since then, Girl Scouts has grown into an important organization with millions of girls and adult leaders in the U.S. and Canada alone.

Here's a challenge.

First, what time is it right now? _____
Now, see how long it takes you to find out two things: 1. What is the Girl Scout motto?

2. What is the Girl Scout slogan?

How long did it take? _____
How did you find out? _____

Dear Diary:

Answers appear at the back of the book.

March 13
Uncle Sam Day

Uncle Sam is a symbol, a pictured character, who represents the U.S. government. But Uncle Sam was also a real person. His name was Samuel Wilson, and he was born in 1766. During the War of 1812, he worked packing and inspecting food boxes for the U.S. troops in Troy, New York. The boxes were marked "U.S." for United States, but it became a popular joke among Sam Wilson's workers that "U.S." stood for "Uncle Sam," Wilson's nickname. As the joke spread, Uncle Sam became a nickname for the U.S. government, and still is.

One of the first cartoons showing Uncle Sam was published on March 13, 1852. It was drawn by Frank H. T. Bellew.

Draw Aunt Sam.
We all know what Uncle Sam looks like. How about using your imagination to create Aunt Sam?

March 14
Make Shamrocks Today

St. Patrick's Day is March 17, three days away. Make little paper shamrocks to give to your friends.
1. Fold a small square of green paper in half (see a and b) then in half again (c). You end up with a smaller square.

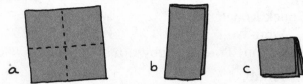

2. Cut out a shape like below, (d) making sure you cut away the open sides of the paper. Now unfold the paper (e).

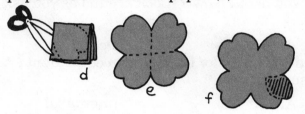

3. Cut part of one leaf away leaving only a paper stem (f).
4. Give it to your friend with a safety pin taped on the back so he or she can wear it on St. Paddy's Day for good luck.
5. To make a St. Paddy's card, pin the shamrock to a rectangle of stiff paper and write your greeting to the side of it.

Dear Diary:

Dear Diary:

March 15
Buzzard Day

Today, right on schedule, the buzzards will arrive in Hinckley, Ohio, as they have every March 15 for as long as Ohioans (or anybodyelsians) can remember.

Birds are amazing. How the buzzards know how to get from their winter home in Kentucky or the Smoky Mountains back to Hinckley is incredible enough, but every year like clockwork on March 15!?!

The swallows of San Juan Capistrano will baffle us in the same way on March 19.

Help the buzzards find their way home.

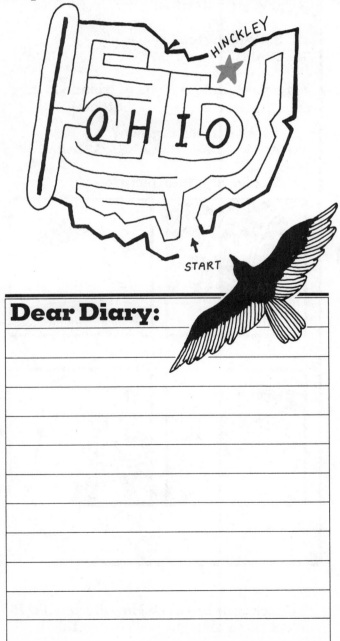

HINCKLEY

START

March 16
Rocket Shot

From the time he was 16, Robert Goddard (1882-1945), an American scientist, worked on figuring out how to send a ship into outer space. He continually experimented and then on March 16, 1926, Dr. Goddard, his wife, and two assistants went to his Aunt Effie's farm near Auburn, Massachusetts. There they fired the first liquid-fuel rocket in history. It looked nothing like rockets you're used to seeing—it was less than 12 feet high including the launching pad—but it was truly the first rocket of the space age.

Build a space rocket.

a rocket's shape is basically a cylinder with a cone on top. →

USE YOUR IMAGINATION to construct a fantastic space rocket from scrap materials.

Tape the parts together then paint with tempera.

Add some liquid detergent to the paint so it will stick to the tape.

SOAP

TEMPERA

← Paper cone

Oatmeal Box or cardboard ← tube

Cottage ← Cheese container

↖ cardboard fins

Dear Diary:

Dear Diary:

St. Patrick's Day

Top o' the morning to you—today's the day of the patron of Ireland, St. Patrick, who lived around the year 400. He was born in Britain but was captured by pirates at the age of 16 and sold as a slave in Ireland. He escaped about six years later but after years of study returned to Ireland to teach the people Christianity. He also taught many people to read and write.

St. Paddy's Day is celebrated as a happy holiday by millions of folks, not only the Irish. On March 17 most everybody claims to have Irish branches on his or her family tree. (add "O" to the beginning of your last name and it will sound as Irish as O'Brien—O'Smith, O'Marshall, O'Stein.) Most everybody wears a shamrock or *something* green because that's the color of Ireland, the Emerald Isle. Lots of cities have parades, and people wish each other the luck o' the Irish. Good Luck!

Dear Diary:

Answers appear at the back of the book.

Take a green quiz.

Find a green pen or pencil then answer the questions below.

1. Circle the two colors that, mixed together make green.

(Try it out with paint or food coloring in some water.)

RED   BLUE   YELLOW

2. Which creature is green?

KING KONG   THE HULK   DRACULA

3. Which stone is green?

EMERALD   DIAMOND   RUBY

(The most famous stone in Ireland is the _____ Stone.)

4. Which food is green?

POTATOES   BAKED BEANS   ASPARAGUS

5. Identify these pictures:

Check your answers. How did you do? If you got them all right you're an official Irishperson.

March 18
Eve of San Giuseppe

Tomorrow is the Feast of St. Joseph, one of the great holidays of Italy. It's celebrated all over that country and in Italian communities in America as well. Often many people of an Italian town contribute food and flowers to a *banchetto* (banquet), and the feast welcomes rich and poor alike. Three people of the town are chosen to sit at the head of the table and portray the Holy Family.

San Giuseppe, as the feast is called, usually begins tonight with a great pasta supper—spaghetti for example. Below are three kids enjoying a pasta feast. One is holding a strand of spaghetti that is tied to the Italian flag. Using a pencil, trace through the strands to find which one.

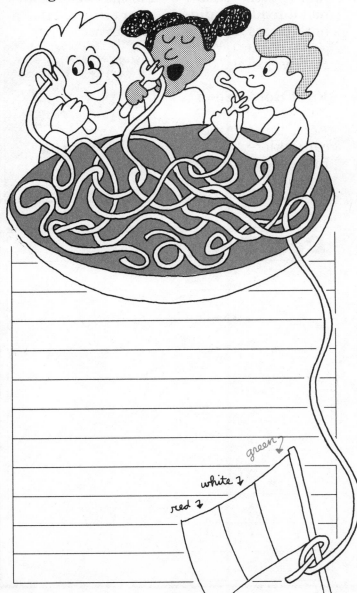

green?

white ?

red ?

March 19
Spring Is Almost Here

The town of San Juan Capistrano, California, has a very special way of knowing when spring arrives. Every year on St. Joseph's Day, which is today, hundreds of swallows return to their nests in and near the famous mission founded in 1776. Like the buzzards of Hinckley, Ohio, the swallows are always on schedule. And, amazingly, they also leave on the same date each year, October 23.

Spring officially begins when the sun "crosses" the equator from south to north, which usually happens on March 20 or 21. (You can find out the exact time from the newspaper.) Day and night are each almost exactly 12 hours long on the first day of spring.

Decorate a window in your house... Use these ideas or make up your own.

CUT spring shapes out of colored paper or white paper colored in

ATTACH to the wooden parts of the window with tacks or hang by string. (If you use cellophane tape don't leave your decorations up for long... tape's hard to get off after a while.)

Dear Diary:

Amazing Daily

SPECIAL SPRING ISSUE

Sun To Cross Equator

The sun is expected to cross the celestial equator sometime today or tomorrow. It will be moving from south to north, thus bringing the first day of spring to the northern hemisphere. Of special interest is the fact that day and night will be equal all over the world. Scientists call this day the vernal equinox.

Now-Ruz Celebrated

People of Afghanistan, Iran, and the Bahai faith celebrate their new year tonight and tomorrow. The holiday is called Now-Ruz. Celebrants plan to take special spring baths, scrub their homes, wear new clothes, and visit friends.

Tonight Now-Ruz festivities begin with a traditional feast made up of seven foods that begin with the Persian letter "S." They are said to represent the seven archangels of God in the Zoroastrian religion.

Goodie Cooke, who writes *Amazing Daily*'s food column, suggests you have a 'Seven-S' supper. Goodie writes:

"How many foods can you think of that begin with the letter *s*? Write them all down, then plan a menu using seven of them. If you want to include your favorite food, change its name to begin with *s*. I changed 'ice cream' to 'S-cream' and 'pizza' to 'succulent Italian pie.' Some adjectives that may help are: simply delicious, scrumptious, and super-duper. I also picked all the *s*'s out of a package of alphabet noodles to make a special *s* alphabet soup, but I wouldn't recommend it as it was very time-consuming. (By the time I had it ready my dinner guests had all gone home.) Well, Happy Spring."

First Robin Seen

According to American folklore, the first robin seen is a sure sign that spring has arrived. The first robin seen in these parts was spotted this morning by this reporter. We tried to interview Ms. Redbreast, but when asked where she had spent her winter vacation she refused to comment. However we believe it was in Florida for she was sporting quite a sunburn.

When you see YOUR first robin of spring mark the occasion with the ROBIN STICKER at the back of the book.

Dear Diary:

March 21
Aries Begins

People born between March 21 and April 20 are born under the sign of Aries, the ram. According to astrologers, they are strong and active and have lots of energy. They like excitement and change. Their worst fault is that they lose interest in some things that take a long time—they're better at starting than finishing projects. They usually have a good sense of humor and are often fine athletes.

List all the people you know born under the sign of Aries. Which ones seem to fit the description?

Make ram's horn mobiles for your Aries friends. See July 22 for more on mobiles.

1. Trace around a plate or other circle on a fairly stiff piece of paper.
2. Cut it out. Then make a spiral cut into it, like this:

HAPPY BIRTHDAY, ARIES FRIEND. LOVE,

3. Print a birthday message along the spiral.
4. Put a string through the center to hang it.

Dear Diary:

March 22
Marcel Marceau's Birthday

Marcel Marceau, alone on a stage in front of thousands of people, doesn't have to say a word to keep his audience spellbound. He is the world's best-known mime, an actor who expresses himself only with movement—no words.

Born in France, Marcel Marceau loved pantomime as a child. He carefully watched the movements of people and animals, and went to see the silent movies of Charlie Chaplin and others. As a young man he studied mime with a famous teacher, and then created his most famous character, Bip, whom millions of people have enjoyed on stage and television.

Play pantomimes.

Get a few friends together for some silent fun. One person at a time acts out something (no talking or props at all) and everyone else tries to guess what it is. For example, pretend to make something.

Pantomime very clearly so your friends can "see" the object you are making. Then hand it to someone who was watching and see if he or she knows what you've made. (After you've mimed making a cake, your friend might think you've made a basketball and pretend to dribble it down the court.) When someone does guess, it's his or her turn to pantomime.

Dear Diary:

March 23
A Day in the Kitchen

Fannie Farmer liked to cook
And on that subject wrote a book
With easy directions
For soups and confections,
For vegetables, cheese, and other selections.
Many folks have learned to cook,
From Fannie Farmer's trusty book.

Fannie Farmer, born March 23, 1857, was the first cookbook author to use standard, exact measurements (a level teaspoon, tablespoon, cup, etc.). Before, recipes had used measurements like "a handful of . . ." Since people's hands were different sizes the recipe varied from person to person.

Ms. Farmer's famous *Boston Cooking School Cookbook* sold over four million copies. Explore your kitchen to see if there's a copy. While you're looking, browse through other cookbooks just for fun. Find a recipe you'd like to try.

Cook today.

Assist whoever is preparing tonight's dinner. Use a new-found recipe or an old favorite. Write down the ingredients, the exact measurements and preparation of the main dish. Use the recipe card.

(name of dish)

Ingredients:

Preparation:

Dear Diary:

what's your favorite food?

COOK BOOK

March 24
March Museum Day

Did you know that you are part owner of an art gallery? Not just any art gallery either, but one of the finest there is anywhere.

The National Gallery of Art in Washington, D.C., truly belongs to the citizens of America. It was established by Congress on March 24, 1937. Since it opened in 1941, millions of people have enjoyed its wonderful collection of paintings and sculpture. If you go to Washington be sure to see your art gallery. It's open every day except Christmas and New Year's, and there's never an admission charge.

Be a museum-goer.

You may not be close enough to Washington to visit the National Gallery today, but there may be a museum near you. Look up "museums" in the Yellow Pages of the phone book. If you can't go today, plan to go soon. Meanwhile make your room into a museum.

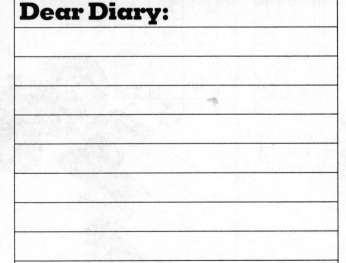

Dear Diary:

MAKE YOUR ROOM INTO

A MUSEUM

① GATHER favorite snapshots, magazine pictures, and your artwok.

② GLUE them to bigger pieces of paper.

③ DECORATE the borders and add titles... just like museum picture frames.

MY BUDDY

④ INVITE friends to see your museum.

March 25
Greek Independence Day

Today is a day of celebration in Greece. It's Greek Independence Day, much like America's Fourth of July.

This is the Greek flag adopted in 1822 while their war of independence, from Turkish rule, was being fought. Color the shaded areas blue. Leave the cross and unshaded stripes white.

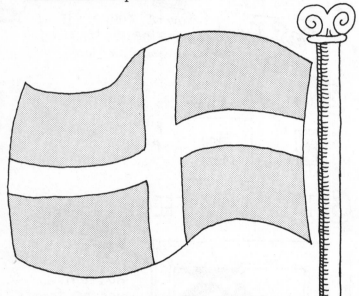

For more information about Greece write: Press and Information Service of Greece, 601 Fifth Ave., New York, N.Y. 10022.

ΔΕΑΡ ΔΙΑΡΥ:

Write a message in Greek.

Whether you know it or not, you read and write in Greek. The ABC's you know (called the Roman alphabet) come right from the *western* Greek alphabet. And did you know that lots of English words come from the Greek language — arithmetic, democracy, drama, hero, history, museum, and mythology are just a few.

This code is based on the *eastern* Greek alphabet.

March 26
Robert Frost's Birthday

I'm going out to clean the pasture spring;
I'll only stop to rake the leaves away
(And wait to watch the water clear, I may):
I sha'n't be gone long.—You come too.

I'm going out to fetch the little calf
That's standing by the mother. It's so young
It totters when she licks it with her tongue.
I sha'n't be gone long.—You come too.

Robert Frost's (1874-1963) beautiful verses have enchanted both grown-ups and kids for years. Poems like "Birches," "Stopping by Woods on a Snowy Evening," and "The Road Not Taken" are well known and well loved.

Most of Frost's poems have to do with nature. He may have even written these lines from "Nothing Gold Can Stay" in March:

Nature's first green is gold,
Her hardest hue to hold.
Her early leaf's a flower;
But only so an hour.

GO FOR A SPRING WALK!
Take along a magnifying glass and look closely for nature's first green: buds on trees, plants just poking out of the ground, flowers getting ready to bloom...

Dear Diary:

US 10c
Robert Frost
AMERICAN POET

March 27
Photography Day

Q: How is a camera like a paintbrush?
A: You can use either one to make art.

Edward Steichen (pronounced "STY-ken"), born March 27, 1879, was a great artist. He first studied painting, but became more interested in photography as an art. In 1947 he became the director of photography for the Museum of Modern Art in New York City.

Be a shutterbug.

You can make art with any kind of camera. Here's one idea. Get above it all (climb a stairway, tree, or ladder) and take an *aerial* photo. These two photos show how to make a trick pic:

Q. Is Danny standing on his head?
A. Nope.

Dear Diary:

If you don't have a camera write for the free pamphlet, "How to Make and Use a Pinhole Camera": Eastman Kodak Co. Dept. 841, 343 State St. Rochester, New York 14650

March 28
Spring Cleaning Day

In many parts of the world, house cleaning is a basic part of each year's spring celebration, probably because it's finally warm enough to open the doors and windows wide and give a good sweeping.

Lots of kids say their favorite way to clean up their rooms is to put the stereo at full blast, pretend the waste can is a basketball hoop (and that wastepaper is a basketball), and then race the clock to see how fast they can finish hoping nobody looks under the bed!

Dear Diary:

March 29
Mutt and Jeff Get Together, 1908

Three cheers for comic strips! On March 29, 1908, Jeff joined Mutt in a San Francisco newspaper, and those two comic characters, drawn by Bud Fisher, became the first successful daily comic strip—"Mutt and Jeff."

What's your favorite strip? Cut it out of the paper and glue it here.

Then cut out other comic strips and cut each square apart. Mix up the squares and combine different squares from different strips to make new strips.

Draw your own comic strip.

Make up two funny characters (people or animals) and draw your own comics here.

Dear Diary:

The famous painter Vincent Van Gogh was born in Holland on March 30, 1853. You've probably seen some of his paintings in books. From 1880 till his death in 1890 he drew and painted over 1,700 works of art. He used bright colors and strong, lively brushstrokes to make his paintings.

Some of his most famous paintings are self-portraits. A self-portrait is a picture of an artist drawn or painted by the artist him or herself.

Draw your self-portrait.

Sit in front of a mirror and really *look* at yourself as you draw.

Dear Diary:

March 31
... Out Like a Lamb

If March comes in like a lion, it goes out like a lamb ... Here's hoping today dawns gentle and lamblike.

Do you know what spring holiday has a lamb, a rabbit, and an egg for its symbols? It's Easter and although it falls on a different date each year, it always comes in the spring because it celebrates new life. Why not prepare for it today!

Put together a spring nature basket.

This is a great gift for somebody you like a lot.

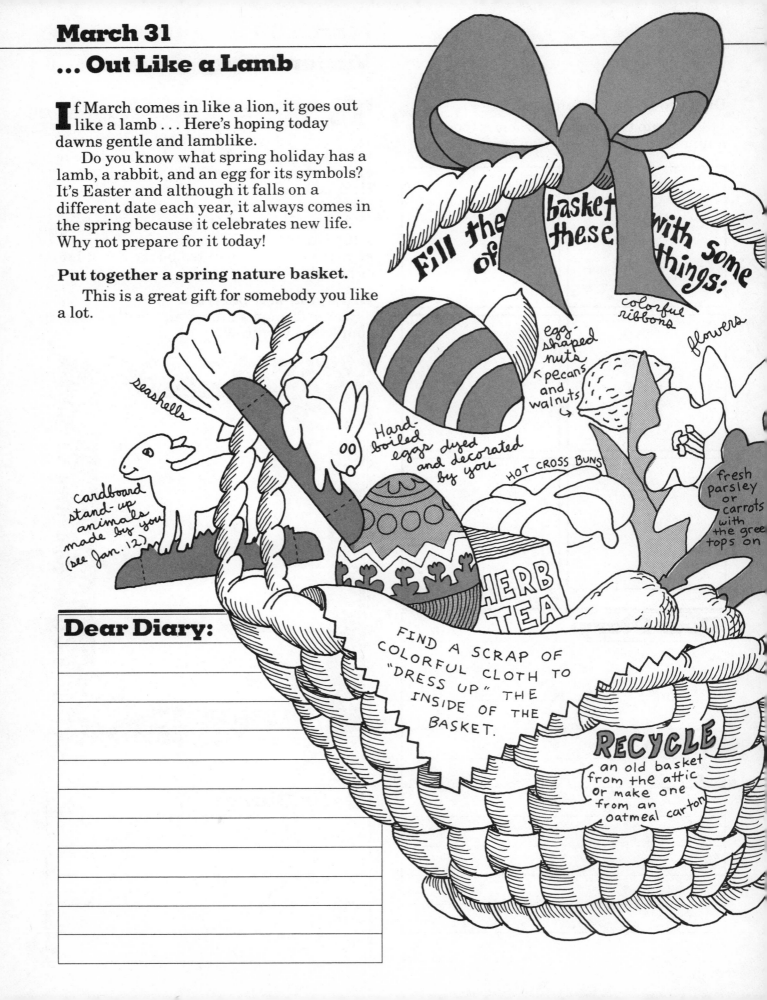

Fill the basket with some of these things:

colorful ribbons

flowers

egg-shaped nuts ← pecans and walnuts

seashells

Hard-boiled eggs dyed and decorated by you

HOT CROSS BUNS

fresh parsley or carrots with the green tops on

cardboard stand-up animals made by you (see Jan. 12)

HERB TEA

FIND A SCRAP OF COLORFUL CLOTH TO "DRESS UP" THE INSIDE OF THE BASKET.

RECYCLE an old basket from the attic or make one from an oatmeal carton

Dear Diary:

April Fool's Day

April 1 is probably the silliest day of the whole year. Friends plan ways to make fools out of each other so be prepared today . . . for fun!

Down with practical jokes. Nobody really thinks it's funny spooning salt on cornflakes because somebody switched what was in the sugar bowl.

Up with impractical jokes.

TRY THESE ON YOUR FRIENDS:

What's long, green and creepy with six legs and big teeth

I don't know. What?

I DON'T KNOW EITHER, BUT IT'S CRAWLING UP YOUR LEG!!!

CUT OUT THE LETTERS BUNNY. CARRY THEM IN YOUR POCKET.

Hey! You got a letter from the Easter Bunny!

WHAAAT!?

HAND HIM/HER ONE OF THE LETTERS AND SAY "APRIL FOOL!"

FRUSTRATING QUESTIONS TO ASK YOUR FRIENDS:

"What's that on your face?"

"Who put that sign on your back?"

BE INTERNATIONAL!

Call your victim "April Fish!" (That's what they say in France instead of "April Fool.")

APRIL FISH?

Dear Diary:

April 2
International Children's Book Day

Libraries all over the world are buzzing with activity today. All kinds of special programs and exhibits are going on as they celebrate International Children's Book Day. April 2 was selected for ICBD because it's Hans Christian Andersen's birthday. He was born in Denmark in 1805 and grew up to write "The Ugly Duckling" and other wonderful fairy tales and stories.

April 3
Rip Van Winkle Day

Today is Washington Irving's birthday. He was the first American writer to be widely read all over the world. Kids remember him most for his stories, "The Legend of Sleepy Hollow," and "Rip Van Winkle." He was born in 1783 and lived for 76 years.

In Irving's story, Rip Van Winkle went to sleep for 20 years. When he woke up everything had changed. He almost didn't recognize his own family. Imagine going to sleep for 20 years and in your diary space write the story of what would happen when you woke up.

MAKE BOOKPLATES.

A Bookplate is a little label that's pasted inside the front cover of a book to identify you as the book's owner. It usually says something like...

THIS BOOK BELONGS TO

(1) On scratch paper plan how you'd like your design to look. USE...

A Symbol   A Drawing

MB your Initials

Whatever makes it specially yours!

(2) Use a ruler to make neat squares or rectangles on the best paper you have.

(3) Carefully cut them out with scissors.

(4) Draw your design and write your name with ink. Felt-tip pens are great. Or print a design with a rubber stamp or a potato (see May 13).

(5) Neatly glue or paste your bookplates inside your favorite books.

EX LIBRIS

(your name)

Dear Diary:

Dear Diary:

April 4
Go Fly a Kite Day

The most kites ever flown on a single kite string were flown on this date in 1976 by 52-year-old Kazuhiko Asaba in Kamakura, Japan. He flew 1,050 kites at once. Imagine even *having* 1,050 kites, much less being able to fly them all on one string! The kite at the top soared 4,000 feet above the earth. Flying kites is a part of spring celebrations around the world, especially in Japan and China.

Fly more than one kite.

Flying several kites on one line is sometimes difficult, but if you've never done it, it's worth a try. Ask a friend to help.

① First get one kite flying well so you don't have to pay much attention to keeping it in the air.

② Take the end of that kite's string and TIE it carefully to the intersection of the two sticks of the second kite.

③ Hold the line steady as you let the second kite go. It will jump around a bit and require some real kite-flying skill.

④ Add other kites in this same way.

There's a special club for kite lovers. For a membership card, send a self-addressed stamped envelope to: Kitefliers' Association International, 321 E. 48th St., New York, N.Y. 10017 (there are no fees or dues).

NEAT KITE TRICK

① CUT a circle out of a stiff piece of paper.

② PUNCH a hole in the center.

③ Using scissors, make a CUT from the edge of the paper to the hole

④ SLIP this disk onto your kite line and the wind will carry it up to your kite.

Dear Diary:

April 5
Movie Star Night

Today is the birthday of three very famous movie stars—Bette Davis, Gregory Peck, and Spencer Tracy. What better reason does anybody need to celebrate the movies?!

The annual Academy Awards presentation always takes place on a Monday early in April. Find out from a movie buff (or the newspaper) what movies and stars are nominated for the awards listed below. Write in who and what film you think will win.

Best Picture _____
Best Director _____
Best Actor _____
Best Actress _____
Best Supporting Actor _____
Best Supporting Actress _____

On Academy Awards Day, May 16, there's a place to write in who actually wins the Oscars this year.

Next time you watch a movie on TV, make it a real event by fixing a bowl of popcorn (see August 11). Instead of butter try sprinkling it with lemon juice or Parmesan cheese and salt. Dee-lish!

Dear Diary:

...GLUE IN A PICTURE OF YOUR FAVORITE MOVIE STAR

April 6
Houdini's Birthday

Harry Houdini could get out of anything (except, maybe, going to the dentist). He could escape from boxes nailed shut, strait jackets, jails, ropes, and handcuffs. Even devices specially designed to hold him never could. Houdini never failed to escape, not even once, so he's remembered as the greatest escapologist of all time.

Houdini, born on this date in 1874, was also considered the master magician of his time after he made a 10,000-pound elephant disappear on stage. He always said his tricks could be easily explained, but a 10,000-pound elephant?!

NOW YOU SEE ME...

NOW YOU DON'T!

Dear Diary:

HANDS OF HOUDINI Card Trick

Houdini entertained his friends with card tricks and simple (to him) feats of illusion. Here's one you can do:

1. Cut this shape out of stiff paper twice. Make sure that both "cards" are exactly the same size.

2. Show them to your audience. Put one on top of the other to show they're the same.

3. Now tell everybody you're going to stretch one card. Put the other one down. Make a show of pulling and stretching the card. Maybe throw in a magic word or two, like: "Longabadonga stretcheroo."

4. Hold the "stretched" card in your left hand this way:

♣ ♥   ♦ ♠

5. Now pick up the other card with your right hand, holding the two cards together like this:

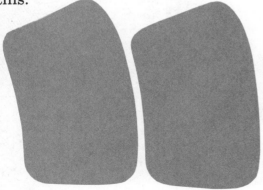

The card will look like it's been stretched! Your audience's eyes are playing tricks on them (optical illusion), but they'll think you've performed a "Houdini."

April 7
World Health Day

WH.O. stands for World Health Organization, and it is an agency of the United Nations. Its purpose is to build a world of healthier people. World Health Day is always observed on April 7.

Good health quiz.

Solve this puzzle by following the clues through the pages of *Amazing Days*.

Take a [ ][ ] H each day. (Feb. 23)

[ ] E [ ][ ][ ][ ][ ] (Feb. 28)

Drink lots of [ ] A [ ][ ][ ][ ] (April 25)

[ ] L [ ][ ] (Jan. 16)

Eat a balanced [ ][ ][ ] T (Mar. 23)

Brush your [ ][ ][ ][ ] H (mar. 9)

Dear Diary:

Answers appear at the back of the book.

April 8
The Flower Festival

In Japan, where many people are of the Buddhist religion, April 8 is celebrated as Buddha's birthday. There are parades and singing and many, many spring flowers. That's why it's known as Hana Matsuri, the flower festival. Legend says that when Buddha was born flower petals fell from the sky so everywhere are huge paper floral decorations and people who visit Buddhist shrines bring fresh flowers.

Make tissue paper flowers.

String them together to make garlands. Decorate windows, doors, and picture frames with the garlands.

Decorate with flowers.

Arrange real flowers in vases and put them where lots of folks will see and enjoy them.

Dear Diary:

PLANT FLOWER SEEDS.

If you live where danger of frost is over now, you can plant your seeds outside. If you live elsewhere, don't take a chance. Here's how to plant your flowers indoors:

① USE a shallow container- a cut-down milk carton, egg carton, or whatever.

② Soil at least 1-inch deep →

③ PLANT seeds by pack directions. Marigolds, zinnias, and cosmos start well indoors.

④ MOISTEN soil well, but don't fill it with water.

⑤ Put the container inside a clear plastic bag and seal it tightly. The bag is a little greenhouse. It keeps the moisture in and heats up so the seeds germinate quickly.

⑥ PUT the whole greenhouse in a sunny window.

⑦ WATCH it every day. After a week or two you may need to add more water. ugh!

⑧ WHAT NEXT? For a sneak preview see April 28.

Keep track of your gardening in *Amazing Days*. When do the seeds come up?

April 9

First Free Public Library in U.S.

Where can you browse for as long as you like then take whatever you like home—for free? *The Public Library*. It's the best deal in town. Just tell the librarian what you'd like to read about (monsters? motorcycles? insects? outer space?) and he or she will make plenty of suggestions.

The first free public library in the U.S. was established in Peterboro, New Hampshire, on April 9, 1833.

Visit your public library.

Do you have a library card yet? They are easy to get. The librarian will want to know your name and age and where you live and then you'll be given a temporary card which will allow you to take almost any book you like for two weeks or more. Your permanent card will arrive in the mail soon after.

RECYCLE favorite pictures, stickers, and cartoons by pasting them on a strip of colored paper to use as a bookmark. (This might be a nice gift to enclose in a birthday card.)

Dear Diary:

April 10

Pets' Birthday Party

Many pets don't get to celebrate their birthdays. Many owners don't even know when their pets' birthdays are. So today's as good a day as any to sing "Happy Birthday" to them. Give them something special to eat, but most important of all, give your pets lots of attention and affection today—the best birthday present of all.

Draw a picture of your pet here.

If you don't have a real one, imagine the pet you'd like to have and draw it. Maybe something completely imaginary like a dragon, dinosaur, or *Bigfoot*!

The American Society for the Prevention of Cruelty to Animals was chartered on April 10, 1866. Founded by Henry Bergh, the A.S.P.C.A. still works to protect animals and offers shelters and adoption services for those that are lost or unwanted.

Dear Diary:

GEE WHIZ! FOR ME?

April 11
Jackie Robinson Day

Did someone say "Jack Robinson?" Jackie Robinson was one of the best all-around athletes ever. In high school and college, he played baseball, football, basketball, *and* ran track. He won a letter in each sport.

In 1947 he joined the Brooklyn Dodgers and became the first black player in American major league baseball. Robinson helped win six National League pennants in the 10 years he played with the Dodgers. In 1955 he helped defeat the New York Yankees in the World Series. He was voted into the Baseball Hall of Fame in 1962.

Make a pennant for your room.

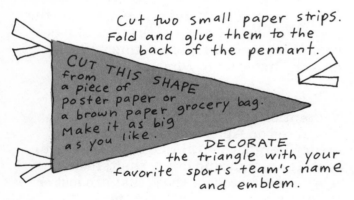

Cut two small paper strips. Fold and glue them to the back of the pennant.

CUT THIS SHAPE from a piece of poster paper or a brown paper grocery bag. Make it as big as you like.

DECORATE the triangle with your favorite sports team's name and emblem.

Dear Diary:

April 12
Picture-perfect Celebration

Imogen Cunningham, born April 12, 1883, was 18 years old when she decided to become a photographer. She bought an inexpensive camera and started taking pictures. She kept taking pictures for 75 years, and what beautiful pictures they are! She's most famous for close-ups of plants and people, but Cunningham said once that she would photograph "anything that could be exposed to light."

Make photo portraits.

FIND a photo booth, the 50-cent type (maybe 75-cent) that gives you four pics. (They're usually in dime stores, "penny arcades," or, for some reason, bus stations.)

Be zany! Wear a costume, a big floppy hat and sunglasses.
Be wild! Make faces. Blow kisses.
If you can't find a photo booth, ask a friend to take silly pictures of you.

Dear Diary:

April 13
Guess-Who's Birthday

Who was an architect, farmer, inventor, scientist, writer of the Declaration of Independence, and president of the United States all rolled into one? Hint: He was born April 13, 1743, in Virginia.

Need more hints? His picture is on the face of a U.S. nickel and his famous home is on the back. In 1783 the mystery person suggested to Congress that the decimal system be used for U.S. currency. His birthday is always followed by National Coin Week, the third week of April. Give up?

Collect nickels.

1. Look through your piggy bank and sort out the nickels. See if you can find a 1943 nickel. (1943 was the 200th anniversary of "guess-who's" birth.)
2. Go to a bank with a dollar bill and ask a teller to exchange it for 20 nickels. How many different years can you find?
3. If you get really interested you can get a nickel folder in which to keep one coin of each different date and "mint." Folders are available at most dime stores or hobby shops.

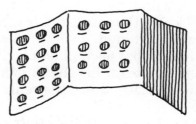

4. Some nickels, because they're old or rare, are worth much more than five cents. For more information about numismatics (the study of collection of coins) write to: American Numismatic Association, P.O. Box 2366, Colorado Springs, Colorado 80901. Ask for the free booklet, "Welcome to Coin Collecting."

Dear Diary:

April 14
Dictionary Day

Do you know what a lexicographer is? Noah Webster was one and you can find out the meaning of the word by looking it up in his dictionary. Webster's first major dictionary was published on this date in 1828.

Play dictionary.

This game needs at least four players, a dictionary, and a pencil and slips of paper for each player. The more the better — grown-ups too.

1. Choose an *It* by the "Eeny, meeny, miny, mo method. *It* finds a word in the dictionary of which he or she is quite sure nobody will know the meaning. *It* reads and spells the word out loud.

2. On a slip of paper each player writes the word and whatever he/she *thinks* the word means. *It* writes down the real definition.

3. All players hand their slips to *It*.

4. *It* numbers the definitions (including the real one) then reads them out loud.

5. Each player then says which definition he/she thinks is the real one.

6. After everyone guesses, *It* gives one point to each correct player. The player with the most points then becomes *It*. The player who reaches 15 points first wins.

Dear Diary:

April 15
Invitation Day

There's a party planned for April 20. Look ahead to see what it's about. You may want to send invitations. Here's one idea:

① CUT a fat bat out of black paper. (You can use these bats for party decorations too.)

② PAINT the eyes with yellow or green tempera paint.

③ PRINT the invitation in white ink (available in most dime stores.)

④ To mail in an envelope, fold the bat's wings in front of him, like a cape. His eyes should still show.

(This bat also makes a fun birthday card for someone born on April 20.)

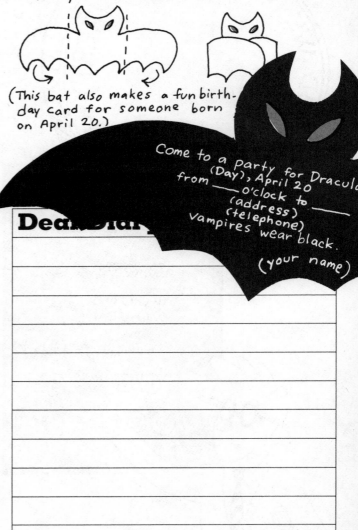

Come to a party for Dracula.
(Day), April 20
from ____ o'clock to ____
(address)
(telephone)
Vampires wear black.

(your name)

Dear Diary:

April 16
Silent Day

Have you ever seen a silent movie? Until 1927 and the first commercially successful talkie, "The Jazz Singer," almost all movies were silent. Silent films aren't often shown anymore, but silent movie stars are remembered and one especially—Charlie Chaplin. His movies are still enjoyed by those who love to laugh.

Charlie Chaplin, born April 16, 1889, has charmed millions of people with his character called "The Tramp" or "The Little Fellow." People laughed and cried over "The Tramp's" misadventures and Charlie never had to say a word to communicate joy, humor, sorrow, or tragedy to his audience.

Play the silent game.

See how few words you can say today. Like Charlie Chaplin, use your hands, eyes, expressions, body, to express yourself. Sometimes you'll have to speak. If today is a schoolday just play this game before and after school and during lunch break. Write down the things you *had* to say in your diary.

April 17
Eat More Pineapple-Cheese Day

In April 17, 1808, the first pineapple cheese was created by Lewis Mills Norton in Troy, Pennsylvania. Good for you, Lew!

Pineapple-cheese Tooth-Ticklers

CUBE your favorite cheese (Cheddar, Swiss, or Muenster are tasty!)

CUBE fresh or canned pineapple.

On a toothpick SPEAR a cube of each.

If you use fresh pineapple you can plant the top - it'll grow into a beautiful plant.

Leave on about 1-inch of the fruit.

where's the cheese?

PLANT almost up to the leaves. PLACE it in a sunny window.

WATER by sprinkling into the leaves. They hold water. Keep them full most of the time.

LOOSE SANDY SOIL

r Diary:

Cut a circle out of cardboard and write this message.→ Wear it with a safety pin.

I AM BEING **SILENT** TODAY TO CELEBRATE THE BIRTHDAY OF CHARLIE CHAPLIN

Dear Diary:

April 18
Paul Revere's Midnight Ride, 1775

Paul Revere was a great silversmith and made such beautiful spoons and teapots and cream pitchers that some silversmiths nowadays copy his designs. In museums you can sometimes see things that Paul Revere made, especially in New England. But the reason most people remember Paul Revere is not that he was a fine silversmith. On

April 18, 1775, Paul made his famous ride in Massachusetts, from Boston to Lexington, to warn Samuel Adams and John Hancock and the people of the countryside that the British soldiers were on their way. The next day the Battle of Concord and Lexington would begin and so too the War of Independence.

Help Paul Revere get to Lexington.

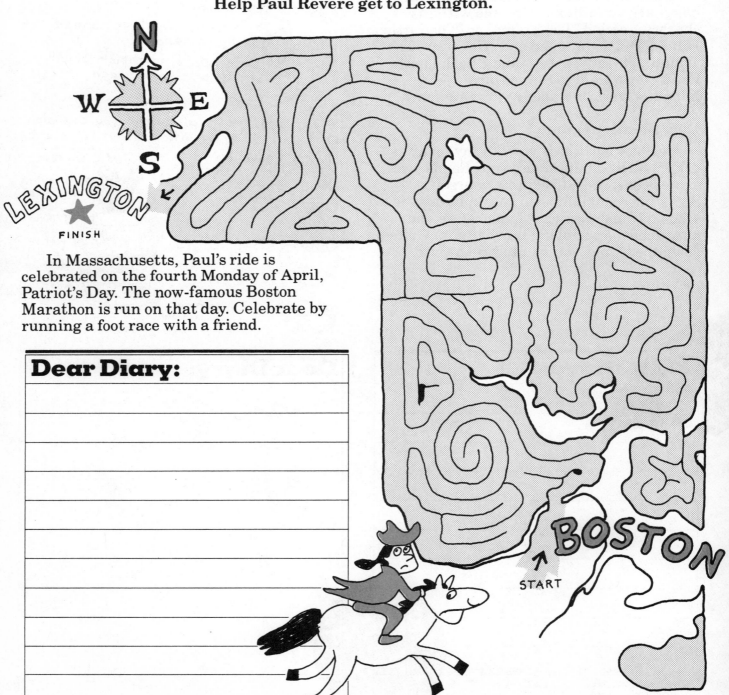

N
W E
S

LEXINGTON
★
FINISH

In Massachusetts, Paul's ride is celebrated on the fourth Monday of April, Patriot's Day. The now-famous Boston Marathon is run on that day. Celebrate by running a foot race with a friend.

START

BOSTON

Dear Diary:

Feast of the Long Loaf

On April 19, 1975, a loaf of bread 400 feet long was baked in Idaho. What a sandwich that must have made!

Make a long, long lunch.

All over America people eat sandwiches made on long loaves of bread (usually not quite 400 feet long!). They're called subs (submarines), torpedoes, hoagies, grinders, po'boys, heroes, and about as many other names as there are places to eat them. Make up a great name for the sandwich you make:

_____

1. First decide whom to invite over to share your sandwich.
2. At a grocery or bakery buy a loaf of bread long enough to make one sandwich to

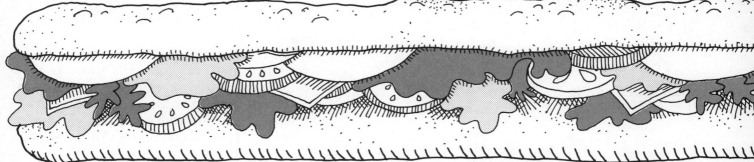

feed everybody you invite—not big around, just long. Italian bread sometimes comes as long as 32 inches!
3. Slice the loaf lengthwise leaving a "hinge of crust" and open it up flat.
4. Spread the bread with your favorite dressing—mustard, mayonnaise, or Russian.
5. Arrange your favorite sandwich ingredients in layers on one side of the loaf. Use shredded lettuce, sliced tomatoes, pickles, onions, and hard-boiled eggs, hot peppers, sliced provolone or other favorite cheese, sprouts, olives, cucumber strips, and whatever else will make it long on taste.
6. Close the sandwich and invite your friends and family to see your masterpiece.
7. Then cut it into as many equal parts as there are hungry guests. Serve your long, lovely lunch with lemonade.

Dear Diary:

"Velcome to my castle..."

That's what to say when you greet your guests for Dracula's house party. (Bram Stoker, who wrote *Dracula*, the most famous of all vampire stories, died on April 20, 1912.)

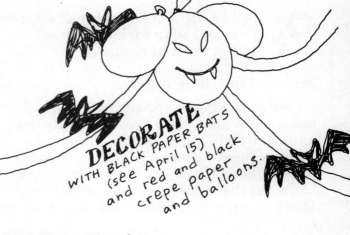

Vant to drink some BLOOD vith me?

DECORATE WITH BLACK PAPER BATS (see April 15) and red and black crepe paper and balloons.

Serve **RED PUNCH**

Serve **STRAWBERRY COFFINS** Sandwich bread cut into coffin shapes and spread with butter and strawberry jam

Serve **BLACK LAGOON MONSTER EYES** pitted prunes stuffed with cream cheese and topped with a raisin

Do **NOT** SERVE GARLIC BREAD. (vampires <u>hate</u> garlic!)

Make extra sets of vampire fangs for your friends who come without them. (March 9)

Remember: vampires have no reflection so cover all the mirrors in your house to save them embarrassment. Drape them with towels.

Stay away Drac!

One way people used to keep away vampires was to scatter mustard seeds on their roofs. Supposedly if a vampire saw some mustard seeds he'd have to stop and count each one. People scattered so many seeds that counting them would take all night (by dawn a vampire has to return to its grave).

Fill a small jar with dried beans (who has mustard seeds anymore?). Count as you go. Write down the correct number and keep it in a secret place. Let all your guests write down their guesses. Give a prize to the one who comes closest to the correct number of beans.

Dear Diary:

Taurus Begins

People born between April 21 and May 20 are born under the sign of Taurus, the bull. According to astrologers they are friendly, warmhearted, down-to-earth people. They like to be comfortable and surrounded by nice things, but they care little for luxury.

People born under Taurus are sometimes slow to do things (they have a lazy streak, but who doesn't?!). But, once they've begun something, they always finish it. They're good at building things and doing research and working out math problems—at least *some* of them are.

They're not talkative, but Taurus people make great friends.

List all the people you know born under the sign of Taurus. Which ones seem to fit the description?

Taurus cards.

This is the symbol of Taurus. Turn it into a picture of a bull by adding a face and body. Use your bull picture on the front of birthday cards for your Taurus friends. Inside write, "It's your birthday, Taurus. *Bully* for you!"

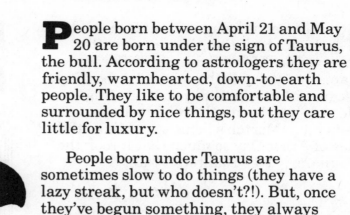

Dear Diary:

April 22
Arbor Day

Arbor Day is a day to plant trees and to think about their importance. It is observed on different dates in different states, but today is the *original* Arbor Day because it's the birthday of J. Sterling Morton, who began the celebration in 1872. Nebraska (Morton's home state) liked the idea of Arbor Day so much that it took the nickname, "Tree Planters' State."

A citrus tree will grow very well INDOORS in a sunny window. If you can't plant a tree OUTDOORS try this ——→

PLANT A CITRUS TREE.

① EAT a grapefruit, orange, tangerine, or lemon - ICK! - well, lemonade then!

② SAVE THE SEEDS

③ DON'T LET THEM DRY OUT. Put them in warm (not hot) water and LET THEM SOAK OVERNIGHT.

④ PLANT SEED ½-inch deep

Keep soil moist.

Rocks for drainage →

Potting soil with sand added.

⑤ BE PATIENT.

⑥ After several weeks one of the seeds you planted is bound to show its green head.

SING HAPPY BIRTHDAY!

NAME IT!

Keep a record of its growth in this journal.

KEEP IT MOIST AND SUNNY and you may watch it grow for the REST of YOUR LIFE!

April 23
Shakespeare Day

William Shakespeare was born in England on this date in 1564. He grew up to be a wonderful poet and perhaps the greatest playwright of all time. He wrote *Hamlet, Macbeth, Romeo and Juliet,* and many other plays which, even though they are 400 years old, are still performed quite often.

Put on a play.

Get together some friends who like to act (and who doesn't?) and turn your favorite story into a play. Use your house and yard as a stage. A second floor window becomes Juliet's balcony, a staircase becomes a snow-covered mountain, a closet becomes a pirate's cave. USE YOUR IMAGINATION. Have fun - after all it is a PLAY!!!

If you want to try a real Shakespeare production look into <u>Tales</u> <u>from</u> <u>Shakespeare</u> by Charles and Mary Lamb (especially for kids!).

April 24
First Soda Fountain Patented, 1833

Come on down to the so-dee fountain," kids used to say to each other. Some towns still have soda fountains in dime stores and pharmacies. They used to be popular hangouts for kids after school in almost every town. What was the big attraction? Well, come on down to the so-dee fountain and see.

Fix a soda fountain treat.

1. Start with two scoops of vanilla ice cream in a tall glass.

2. Add sliced strawberries.

3. Add some club soda.

4. Add a straw *and* a spoon, and dig in.

Experiment. Use sherbet, other sliced fruits, fruit juice instead of milk, or soda, cinnamon or nutmeg on top or powdered chocolate drink. Add nuts!

Dear Diary:

Dear Diary:

Amazing Daily

MAYFLOWERS EXPECTED

Amazing Daily's weather forecaster, Ms. April Showers, predicts more rain this month. Cloudy today, wet tomorrow, baby showers expected on Tuesday, floods on Wednesday. "When it rains it pours," says Ms. Showers. "If you live in a two-story building, better stay upstairs for awhile. But remember, April showers bring Mayflowers!" Ms. Showers could not explain what spring rain has to do with the Pilgrims. "Leave well enough alone. Every cloud has a silver lining," says our trusty forecaster, known for her thoughtful and original way of speaking.

Cover a card table with a blanket to make a rainy day fort.

Lightning—Near or Far?

According to Dr. Felicity Flannegan, anyone can figure out in a flash how far away lightning is. Says Flannegan, "When you see the light start counting — one-one thousand, two-one thousand, three-one thousand, and so on till you hear the thunder. If you get to three-one thousand, the lightning was about three miles away; six-one thousand, it was about six miles away; etc. If you don't even get to one-one thousand, just be glad you weren't standing on the roof!"

April 26
A Day in the Park

Two very important men associated with the Great Outdoors have birthdays today.

John James Audubon, famous for his book, *Birds of America*, was born in 1785. He devoted his life to drawing and painting pictures of animals, especially birds, with incredible attention to detail. His pictures became so well known that his name itself came to be associated with caring for wildlife; one of the largest conservation organizations in America is called the National Audubon Society.

Frederick Law Olmsted, America's first landscape architect, was born in 1822. He is most famous for designing Central Park in New York City, but he also designed the grounds of the U.S. Capitol in Washington, D.C., and parks in other great cities in the U.S. and Canada. People still enjoy the parks and public places Olmsted designed.

Dear Diary:

Dear Diary:

April 27
Dot-Dash Day

Visit a park. Be a bird-watcher.
Take this list with you and check the birds you see or hear.

☐ Goldfinch
(bright yellow with black wings)

☐ Woodpecker
(ratta-tat-tat-tat)

☐ Catbird
(gray; sounds like a cat)

☐ Chickadee
(says its name: chick-a-dee-dee-dee)

☐ Blue jay

☐ Robin

☐ Pigeon

☐ Crow

☐ Sea gull

☐ Duck

☐ Swan

Not many people know that the inventor of the electric telegraph was an artist. But that's exactly what Samuel F. B. Morse was. Born April 27, 1791, he became a fine portrait painter and was 40 years old before he even got interested in things electrical.

Still, he's best remembered for inventing the telegraph and creating the International Morse Code, both of which are still used today.

•—	—•••	—•—•	—••	•	••—•	——•	••••	••
A	B	C	D	E	F	G	H	I

•———	—•—	•—••	——	—•	———	•——•	——•—	•—•
J	K	L	M	N	O	P	Q	R

•••	—	••—	•••—	•——	—••—	—•——	——••
S	T	U	V	W	X	Y	Z

Send a Morse code message.

At night, you can send a Morse message with light. You need two flashlights.
1. Cover one with red cellophane (a rubber band will hold it in place).
2. Put the lights side by side pointing toward your friend who's receiving the message.
3. Flash red for a dot, white for a dash.
4. Go slowly so your friend can write down the letters as he "reads" them.

Leave three dots' worth of time between letters, five between words.

Dear Diary:

April 28
Spring Gardening Day

Celebrate spring with a garden. It doesn't have to be big to be beautiful. A "postage stamp" flower bed could be only a foot square with three lettuce plants and two marigolds, yet give a summerful of pleasure.

Did you plant flower seeds on April 8? If you did, here's something important to remember: your seedlings have spent their whole lives in a "greenhouse." You must let them get used to being outdoors, where they'll spend the summer, a little at a time.

Open the bag, but leave the little plants inside the greenhouse for at least a day.

Take the plants outside for several hours each day for about a week, but don't leave them out at night.

FINALLY they're ready to be planted in the ground. Summer's not far away now!

Dear Diary:

April 29
Almost Lei Day

May Day, Lei Day,
Aloha's-what-you-say Day

The day after tomorrow is Lei Day in Hawaii. Lei (pronounced "lay") is the Hawaiian word for garland. In the fiftieth state garlands of flowers are given to say "welcome" or "farewell."

Leis were originally made of brightly colored feathers and worn by Hawaiian kings and queens. They've also been made of seashells, nuts, leaves, and berries. On Lei Day many people wear leis, and there are shows, festivals, and even contests for the most beautiful and unusual leis.

MAKE a LEI!
1. String together real flowers. Use clover, dandelions, violets, or any kind you can find.
2. Cut the stems fairly short.
3. Double-thread a needle with strong thread. Push the needle up through the stem and through the center of the flower.
4. Add another flower. Repeat. Repeat. Repeat . . .
5. When the lei is long enough to fit easily over your head, tie the two ends together with a strong knot.

Dear Diary:

April 30
Walpurgis Night

People who study folklore say that Walpurgis Night (or May Eve) is the first of three great festivals that fairies celebrate in the year: Midsummer Eve, June 23, and Halloween (October 31) are the other two. Usually on May Eve the fairies dance and sing to welcome back warm weather.

Tonight, in Sweden, huge bonfires will be burned on the tops of hills and mountains. Back in Viking times the fires were lit to frighten away the demons of darkness. Now people dance around them, singing spring songs.

MAKE A MAY BASKET

make a little basket tonight for each person you want to surprise on May Day.

① CUT A PIECE OF PAPER like this. COLOR a rainbow around the top.

② ROLL it into a cone.

③ TAPE or STAPLE it to hold it's shape.

④ TAPE or STAPLE a ribbon, string, or paper handle so the baskets can be hung on your friends' doorknobs.

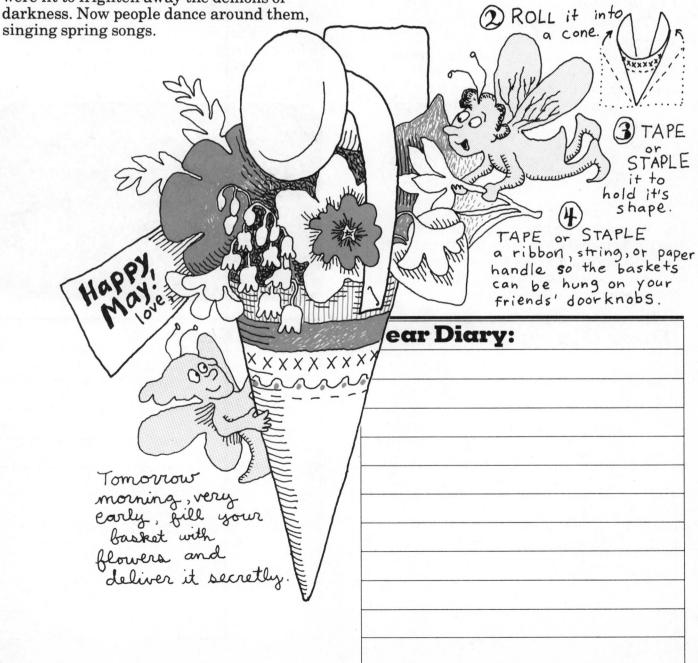

Happy May! love

Tomorrow morning, very early, fill your basket with flowers and deliver it secretly.

ear Diary:

May 1
May Day

After you've left your May baskets on doorknobs (maybe your brother's, sister's or parent's bedroom knob) find an early-bird grown-up to help make a "May breakfast." May breakfasts are popular in New England where people get together with family and friends to enjoy a meal and celebrate spring. These are often held in community halls, schools, and such, but your own kitchen will do just fine.

Fry bananas.

These bananas make your May breakfast really delicious.
1. Slice each banana in half lengthwise.
2. For each whole banana, melt half a tablespoon of butter in a frying pan.
3. Arrange the banana slices in the pan like this:

4. Fry them over medium heat.
5. When they're brown and caramelly on the bottom (10-15 minutes) turn them with a spatula and fry the other side.

Also, be sure to wear your lei (from April 29) at your special breakfast.

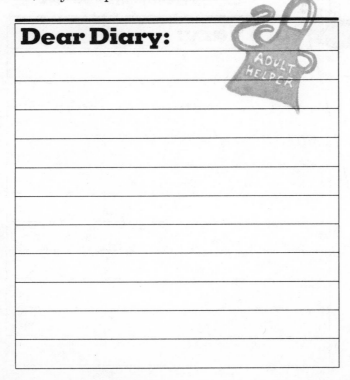

Dear Diary:

May 2
Backwards Day

Leonardo da Vinci was *anything* but backwards, and in fact, he has been called "the man 500 years ahead of his time." Born in 1452 in Italy, (he died on May 2, 1519) Leonardo grew up to be both a scientist and an artist, and one of the most brilliant men in history. He painted the famous *Last Supper* and the *Mona Lisa*. He kept notebooks, 5,000 pages of them, filled with his thoughts, observations, sketches, and designs. Among the things he designed way back then were airplanes, helicopters, and submarines.

No one is sure why, but Leonardo wrote in his notebooks *backwards*. Maybe he didn't want others to read his private writings.

Try Leonardo's backward writing! Hold Amazing Days up to a mirror and write. Nobody will be able to read it but YOU.

Dear Diary:

May 3
Sun Day

When was Sun Day on a Wednesday? In 1978, when Sun Day was held for the first time. The idea was to make people aware of the many ways solar energy could be used. All over North America homes and businesses that are heated and cooled by the sun's energy were opened to the public. There were also sunrise celebrations, kite-flying events, and all sorts of fun to salute our nearest star, the sun.

Watch the sun set tonight. What time did it disappear? _____
Look back to January 10 and 23, Compare the times.

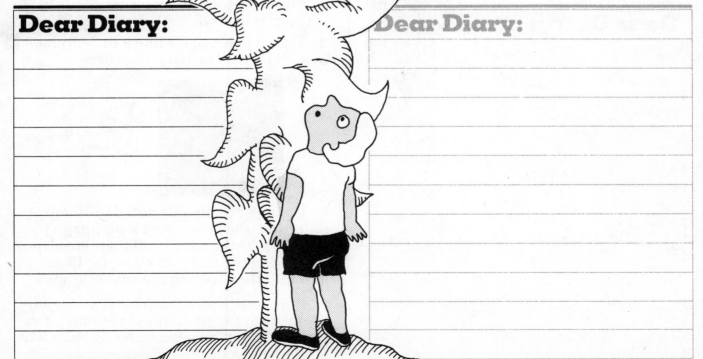

PLANT A SUNFLOWER
a sunflower actually turns to follow the sun, facing east in the morning and west in the afternoon. If all danger of frost is over, plant your sunflower seeds OUTSIDE in a very sunny spot. If the weather's still too cold, plant them in a pot on a sunny windowsill and transplant them outdoors later. SUNFLOWER SEEDS ARE SOMETIMES SHELLED AND TOASTED TO EAT. YOU can find them that way at the grocery. For a treat, sprinkle them on a grilled cheese sandwich or a green salad!!!

May 4
Invisible Ink Day

During the American Revolution invisible ink was often used by people who wanted to make sure their messages stayed secret. John Jay, an American leader, wrote to his brother in London, writing secret info in invisible ink between the lines of an innocent-looking letter. According to some sources, May 4, 1776 was the first day invisible ink was used in diplomatic correspondence. But, we can't be sure; after all, it was *secret*!

Write an invisible message.

1. For ink use lemon juice, orange juice, grapefruit juice, milk, or grated-onion juice (smelly message!).
2. Use a very clean drawing pen or a toothpick to write. Dip it in the ink after every three or four letters you write. Don't use shiny paper. The ink won't soak in and become invisible. Let ink dry.
3. Hold the message next to a 60-watt (or higher) light bulb and your words will appear. When you send a message to a friend, be sure they know how to make the writing visible.

Dear Diary:

Dear Diary:

May 5
Feast of Flags

Today is Kodomo-no-hi, Children's Day in Japan, also called the Feast of Flags (or Banners). Tall poles are set up near Japanese houses and red and black flags in the shape of fish are flown from them. They look a lot like kites. There's one flag for each boy in the family; the biggest one, at the top, may be as long as 15 feet and is for the oldest son. This day used to be called Boy's Day (March 3 was Girl's Day). Now that it's Children's Day, maybe families will start flying flags for girls too!

Make a banner.

① CUT the bottom from a brown paper grocery bag.

② Make one cut through the bag and flatten it out to a long rectangle.

③ FOLD top of banner over a coat hanger and fasten with tape.

④ Use wrapping paper, newspaper, foil, etc. to cut out main shapes for your design.

Tempera paint is great too.

Make any design you like

use your initials.

Trim this edge.

Dear Diary:

May 6
Penny Black's Birthday

Here's a question to stump the smartest history buff you know: Penny Black, born May 6, 1840, in Great Britain, started something that quickly spread to almost every country in the world, eventually becoming the world's most popular hobby? Who was she?

The question is a tricky one. "Penny Black" was the world's first postage stamp. It was printed in black and cost a penny and was first issued on this day in 1840. And what's the world's most popular hobby? Why stamp collecting, of course!

So YOU're Penny Black!

ONE PENNY

Start a stamp collection.

1. Look through the mail delivered to your home today. Any stamp on an envelope that is going to be thrown away can be the first stamp in your collection.

2. Cut the whole stamp corner of the envelope off.

3. Trim it down so it's like a little frame around the stamp and glue it here:

My First Stamp

4. If you get really interested in stamp collecting (the fancy word is *philately*) you'll want to take the stamps off their envelopes by soaking them in cold water for 15 minutes, then peeling the envelope away.

5. Philatelists use stamp hinges instead of glue to put their stamps in albums. You can buy stamp hinges at a hobby shop. They don't cost much.

6. Collect stamps on a special subject—animals, outer space, famous people, history, or whatever interests *you*. Use *Amazing Days* as your first album.

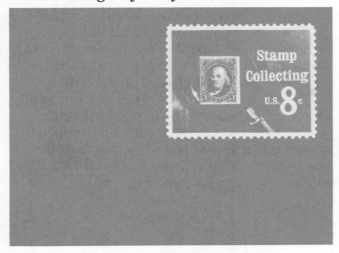

7. Go to your local post office. The folks there will be of help.

8. Let your friends and relatives know you collect stamps. They may save envelopes for you.

9. For more information write to: Detjen Philatelic News Service, P.O. Box 150, Clinton Corners, New York 12514. Ask for the free pamphlet "The Fascination of Stamp Collecting."

Today definitely has rhythm. It's the birthday of composers Johannes Brahms (1833) and Peter Ilyitch Tchaikovsky (1840) and poets Robert Browning (1812) and Archibald MacLeish (1892). What composers and poets have in common is a love of sound and rhythm.

What *is* rhythm? Put your hand on your heart and feel the steady beat, beat, beat. That's rhythm. You can often clap to the rhythm of music and poetry.

Play "Archibald's Cat," a rhythm game.

1. At least four people sit in a circle.
2. Everybody starts a simple rhythm together: Slap knees twice then clap hands twice. Knees, knees, *hands*, *hands*, knees, knees, *hands*, *hands* . . . and so on.
3. Now one person says "Archibald's cat is an awful* cat" (*or any adjective beginning with A which has two beats—aw·ful).
4. The next person clockwise in the circle must say, "Archibald's cat is a *bossy** cat," (*or any adjective beginning with B which has two beats) and so on through the alphabet always keeping the rhythm.
5. Whoever can't keep up or can't think of an adjective is "out." The last person "in" the game is the winner.

Dear Diary:

Dear Diary:

AN
X... X...
X-tatic
CAT!

May 8

International Red Cross Day

The Red Cross is an international organization that works to relieve human suffering whenever and wherever war or natural disaster strikes.

Jean Henri Dunant, whose birthday is today, founded the Red Cross in 1863. He reversed the colors of his country's flag to create the international symbol of his new organization. To find out what country has a red flag with a white cross, unscramble these letters.

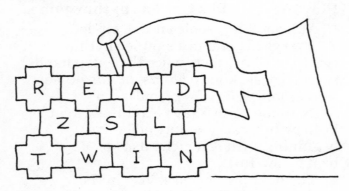

READ
ZSL
TWIN

The famous nurse Clara Barton established the American Red Cross in 1881 and served as its first president.

Of special interest to kids: local Red Cross chapters offer courses in swimming, water safety, and first aid. Call for more info.

Dear Diary:

May 9

Peter Pan Day

All children, except one, grow up," said Sir James M. Barrie. He was referring to Peter Pan, whose story was first told by Barrie, born on this date in 1860.

Peter Pan lives on the magic island of Never-Never Land. Almost all kids, whether they've read *Peter Pan* or not, are familiar with its dangerous, beautiful forests, Mermaid Lagoon, pirate ship docked in a hidden inlet, Indian camp, and the underground home of the Lost Boys. That's because Barrie managed to capture the adventure that lives in all kids and make it into a story (and a play) that still enchants kids and grown-ups alike.

Make your own map of Never-Never Land.

Be sure to show where the pirates hid their treasure and where the mermaids live; Peter too. Draw the map with waterproof black ink (India ink is great) on onionskin paper or the thinnest paper you can find. Let your drawing dry completely. An hour later make a cup of strong tea. Crumple the map, then flatten it out in a shallow pan and pour the tea over it. Let it stay in the tea for about 15 minutes; the tea will make the crumpling show up and darken the whole map, making it look really old. Let the map dry on a sunny windowsill.

The first Mother's Day was held on May 10, 1908, in Grafton, West Virginia. It was Anna Jarvis's idea, and the first celebration was a church service in memory of her own mother who had died three years earlier. The idea caught on quickly all over America, and in 1914 President Woodrow Wilson proclaimed the second Sunday of May as Mother's Day. And so it's been ever since.

Interview your mom.

Sit down and really talk to your mother. Find out things you don't know and write them in the diary space below. Where was she born, what year? What was her maiden name? What was she like as a girl? What games did she play? Did she get in trouble with *her* parents? What for? What jobs has she had? What's her job like now? If she could change anything about her life, what would it be? What are her plans for the future?

Glue a snapshot of your mom here, or draw her portrait.

Dear Diary:

Dear Diary:

May 11
Feast of the Ice Saints

Brrr! For centuries people in central Europe have noticed a sudden drop in temperature on May 11, 12, and 13. And because those are the feast days of the Christian saints Mamertus, Pancras, and Gervais, they're called the Ice Saints. So if it suddenly gets chilly outside you can thank St. Mamertus, the first of the Ice Saints. At least that's what farmers in France and Germany say.

FEAST ON ICE

How can ice be a feast? When it's fruity ice it can! Try this! Fill an ice tray with fruit juice. Orange, grape, cranberry, pineapple, or lemonade. The freezer does the trick, but don't even peek for 8 hours. Put the fruity cubes in a glass. Add more juice for a frosty treat.

Pay particular attention to the weather over the next three days and record the temperatures in your diary.
Are you ready for a cool spell?

Dear Diary:

May 12
Mr. Lear's Limerick Day

There was a young lady whose nose
Continually prospers and grows;
When it grew out of sight,
She exclaimed in a fright,
"Oh! Farewell to the end of my nose!"

That silly rhyme was written by the lord of limericks Edward Lear, born in England, May 12, 1812. He published *A Book of Nonsense* in 1846—a whole book of limericks with his own funny illustrations. As well as writing nonsense, Lear was a writer of travel books and a landscape painter. He was even Queen Victoria's drawing teacher!

Write something silly.

First read the limerick above several times till you get used to the rhythm. Remember, a limerick always has *five* lines; the first two lines rhyme, the second two lines rhyme, and the fifth line rhymes with the first two.

There once was a kid from _____ ,
Who liked to eat honey and _____ .
  When asked why, he replied,
  "cause it sticks well inside,
And I don't want my stomach _____ ."

Dear Diary:

BRRR

May 13

Homage to the Prints Day

On this date in 1821 the Washington Press, America's first practical printing press, was patented by Samuel Rust of New York City. It was such a good design that over 150 years later machines of this type are still used in some places.

Make prints with potatoes.

1. Carefully cut a potato into pieces about 1½ inches thick.

2. Now cut those pieces into simple shapes.

3. Pour tempera paint into a dish and in it soak several layers of paper towels. This will be your "paint pad."

4. Press a potato stamp onto the paint pad and print it on paper.

5. Make pictures using all your stamps. Decorate wrapping paper, cards, book covers, or anything.

Dear Diary:

Who's the ruler of the vegetable garden?

The potato prints (prince)

May 14

Fahrenheit Day

The Ice Saints are gone now and with them, we hope, the last of cold weather (at least till fall). Did you check the temperature? If you did you probably used a mercury thermometer like the one invented in 1714 by German physicist Gabriel Daniel Fahrenheit whose birthday is today. Fahrenheit also created the temperature scale that bears his name.

The U.S., Canada, and England still use the Fahrenheit scale, but most countries use Celsius, named for the Swedish astronomer who introduced *that* scale in 1742.

Some Equivalents

Here's a simple but useful gift for someone who likes to cook—a little chart that shows oven temperatures in Fahrenheit (F) and Celsius (C). Print the information clearly on an index card and add your own decorations.

Oven Temperatures in Degrees		
	F	C
very slow oven	250-275	120-135
slow oven	300-325	150-165
moderate oven	350-375	175-190
hot oven	400-425	200-220
very hot oven	450-475	230-245

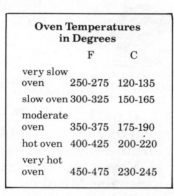

Dear Diary:

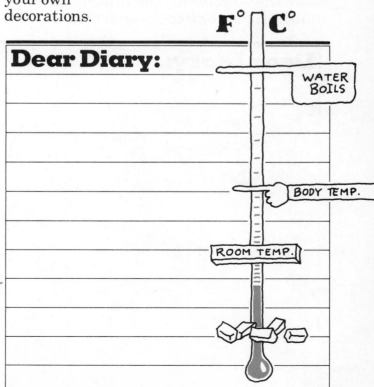

F° C°

WATER BOILS

BODY TEMP.

ROOM TEMP.

May 15
Over the Rainbow Day

The Wonderful Wizard of Oz, was written in 1900 by L. Frank Baum (who was born on this date in 1856). It became popular right away and kids clamored for more. So Baum wrote 13 more Oz books, and after he died in 1919 other writers continued to make imaginary trips over the rainbow.

Make a pair of Oz shoes.

Not ruby slippers; rainbow sneakers!

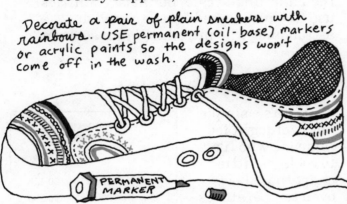

Decorate a pair of plain sneakers with rainbows. USE permanent (oil-base) markers or acrylic paints so the designs won't come off in the wash.

PERMANENT MARKER

If you love *The Wizard of Oz* here's something you might be interested in: The International Wizard of Oz Club, Fred M. Meyer, Secretary, 220 North 11th St., Escanaba, Michigan 49829.

Write for information. (Among other things, the club offers full-color maps of Oz.)

Dear Diary:

May 16
Academy Award Day

There are many people who claim to have given the Academy Awards statuette the name "Oscar." Here's one of the popular versions of the story: When the little statues were delivered to the Academy of Motion Picture Arts and Sciences, the secretary there took one look at them and said, "Why, they look just like my Uncle Oscar!" The award has been called Oscar ever since.

Although they are usually on a different day each year, the Academy Awards were first presented on May 16, 1929. Here's a place to write in who won Oscars this year:

Best Picture _____

Best Director _____

Best Actor _____

Best Actress _____

Best Supporting Actor _____

Best Supporting Actress _____

WRITE A LETTER TO YOUR FAVORITE MOVIE STAR. In your public library there's a book called <u>who's who in America</u> with addresses of most celebrities.

If you want an autograph, <u>ask</u>, and enclose a self-addressed stamped envelope or postcard.

Dear Diary:

May 17
Botticelli Day

Today is Sandro Botticelli's birthday. He was an Italian Renaissance painter who lived in Florence and painted *Birth of Venus* and other pictures. His birthday is a good excuse to play "Botticelli," a really challenging name game. Any number can play.

"**IT**" thinks of a famous person or fictional character

"**IT**" answers with an example of a dog whose last name begins with "T."

Dear Diary:

May 18
World Good Will Day

World Good Will Day used to be called Peace Day. It's the anniversary of the opening of the first Hague Peace Conference held back in 1899, when representatives from many countries came together in Holland to organize for better international relations and make laws to govern all nations. The United Nations now carries on the quest for peace begun so many years ago.

Make peace sign cookies.

① LOOK AHEAD to October 13 for a good cookie recipe.

② CUT rolled-out dough with a juice glass to make round cookies and bake according to the directions.

③ MIX TOGETHER a small package (3 ounces) of CREAM CHEESE (at room temperature) with a tablespoon of honey. SOFTEN with a dash of milk.

④ MAKE a cone of wax paper. Secure it with tape. The hole at the end should be no bigger than this → ○.

⑤ PUT the cream cheese icing into the cone with a spoon.

⑥ SQUEEZE out icing to decorate each cookie with a peace sign.

Add your own symbols to this collection.

Dear Diary:

Amazing Daily

May 19   *All The News That's Fit To Tickle*

1ST FROG JUMPING JUBILEE HELD, 1928

Calaveras County— Hundreds joined the festivities as the first actual frog jumping contest got under way in California on this day in 1928. It was held to celebrate Mark Twain's famous story "The Celebrated Jumping Frog of Calaveras County," and has become an annual event. Frances F. Frogg, a well-known jumper hopped all the way from Florida for the event and was interviewed by the *Amazing Daily* at the time. When questioned about her home-swamp she replied, "Knee-deep."

Frog Festival Planned

Rayne, Louisiana— The town that calls itself "the frog capital of the world" is planning its annual frog festival for the fall. As always it will feature a beauty contest culminating in the selection of the Frog Queen. We've heard of the frog *prince*, but this is ridiculous!

Friends of Frogs Say, "Fry Fruit"

San Francisco—The radical group, Friends of Frogs, said today they will not rest till frogs' legs have been removed from menus across the country. "Frogs' legs belong on frogs, not on plates," said one member who was crocheting a tiny pair of stockings for "a friend." An FOF spokesperson said, "If you must fry something, fry fruit. Apples are very good fried in butter."

May 20
Dolley Madison's Birthday

Dolley Madison, one of the most popular First Ladies ever, was born Dolley Payne on this date in 1768. She married James Madison (fourth President of the United States) in 1794. She was a remarkably charming person who loved to entertain.

When the British invaded Washington during the War of 1812, it was Dolley Madison who gathered up many state papers (including the original Declaration of Independence) and the most famous portrait of George Washington, and fled the city. Without her, these would surely have been destroyed.

In a happier moment, it was Dolley Madison who began the custom of rolling colored hard-boiled eggs on the White House lawn on the Monday after Easter.

PLAY EGG-ROLLING. (No, it's <u>not</u> playing with your food in a Chinese restaurant!)

1. You and your friends each need a hard-boiled egg. Make a starting and finishing line on a nice grassy lawn.
2. Place all eggs on the starting line with each egg-roller on his or her hands and knees, bent over with nose touching egg.
3. The object is to roll the egg across the finish line using only your nose - no hands allowed. First one across wins. Now go to the winners house, make deviled eggs, and have a PICNIC!

Dear Diary:

Dear Diary:

May 21
Gemini Begins

People born between May 21 and June 21 are born under the sign of Gemini, the twins. According to astrologers they are lively, energetic fun people who will do most anything on the spur of the moment. They are restless too, and always ready to try new things.

Gemini people are witty and have a special talent for communication. That's why they're so good at dealing with people and usually have lots of friends around.

List all the people you know born under Gemini. Which ones seem to fit the description?

BE A TWIN FOR A DAY.

Pretend you're your best friend's twin. Get together and go through your wardrobes. Put together nearly identical outfits. See if you can add a distinctive touch — matching kerchiefs or hats.

HI. WHAT'S NEW? SEEING DOUBLE?

Comb your hair the same way. Practice saying things at the same time. Dot your faces with the same freckles — use an eyebrow pencil.

Dear Diary:

May 22
Mystery Day

It's no mystery. It's very clear that today is the birthday of Sir Arthur Conan Doyle, born in 1859. He wrote stories about a very famous detective. Do you know who it is? There are several clues on this page. Can you solve the mystery? Doyle's famous detective was _____.

Send a mystery message to a friend.

1. Put together a sentence that contains all the letters of your first and last name. The letters may be in correct order, backwards, or jumbled up. (Jumbled letters are the hardest to figure out.) For instance:

Yellow rOses UndeRNeath A Mimosa trEe.

(Read only capital letters.)

2. Cut the letters out of a newspaper or magazine to form your words; this way nobody will recognize your handwriting.
3. Make the letters of your name different from the rest: all capitals or in colored letters.
4. End your message with, "Call me if you know who I am," and mail it or secretly deliver it to your friend.

May 23
Mary Cassatt's Birthday

Mary Cassatt, born in 1844, always wanted to be an artist. She studied art in Philadelphia, her hometown, then in her twenties, she moved to Europe to devote her life to painting. After living and working in Paris for several years, Mary Cassatt met Edgar Degas who asked her to join his group of artists (known as the Impressionists) and to show her paintings with theirs. In the 1870's the Impressionists' paintings were lighter and more colorful than most other paintings being shown, and they were painted of everyday people and places, not kings, palaces, stories, or history. Cassatt concentrated on paintings of mothers and children and scenes of family life with rare sensitivity.

Celebrate Mary Cassatt's birthday by making a drawing (or painting) from your family life—suppertime, a family picnic, playing, or working together.

Dear Diary:

Dear Diary:

Answer appears at the back of the book.

May 24
Commonwealth Day

This is the United Kingdom's flag.
Color the cross and *X* red.
Color the shaded field blue.

Commonwealth Day, Victoria Day, and the Queen's Birthday are all names for May 24 in England and Canada. Queen Victoria was born on this day in 1819. She was greatly loved and had the longest reign ever (64 years) of a British monarch, so her birthday became a day to celebrate the unity of the United Kingdom. In London there are wonderful parades featuring the colorful Royal Guard. Buildings are gaily decorated, and in the evening there are banquets, toasts, and of course, fireworks.

Dear Diary:

GREAT BRITAIN (Finish)

EUROPE

AFRICA

Find your way from Capetown, South Africa, to Great Britain...

(START) CAPETOWN

May 25
Africa Freedom Day

On this date in 1963 the Organization of African Unity was founded, and May 25 became a day for the people of Africa to celebrate. In many places on the huge continent, there are parades, special sports events, speeches, and songfests to celebrate.

Try African soup for supper.

Peanuts were brought to America from Africa. In the Congo, where the dialect Lonkundo is spoken, the peanut is called *nguba*.

1. Put four heaping tablespoons of *nguba* butter in a saucepan. Heat gently. Stir to keep it from sticking.

2. Add two cups of hot water. Stir till smooth.

3. Add some grated *batungula* (onion) to suit your taste. Also add some paprika. Heat the soup thoroughly.

4. Add a gob of sour cream to each bowl and top with fresh parsley or chives.

Here are some Lonkundo words for other foods:

bananas—*mankondo*   beans—*babinsi*
oranges—*ilala*   greens—*banganju*
sweet potato—*baenge*

Dear Diary:

May 26
Play Day

Play May Day on Play Day. May Day is a rhyming game. Any number can play.

① Each player takes a name that rhymes with May: Kay, Fay, Gay, Edna St. Vincent Millay, Jay, Ray, Sashay, Mr. Monet, (made up names are fine too)

② Players sit in a circle.

③ Any player may begin by saying his or her name, then asking a question of another player. The last word of the question must rhyme with May.

> I'm Jay. Oh, Ray, Would you like to play croquet?

> I'm Ray. No, Jay. I don't play croquet. Fay, did you send me a bouquet?

> I'm Fay. Yes, Ray, I sent the bouquet. Jay, where were you on Tuesday.

. . . and so on. This game makes for a lot of laughs as players get tongue-tied and forget each other's phony names. If a player calls another player by the wrong name or asks a question that doesn't rhyme, he or she must quickly say four words that rhyme with May or be out of the game. Last player *in* wins. Okay?

Dear Diary:

> I'm Jay. On Tuesday I flew to the Milky Way. Oh, Ray, may I borrow your beret?

May 27
Isadora's Birthday

Isadora Duncan was born by the ocean, in San Francisco, in 1878, and became the first "modern dancer." She said she learned to dance by following the rhythm of the waves.

"To dance is to live," Duncan said. Unlike ballet, her dance stressed natural movements. She danced barefoot, and wore loose, flowing clothes sort of like the chiton (pronounced "ky-ton") that the ancient Greeks wore.

Make a GREEK chiton.

This simple costume was everyday garb. Men and children wore it short, women long.

(1) START with a single-bed sheet.

(2) FOLD it over so it's about the length from your shoulders to your knees.

(3) FOLD it in half →

(4) USE two large safety pins to fasten it at the shoulders.

(5) PUT IT ON like this ⟶

(6) CHANGE the length by blousing it out at the waist.

(It's fun to wear a chiton over your bathing suit at the beach or pool. Try making it from a beach towel.)

May 28
Sierra Club Founded, 1892

As the weather gets warmer, and the calendar gets closer to summer vacation (applause, applause), everybody gets more interested in the great outdoors. Sierra Club members, people dedicated to clean air and water, wise land use, and energy conservation, have always been interested. The club has become one of the best-known groups of great-outdoors-lovers in the world.

With World Environment Day coming up on June 5, today's the perfect time to send for a free copy of the Sierra Club's newsletter, "Somebody Do Something." It's filled with ideas for things you can do in the battle against pollution. Write: Sierra Club, 530 Bush St., San Francisco, California 94108.

Ask for a copy of "Somebody Do Something," and enclose a self-addressed stamped envelope.

You can also write the U.S. Environmental Protection Agency, Washington, D.C. 20460. Ask for "What You Can Do To Recycle More Paper," "Bicycle for a Better Environment," and "Our Endangered World."

Dear Diary:

Dear Diary:

Little Rhody's and the Badger State's Birthday

Did you know states have birthdays too? Well they do—the date of their statehood—and you can help to celebrate your state's birthday.

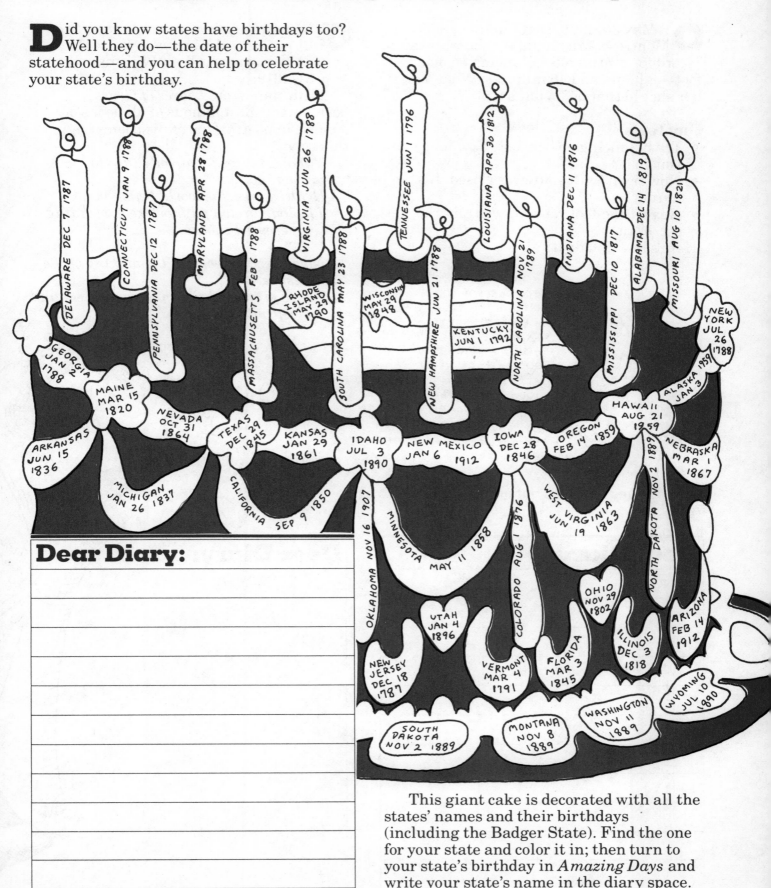

Dear Diary:

This giant cake is decorated with all the states' names and their birthdays (including the Badger State). Find the one for your state and color it in; then turn to your state's birthday in *Amazing Days* and write your state's name in the diary space.

May 30
One-Foot Day

On May 30, 1975, Don Carter of Montrose, Michigan, set the world's record for continuous balancing on one foot—8 hours and 46 minutes. What a feat! (Or should that be "What a foot!"?)

Foot feats.
- Try balancing on one foot. How long can you do it?
- Now try it with your eyes closed. It's harder!
- Have a one-foot race. On your marks, get set, Wait!

Here's how you do it:

As many friends can race as want to, but there must be a judge to watch carefully. From the start to the finishing line only ONE FOOT (either right or left) may touch the ground. In other word... HOP! If anyone's other foot touches, he or she must go back and start over.

Q: What has four legs but only one foot.
A: A bed.

Dear Diary:

May 31
Outdoors Day

Give me the splendid silent sun with all its beams full-dazzling," wrote the great American poet Walt Whitman, born May 31, 1819.

Whitman wrote *Leaves of Grass*, perhaps the most famous of all books of American poetry. One of his poems begins this way:

"Afoot and light-hearted I take to the open road,
Healthy, free, the world before me,
The long brown path before me leading wherever I choose.
* * *
Now I see the secret of the making of the best persons,
It is to grow in the open air and to eat and sleep with the earth."

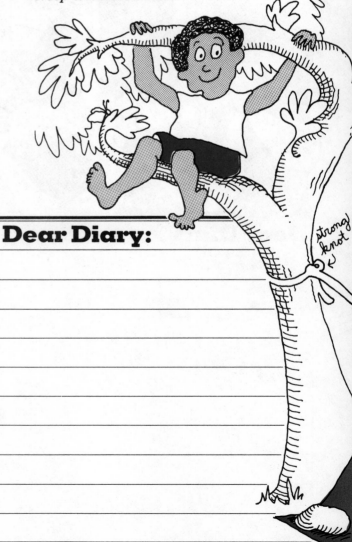

strong knot

Dear Diary:

Nathaniel Ulysses Turtle Day

Celebrate Walt Whitman's birthday outdoors.

Start out with a picnic breakfast: A handful of granola or any favorite cereal, a piece of fruit, and a peanut butter and jelly sandwich made on a muffin. Have a picnic lunch and dinner too.

RIDE YOUR BIKE.
CLIMB A TREE.
SWIM.
GARDEN.
PLAY OUTDOOR
HIKE.
whatever you want to do, do it outside.

If you can, spend the night outdoors. Here's a simple tent:

Lay a heavy cloth on the ground under your sleeping bag or blanket

blanket and clothesline

stone or something heavy

Members of Turtles International celebrate the birthday of Nathaniel Ulysses Turtle on the Turtle's New Year—that's today. The grand old Turtle (nicknamed NUT because of his initials) turned 9,947 years old in 1979 according to Lloyd Hardesty, Grand Imperial Turtle, who has been known to pull a few legs.

The goal of Turtles International is "more smiles to the mile." Happy birthday, NUT!

TEMPT YOUR TASTEBUDS WITH A **TURTLE TURNOVER.**

1. Place a cookie on a saucer and put a scoop of ice cream or sherbet on top.
2. Top it with another cookie the turtle's shell
3. Add a whole strawberry for a head, and thin orange peel slices, licorice stick pieces or something else skinny for legs and tail.

This day is for real. For more information about Turtles send a self-addressed stamped envelope to: Turtles International (it really exists), P.O. Box 96, Westchester, Illinois 60153.

Dear Diary:

June 2
Another Washington's Birthday

What? Another Washington's Birthday? Yes, but this time it's Martha's.

Born June 2, 1732, Martha Dandridge married George Washington in 1759 and later became the very first First Lady. As a Virginia plantation mistress Martha had many skills. She was a weaver, seamstress, gardener, nurse, musician, and cook. She made wine, cordials, syrup, medicine, perfumes, and even toothpaste. Besides all of that, she supervised all the meals including breakfast, which was served promptly at seven every morning. Tea, honey, and hoecakes (like pancakes only cooked on the blade of a hoe in the fireplace) was George's favorite breakfast.

First Ladies' Firsts

How many of these First Ladies' first names do you know?

_____Adams	(wife of John Adams)
_____Madison	(wife of James Madison
_____Lincoln	(wife of Abraham Lincoln)
_____Roosevelt	(wife of Franklin Roosevelt)
_____Kennedy	(wife of John F. Kennedy)
_____Johnson	(wife of Lyndon Johnson)
_____Ford	(wife of Gerald Ford)
_____Carter	(wife of Jimmy Carter)

Dear Diary:

UNITED STATES POSTAGE
MARTHA WASHINGTON
1½ CENTS 1½

Answers appear at the back of the book.

June 3
Josephine Baker's Birthday

Picture a thin, beautiful black woman promenading down the most elegant street in Paris led by a pair of leopards or two white swans! That was Josephine Baker, (1906-1975) an American who became the "toast of Paris" in the 1920's. Parisians called her *La Ba-Kair*. She performed in the French music halls wearing elaborate sequined costumes and plumed headdresses that were sometimes four feet high! After World War II, she adopted many orphans of different nationalities and called them her "rainbow tribe." She loved people, and people the world over loved her.

Create a La Ba-Kair headdress

Start with an old hat, one of your mom's or dad's, a baseball cap, or any hat that's okay to poke holes in.

GATHER TOGETHER all kinds of decorations: bows, ribbons, artificial flowers, leaves, and birds, costume jewelry, flags, feathers, small toys, EVERYTHING!

FASTEN the decorations to the hat any way they'll stay. Use paper clips, brass fasteners, glue, sew also.

Dear Diary:

June 4
Salad Day

In June 4, 1070 some brave, hungry person in Roquefort, France discovered that sheeps' milk cheese with blue-green mold all through it was not only edible but delicious! Have you ever eaten Roquefort or blue cheese dressing on a salad?

Make a kitchen sink salad.

It's called that because it has everything *but* the kitchen sink in it.

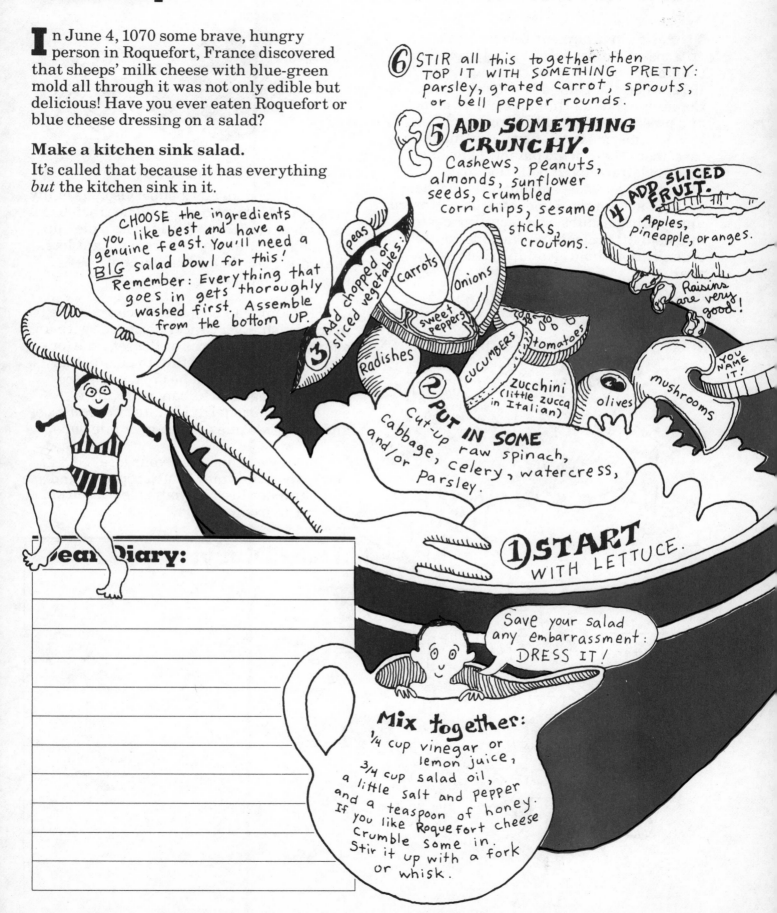

CHOOSE the ingredients you like best and have a genuine feast. You'll need a BIG salad bowl for this! Remember: Everything that goes in gets thoroughly washed first. Assemble from the bottom UP.

⑥ STIR all this together then TOP IT WITH SOMETHING PRETTY: parsley, grated carrot, sprouts, or bell pepper rounds.

⑤ ADD SOMETHING CRUNCHY. Cashews, peanuts, almonds, sunflower seeds, crumbled corn chips, sesame sticks, croutons.

④ ADD SLICED FRUIT. Apples, pineapple, oranges.

Raisins are very good!

③ Add chopped or sliced vegetables:
peas, Carrots, Onions, sweet peppers, Radishes, CUCUMBERS, tomatoes, Zucchini (little zucca in Italian), olives, mushrooms, YOU NAME IT!

② PUT IN SOME cut-up raw spinach, cabbage, celery, watercress, and/or parsley.

① START WITH LETTUCE.

Save your salad any embarrassment: DRESS IT!

Mix together:
¼ cup vinegar or lemon juice, ¾ cup salad oil, a little salt and pepper and a teaspoon of honey. If you like Roquefort cheese crumble some in. Stir it up with a fork or whisk.

Dear Diary:

June 5
World Environment Day

World Environment Day is a time for people around the world to reaffirm their concern for the earth. Since June 5, 1972, when the United Nations held its Conference on the Human Environment and proclaimed World Environment Day, kids in America have shown how much they care about their home planet. They have written letters about pollution to businesses and government officials, held ecology-awareness demonstrations, started anti-pollution clubs, run recycling centers, and held litter cleanups. Various youth organizations hold cleanup drives every year.

Hold a litter cleanup race.

You'll need an adult supervisor, as many kids as possible, and at least one trash bag for each participant. The idea is to pick up as much litter as you can from vacant lots, sidewalks, etc., in a set amount of time—say, one hour.

The adult can begin the race and time it to the finish. Every racer heads out with an empty bag and returns at the set time (or when his or her bag is full, to get another bag). The bags should be piled in a place where garbage trucks can get to them easily. (Variation: Divide into two *teams* and make two piles. The bigger pile wins.)

When you finish, call your local newspaper; they may send a reporter and photographer to cover your celebration of World Environment Day.

Dear Diary:

June 6
Recycling Day

Set up a RECYCLING CENTER in your own room.

Lots of things that could be used again probably get thrown away just because you don't have a place to keep them.

FIND a big cardboard box that will fit somewhere in your room. Grocery stores have lots of empty boxes. Ask for one.

DECORATE the box with magazine pictures and cut-out letters... a good way to recycle an old magazine.

INSIDE KEEP THINGS TO RECYCLE: Shirt cardboard and cardboard tubes, empty containers, spools, egg cartons, empty jars, used ribbons, greeting cards, etc...

① Mix together the same amounts of white glue and water.

② Use a paintbrush to apply the mixture.

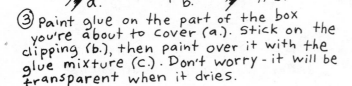

a.   b.   c.

③ Paint glue on the part of the box you're about to cover (a.). Stick on the clipping (b.), then paint over it with the glue mixture (c.). Don't worry - it will be transparent when it dries.

June 7
Funny Fashions Day

All through history there have been certain people who set styles in clothes. Nowadays, fashion magazines show the latest styles; in the early 1800's an English dandy named George Bryan Brummel (born June 7, 1778) was the fashion leader. Beau Brummel, as he was nicknamed, spent hours getting dressed each day, and a lot of his efforts went into arranging his elaborate neckwear. Because of his example, fancy neckwear became the height of fashion.

Have a funny fashions costume party.

Invite your friends over and tell each to wear a crazy costume. Be sure to tell them that the craziest outfit wins a prize. Ask a grown-up to judge the funny fashions. Award the winner a "designers scarf"—with a marker put your name or initials on an inexpensive bandanna or a square of scrap fabric. Also, declare the winner "Beau Brummel" and give him or her first choice of refreshments.

Dear Diary:

Dear Diary:

June 8
Three Cheers for Architects Day

An architect is a designer of buildings, and Frank Lloyd Wright (1867-1959) was one of the finest, most imaginative architects of this century. He thought it very important to blend a building into its natural surroundings. One of his most famous houses has a name, "Falling Water." Built in 1936, this house in Bear Run, Pennsylvania, has trees growing through the roof, large rocks jutting through the walls and floor, and a stream running underneath, spilling over rocks as a waterfall.

Wright designed buildings all over the world, and often designed the furniture and stained-glass windows in them. The Guggenheim Museum in New York City was one of his last major buildings.

Build a secret hideaway.

A hideaway can be built inside or outside; the trick is to build it in an out-of-the-way place of materials that look the same as what's around them.

① **PUSH** 2 "Y-sticks" firmly into the earth.

② **PUT** a strong stick between the Y's.

③ **LEAN** sticks and branches against top stick.

④ Leaves, grass, weeds, and twigs **PILED** over the branches make a roof.

Dear Diary:

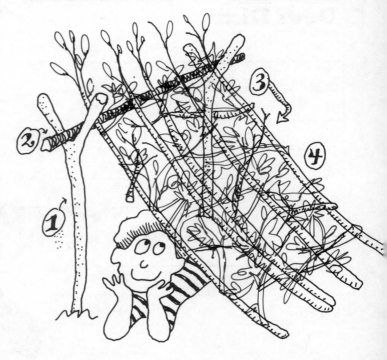

June 9
Home, Sweet Home Day

> Mid pleasures and palaces
> Though we may roam,
> Be it ever so humble
> There's no place like home.
>
> A charm from the skies
> Seems to hallow us there,
> Which, seek thro' the world, is
> Ne'er met with elsewhere.
>
> Home, home,
> Home, sweet home,
> There's no place like home,
> Ah, there's no place like home.

John Howard Payne, born June 9, 1791, wrote those famous lyrics as part of an opera, *Clari, or the Maid of Milan.*

As important to us as our homes are, many of us don't know the history of the buildings we live in.

Be an investigator.

Find out when your home was built. How many other people have lived in it? Are there interesting stories about it? Ask your parents, neighbors, or anybody that might know something. Write down a short history from what you find. Also draw a picture of your home.

Dear Diary:

June 10
Long Live Lefties Day

Judy Garland (born Frances Gumm on this date in 1922) was left-handed. So was Leonardo da Vinci, Michelangelo, Charlie Chaplin, and Babe Ruth, just to name a few.

Celebrate your left hand.

Give your right hand a rest and use your left hand all day.

Shake hands left-handed. Wave with your left. Shoot marbles......... Hold your fork, and your toothbrush all with your left hand.

Collect left-handed autographs from your left and right-handed friends.

Write in your diary space left-handed.

(If you're naturally left-handed do all these things with your right.)

Dear Diary:

June 11
Kamehameha Day

King Kamehameha I is the only king ever to be honored by an American holiday. He united the islands in the Kingdom of Hawaii which, in 1959, became the fiftieth state. Kamehameha Day is a favorite festival throughout the state, celebrated with luaus, pageants, and songfests.

Most Hawaiians speak English, but they often use native Hawaiian words to flavor their speech.

Speak Hawaiian.

The Hawaiian alphabet has only 12 letters:
    A E H I K L M N O P U W

Ae (I) . . . . yes
Aloha (Al-lo-ah) . . . welcome; good-bye; love
Haukalima (How-kah-lih-mah) . . ice cream
Holoku (Ho-lo-koo) . . . . dress; gown
Humahumanukanukaapuaha
    (Hoo-ma-hoo-ma-noo-ka-noo-ka-
    ah-poo-ah-ah) . . . . a very small fish
    (with a very large name)
Kamaaina (Kah-mah-ai-nah) . . . . one who
    belongs to the Islands
La Hanau (La ha-now) . . . . birthday
Mahalo (Mah-hah-lo) . . . . thank you
Makana (Mah-kah-nah) . . . . gift
Malihini (Mah-li-hee-nih) . . . . . . newcomer
Mele Kalikimaka
    (Mel-ah Kah-lee-kee-mah-kah) . . . .
    Merry Christmas (in June?)
Paikikala
    (Pie-kih-kah-lah) . . . . bicycle
Paluna
    (Pah-loo-nah) . . . . balloon
Pau (Pow) . . . . finished
Wikiwiki
    (Wicky-wicky) . . . . hurry up

If you want to know more about Hawaii, write to: Chamber of Commerce, 735 Bishop Street, Honolulu, Hawaii 96813.

Dear Diary:

Eight islands
in the Pacific Ocean
form Hawaii,
"The Aloha State"

June 12
Baseball Day

If you're a baseball fan or player, it's your turn at bat! On this date in 1939 the Baseball Hall of Fame was opened in Cooperstown, New York. Cooperstown was the home of Abner Doubleday who supposedly laid out the first baseball diamond and formulated the rules of the game.

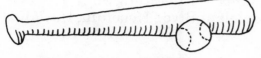

Get up a game of baseball.

While you're at it, astound your friends with your extensive baseball vocabulary. Here are some funny terms players use:

Ace: a great pitcher
Pepper game: practice before the real game
Monkey suit: uniform
Pull a rock: make a mistake
Foot in the bucket: batter's front foot pointing away from the pitcher
The hot corner: third base
Ducks on the pond: bases loaded
Gopher ball: a home run hit
Southpaw: left-handed pitcher
Take-charge guy: player who cheers team members on

Dear Diary:

June 13
Get Ready for Father's Day

While fathers have been around for a long time, Father's Day is a lot more recent. The idea for a special day to honor them began about the same time as one for mothers (1908) but Father's Day was not established permanently until 1972. Now Dad has his day every year on the third Sunday of June.

Interview your dad.

Ask him some of the same questions you asked your mom (see May 10). Find out all about him and write a short biography in today's diary space.

Draw his portrait or glue a snapshot here.

Dear Diary:

June 14
Flag Day

It's a grand old flag, it's a high flying flag, and forever in peace may it wave . . ." On June 14, 1777, the Continental Congress made the Stars and Stripes the official flag of the United States. Look around your neighborhood; is anyone celebrating Flag Day today? How many flags are flying?

Decorate for Flag Day.

Decorate your meals with flags on toothpicks.

Decorate doors and windows with paper chains and stars in red, white, and blue.
(Staple or glue stars to chain)

Decorate your bike with ribbons and stars on the handlebars.
(While you're decorating start planning a "Fourth" Celebration - see July 4.)

Dear Diary:

June 15
Smile Power Day

Smile Power Day was started by Dr. Robert M. Gibson, a dentist in Hawaii, to encourage people to smile more often. He also started the Smilepower Institute to teach folks more about "the miracle of smile power."

For more information write to: The Smilepower Institute, Suite 717, 1441 Kapiolani Blvd., Honolulu, Hawaii 96814.

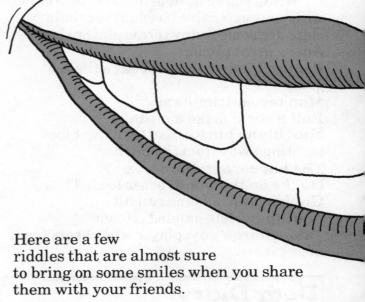

Here are a few riddles that are almost sure to bring on some smiles when you share them with your friends.

Q. What's the longest word in the English language?
A. Smiles. There's a mile between those two *s*'s.

Q. What's the easiest thing in the world to break?
A. It's very easy to crack a smile.

Q. What did the grizzly say as he sat on the hunter?
A. Grin and *bear* it.

Q. When you give it to someone else you're almost sure to get it back. What is it?
A. A smile.

Q. What has a mouth but can't smile?
A. A river.

Q. What flowers are like smiles?
A. Tulips (two lips).

Q. What do you see when you smile in a mirror?
A. A smile.

Q. When does a photographer *not* need a flashbulb indoors?
A. When he flashes a smile.

Q. What can you put on without lifting a finger?
A. That's right.

Q. How is a smile like the obvious answer to this riddle?
A. It's right under your nose.

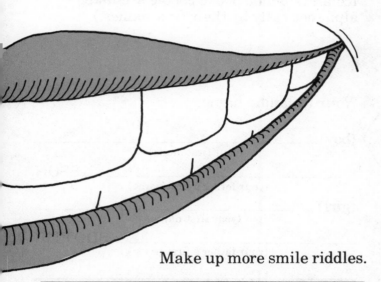

Make up more smile riddles.

June 16
First Woman in Space Day

Valentina V. Tereshkova became the first woman in outer space on June 16, 1963, when she blasted off to make 48 revolutions around the earth. Her spaceflight lasted almost three days.

Tereshkova, a Russian cosmonaut, trained as an airplane pilot and parachuted for a hobby before she volunteered for spaceflight training school. During her flight (over 100 miles above the earth) she operated her ship by manual controls, and on reentering the earth's atmosphere she parachuted to safety.

Make a space capsule that blasts off.

① CUT two slits exactly opposite each other in a paper cup. The slits should be the same length, slightly more than half the height of the cup.

② Decorate like a space capsule.

③ To make it blast off USE a piece of string about 18-inches long. Hold the string loosely so it goes through both slits.

④ 3..2..1... Blast off! SNAP the string tight -- QUICKLY!

Dear Diary:

Dear Diary:

June 17
Iceland's Republic Day

Today is a joyous occasion in Iceland, the date on which this country became completely independent of Denmark in 1944. No one in that island nation works today. City streets are even closed to traffic.

This is the flag of the Land of Frost and Fire. Its colors explain Iceland's nickname. Color the background blue (for mountains). Leave the outline of the cross white (for glaciers). Color the cross red (for the fire of Iceland's 200 volcanoes).

Figure out your Icelandic name.

In Iceland, the system of names is very different from that in America. If a man named Petur Nielsson has a son, the boy is given a first name (say, Jon) and for his last name takes his father's first name plus "sson," Jon Petursson. If Jon ever has a son *his* last name will be Jonsson.

If Petur Nielsson has a daughter her last name will be Petursdottir — "sdottir" is added to the father's first name for girls. When a girl grows up she always keeps her own name, whether she marries or not. (In Iceland's phone books people are listed alphabetically by their *first* names.)

Your Icelandic name:

(boy)_____
          (your first name)

_____ SSON
     (your father's first name)

(girl)_____
           (your first name)

_____ SDOTTIR
     (your father's first name)

Dear Diary:

_____
_____
_____
_____
_____
_____
_____
_____
_____
_____
_____
_____

June 18
International Picnic Day

Whether you take your lunch in a backpack and hike to a favorite spot in the woods or just gather some goodies in a basket and head for the backyard or playground, a picnic is one of the great traditions of summer. If it's raining, you could even have your picnic in the living room.

HAVE A PICNIC.

Take along a kite, horseshoes, Frisbee, or whatever you want to have fun with on your outing

Create some of your favorite sandwiches, plus raw carrots and celery sticks, chips or nuts, some cheese, washed fruit, cookies, plates, napkins, and something to drink.

Pack your picnic in a basket. A heavy duty shopping bag works just fine.

AMAZING DAYS SPECIAL PICNIC SANDWICH SPREAD:

① **CHOP** contents of one small jar of pimientos.

② **GRATE** sharp cheddar cheese till you have 2 cups.

③ **COMBINE** cheese and pimientos and add enough mayonnaise to soften.

④ **SALT** and pepper to taste.

Ask your Aunt Mabel along so there's sure to be at least one ANT there.

Hey, isn't anybody gonna eat?!

Dear Diary:

June 19
Take-a-Chance Day

If you flip a coin what is the chance of its coming down heads? The French mathematician and philosopher Blaise Pascal, born June 19, 1623, was fascinated by this question and worked out a complex theory of probability that is still used by mathematicians, weather forecasters, and others. The probability of that coin coming down heads is one time out of every two times you flip it. The other time it will *probably* come down tails.

PLAY PENNY PINBALL!

Draw the "tree" below larger on a piece of paper. Trace around a penny to make the circles.

① Starting at the bottom, FLIP A PENNY. If it comes down heads go up the left branch and put your marker (maybe a button) on the first circle you get to. If it comes down tails go up the right branch.

② FLIP three more times to continue climbing.

★ PLAY with a friend by taking turns flipping the penny and keeping track of your scores. Climb the tree five times each. Keep track of your points. The player with the most wins.

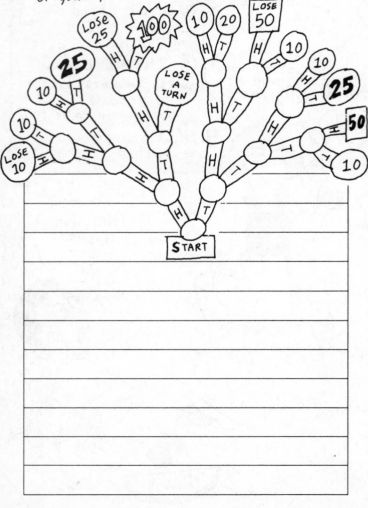

June 20
Great Seal Adopted, 1782

The Great Seal of the United States is *not* an animal that sometimes is seen spinning a ball on its nose. It is an emblem used to authenticate important documents and to represent the U.S. government. It was adopted on this date in 1782.

Thirteen must be a *lucky* number for the U.S. There are 13 stripes on the shield, 13 stars above the eagle's head, 13 arrows in one talon, and 13 olives and 13 leaves in the other. Of course, 13 was used because that was the number of original American colonies. You can see the Great Seal on the back of a one-dollar bill.

Design you own Great Seal.

Your own seal can be a design made up of your favorite animal (real or imaginary), objects, shapes, slogans, initials, colors — all special to you. Try to keep it uncluttered and simple so it will be easy to draw on stationery, book covers, T-shirts, posters, and whatever else you want to identify as yours.

Dear Diary:

June 21
Summer Solstice

At the summer solstice, which falls on or around June 21, the earth is tilted in such a way that the North Pole is as close to the sun as it ever gets. As a result, the day is the longest of the whole year and the night is the shortest.

What time does the sun actually set tonight?_____
Compare this time with the time you wrote down on March 21.

Know your seasons. Can you guess these hinky-pinkies?

A hinky-pinky is two rhyming words together. The first word of each of these is the name of a season.

Q: A Fourth of July musician?
A: Summer drummer.

Q: A football game?
A: Fall ball.

Q: A skier without sunglasses?
A: Winter squinter.

Q: A honeybee in April if you sit on him?
A: Spring sting.

Make up more hinky-pinkies. Just put together two words that rhyme, then make up a question or definition that fits.

Dear Diary:

June 22
Cancer Begins

People born between June 22 and July 23 are born under the sign of Cancer, the crab. According to astrologers they are home-loving, traditional, and patriotic people who love the past. They love parties and amusements too.

Don't be surprised when your Cancer friends get crabby; they're very moody and sensitive. They're great friends, but their worst fault can be holding a grudge against their imagined enemies. When Cancer people try, they can accomplish wonderful things since they stick to a task till it's done. They're often very artistic.

Check out astrology.

Look through the newspaper today and find the astrology column—almost every paper has one. See what tomorrow's forecast is for your sign. Clip it out and glue it here.

Tomorrow write down whether the forecast came true or not.

Try this every day for a week. What do you think?

Dear Diary:

June 23
Midsummer's Eve

In almost every country in Europe, tonight is thought to be the most magical night of the year. "On Midsummer Eve, when the bonfires are lighted on every hill in honor of St. John, the fairies are at their gayest," wrote Yeats in *Irish Fairy and Folk Tales*. Herbs and flowers are picked this night to bring health and blessings to those who keep them. To wash one's face in this evening's rain or dew is supposed to make the skin lovely and the body strong and healthy. (Mexicans and Spaniards take a midnight swim for this reason.) Wishes made tonight are likely to come true, and it's a perfect night for fortune-telling.

Dear Diary:

Look into the future.

1 For this method of fortune-telling you need a thin chain with some sort of pendant hanging from it. Any kind of jewelry "drop" will do

2 SIT IN A CHAIR COMFORTABLY.

3 Hold the chain between your thumb and first finger allowing the pendant to hang down above one knee without touching anything else. Just hold it till it begins to move in a circle. This may take a few minutes.

4 Once it is moving look to see if it is circling clockwise

or counterclockwise

5 Whichever direction it first moves for YOU means **YES**. The opposite direction means NO.

You may now ask any yes or no question, even about the future. The pendant will circle in one direction or the other to answer. If it stops moving or moves haphazardly the answer is UNDECIDED.

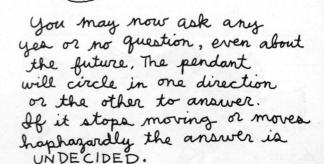

June 24

Midsummer Day/ St. John's Day

For people named John, Johann, Jack, Jonathan, Jean, Jan, Juan, Joan, Joanna, Juanita, Jeanne, Jane, and any other variation of *John*, today is like a second birthday. It's called a name-day. Because it's St. John's Day, people with his name (and there are a lot of them!) are entitled to special treats. In Spain their friends give them small cakes in the shape of the letter *J*.

MAKE J COOKIES
FOR ALL YOUR "J" FRIENDS - AND YOURSELF!

① **CREAM** ½ cup brown sugar with ½ cup BUTTER (at room temperature).

② **BEAT** in two eggs.

③ **STIR** in 2 ¾ cups unbleached white or whole wheat FLOUR, 2 tsp.→ BAKING POWDER, and 1 tsp. vanilla.

④ ❄ **CHILL** dough at least one hour.

⑤ With floured pinch off a little dough and roll between your palms to make a "snake" about ½-inch thick.

⑥ **FORM** "snake" into a J and arrange on a greased cookie sheet. Each J should be about the same size and thickness so they will bake in the same amount of time - **7-12 minutes at 375°**.

Dear Diary:

_____
(your name)

MAKES SMASH APPEARANCE ON TV

Critics raved last night over the surprise appearance of _____ _____ _____ _____ on television. _____ starred in a TV special called _____ _____ _____ all about _____ _____ _____ _____

Special TV Poll
In celebration of the first color television broadcast ever, on this date in 1951, *Amazing Daily* is conducting this "TV Favorites" poll. Please fill in your favorites in the categories listed below:
Show (any kind) _____
_____

Comedy _____
Cartoon _____
Actor _____
in _____
Actress _____
in _____
Favorite time to watch TV _____
Commercial _____
Old movie seen on TV _____

Do you watch the news? Yes ☐ No ☐
News program _____

News personality _____

What sports do you watch on TV _____

Least favorite show

June 26
Babe's Day

The person many sportswriters consider the greatest all-around woman athlete of all time was Babe Didrikson Zaharias. And what an athlete she was!

Babe began her career as a one-person track team, setting world records in the 80-meter hurdles, javelin throw, and high jump. She also threw a baseball 272 feet, 2 inches for another world record. She played baseball, tennis, and basketball (once she scored 106 points in a single game). She even boxed! Finally she concentrated on golf and won 17 tournaments in a row in the 1940s.

"The Babe" was born on June 26, 1911, in Port Arthur, Texas.

Hold a neighborhood sports event.

Get up a big game today—baseball, croquet, relay races, volleyball, whatever.

Make a certificate to award the winning team or player:

BEST IN THE NEIGHBOR-HOOD _____

Set up a lemonade and snack stand for the people who come to watch.

Dear Diary:

Dear Diary:

June 27
Helen Keller's Birthday

Helen Keller (1880-1968) was less than two years old when she suffered a serious disease that left her both deaf and blind. For almost five years she lived without language, cut off from the world most children know. But, thanks to her lifelong teacher, Anne Sullivan, Helen Keller *did* learn to read and write (in Braille, see January 4) and even speak. She went to college and graduated with honors; she wrote many books; she actively worked to improve conditions for blind and deaf people; and she proved that handicapped people not only have a place in our world, but can make vast and beautiful contributions to it.

June 28
A Musical Day

What is a musical anyway? "Musical" is short for musical comedy—that great American theater form that has a story, songs, dances, and orchestral music all tied up in one very popular package. Musicals that start out on the stage often get made into movies that finally show up on TV. Some titles of musicals you may have seen are hidden in this word-search puzzle. *The Wiz, Grease, Funny Girl, Hello, Dolly!, South Pacific*, The King and I*, West Side Story, My Fair Lady, Gypsy, Peter Pan, The Sound of Music*, The Music Man, Hair, Oklahoma!*, Annie.*

```
T M Y F A I R L A D Y L M W C
P H P S T U V W N Y Z T B E D
T H E K I N G A N D I H Q S S
T U T S X O Z A I C D E F T H
O J E L O N O P E H S W U S W
K Y R S O U T H P A C I F I C
L A P C D K N G H I J Z L D N
A P A R S E U D W R Y Z A E C
H E N G G S J K O M N O P S R
O T U V R X Y Z A F C D E T G
M I T H E M U S I C M A N O J
A L M N A P Q R S T U U W R Y
Z G Y P S Y F G H I J K S Y N
O P Q H E L L O D O L L Y I T
F U N N Y G I R L D E F G H C
```

Dear Diary:

Dear Diary:

*These musicals have music by Richard Rodgers, one of the greatest composers of the musical theater, born June 28, 1902.

Answers appear at the back of the book.

June 29
São Pedro

In the port cities and fishing villages of Portugal and Brazil there's much gaiety and excitement today as the watermen brightly decorate their boats in preparation for the blessing of the fleets. It is São Pedro, St. Peter's Day, feast of the saint of fishermen. There will be joyous music and fireworks tonight as the boats set sail in a floating parade.

MAKE A TOY BOAT.

① START by making a "soldier's hat" from a rectangle of paper.

(one flap forward, one back)

a   b

② Now OPEN the hat and make the two ends (a and b) touch each other. It should look like this:

③ TURN the bottom corners up to meet the point ★ at the top.

④ OPEN the new, now smaller "hat" making the two ends touch each other as you did before.

C   D   C   D

⑤ Now PULL points C and D away from each other and you have a toy boat, ready to decorate and sail.

Dear Diary:

June 30
Halfway Day

TODAY is the last day of June and we're exactly halfway through the year - six months gone and six months left to go. DO EVERYTHING "BY HALVES." Usually doing something "by halves" means not doing it well (IT'S NOT A COMPLIMENT!) but these halfway measures are just for fun.

Eat half a grapefruit for breakfast and have half-and-half on your cereal.

Wear one black sock and one orange sock. If anyone notices, laugh half-heartedly and say "I have half a mind to call you color-blind. Ha ha."

HALF

HA is ½ of HALF

At half past noon
halfway through the day
half a sandwich with a friend.

MAKE UP HALFWAY ANIMALS - camephant, giraffalo, rhinonkey. DRAW their pictures

Dear Diary:

July 1
Dominion Day

If you were in Ottawa (Canada's capital) today, you could join in picnics, parades, and sports events to celebrate Dominion Day, the day the provinces were united into the Dominion of Canada in 1867. Then, if you took a car ride south to Washington, D.C., you'd probably arrive just in time to do it all again on the Fourth of July!

Find your way from Ottawa to Washington, D.C.

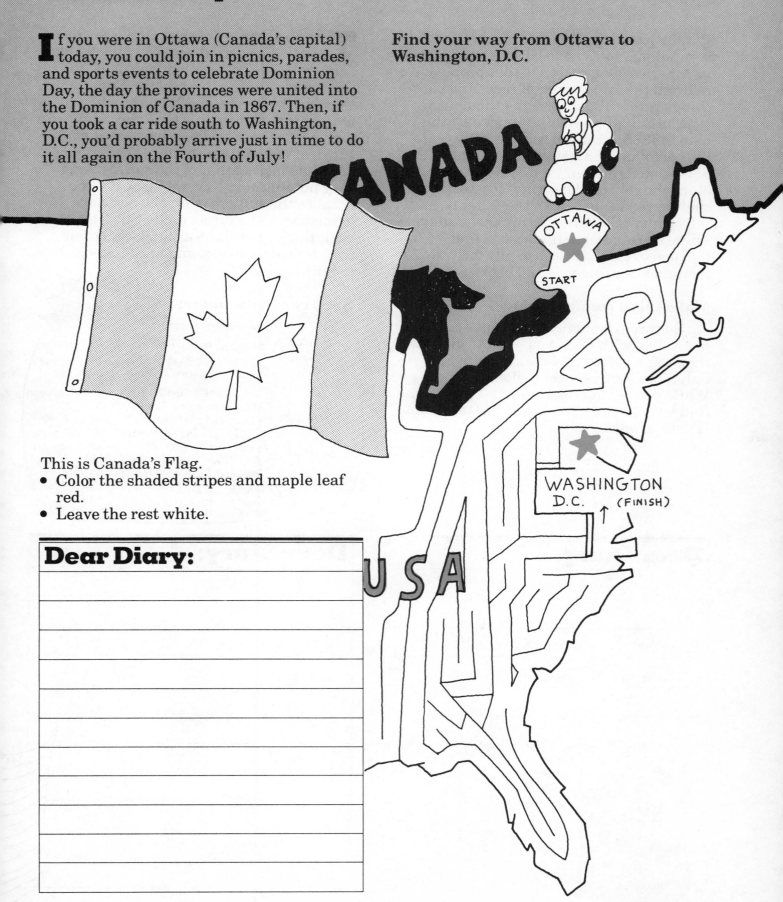

This is Canada's Flag.
- Color the shaded stripes and maple leaf red.
- Leave the rest white.

Dear Diary:

July 2
Rummage Day

In the past few years flea markets and rummage sales have become very popular in America. One reason is that people have realized the importance of recycling old things rather than throwing them away.

The Salvation Army, founded on this date in 1865, has been recycling for years. Lots of folks donate used stuff to the Salvation Army—toys, furniture, clothes. Men who rely on the "army" for work and shelter, repair and clean these items, and sell them in Salvation Army thrift stores. These stores are great places to find inexpensive clothes (especially for costumes) and secondhand books.

Make this a rummage day.

Go through old toys and clothes. Fill a box or bag with what you want to give away, then ask a grown-up to take you to a Salvation Army center to donate them. While you're rummaging, you'll probably find lots of things you had forgotten about. (That's always fun!)

July 3
Dog Days Begin

The hottest part of the summer begins today. The period between July 3 and August 15 has been called "dog days" for thousands of years, first by the Egyptians, then by the Greeks and Romans who noticed that during this time the bright star Sirius (the Dog Star) rose just about at sunrise. The ancients believed that Sirius added its heat to that of the sun, causing very hot weather. Now we know it's hot because the sun's rays hit the northern hemisphere at a direct angle this time of year. But dogs still lie around with their tongues out, panting, and most folks just try to keep cool.

Keep cool with sun tea.

① FILL a big jar with cold water, one glassful at a time. Count them.

② ADD one teabag (or one teaspoon of loose tea) for every _two_ glassfuls of water. Add five or six sprigs of mint if you have it in the garden.

③ FASTEN the lid and place the jar in full sunlight.

④ When it becomes rich tea color (4-6 hours) it's ready. ADD honey, lemon, and ice. Enjoy.

Dear Diary:

Dear Diary:

July 4
Independence Day

Happy birthday, America! The Fourth of July is the day the Declaration of Independence was adopted by the Continental Congress in 1776 and is the most important American national holiday.

Today all over the country people are going on picnics. Watermelon has become the traditional food of the day. Add fresh blueberries on vanilla ice cream to the menu and you'll have a red, white, and blue feast.

Various sports events—swim meets, Little League games, Soap Box Derbies—and many parades will be held. And tonight there'll be fireworks displays in cities and towns from Maine to California.

HOLD A PARADE

OF YOUR OWN! Get all your friends together and stage a neighborhood event.

MAKE paper flags to carry and decorate your bikes with streamers, balloons, ETC. (see June 14)

Make a bow for your dog.

All kids with MUSICAL INSTRUMENTS can form a marching band. The simplest instruments - kazoo, drum, harmonica, even wooden blocks can add a lot of flare to a Parade.

Everybody should wear red, white, and blue clothes _and_ hats (see June 3).

TELL everyone on your block what time the parade will be so you'll have a big audience. To be safe, MARCH on the sidewalk, not in the street.

Turn wagons into floats

We hold these truths to be self-evident, that all people are created equal, that they are endowed by their creator with certain unalienable rights ... life, liberty, and the pursuit of happiness.

Dear Diary:

July 5
Silhouette Celebration

Etienne de Silhouette, born July 5, 1709, was a French finance minister whose hobby was cutting shadow portraits, an inexpensive pastime. His name became identified with this art form as a joke—*à la silhouette* came to mean something done cheaply. Perhaps *because* of the humor, the name stuck and such pictures are still called silhouettes.

Make silhouette cutouts.

① Use black paper. Cut out animals, people, plants, buildings, etc.

② Put the cutouts together to form scenes.

③ Glue the pictures carefully to white paper using white glue. If you like you can add tiny details with a black pen after gluing.

One of the most popular kinds of silhouette is the portrait profile. One person's shadow is projected by a lamp onto a piece of paper. Another person traces the outline of the shadow, then cuts it out. It is then glued to a contrasting colored paper (for example, black on white).

Dear Diary:

July 6
Beatrix Potter's Birthday

Peter Rabbit, Benjamin Bunny, Jemima Puddle-Duck, and Mr. Jeremy Fisher—these are just some of the many characters created by Beatrix Potter, born in London in 1866. Beatrix always loved animals. Her first pet was a mouse named Hunca Munca. Later she kept rabbits, kittens, a hedgehog and even a whole family of snails. *Peter Rabbit* was the first story Beatrix wrote and illustrated. Originally it was part of a letter she sent to a sick friend, a little boy named Noel. Noel and his family loved the story, and years later Beatrix Potter published *The Tale of Peter Rabbit* and then many other picture books that have become classics.

Make a picture book.

① FOLD a piece of paper in half like a card. Fold another the same way and put the two together. Keep folding until your book has the number of pages you want.

② Make a cover of stiffer paper. It should be just a little larger all around than the pages.

③ MAKE UP a story about anything - maybe your pet, real or imaginary. Write one or two sentences and draw a picture on each page..

④ When the book is complete, close the cover and staple 2 or 3 times about ¼ inch from the fold.

Dear Diary:

July 7
Marc Chagall's Birthday

Marc Chagall is one of the most popular artists of the twentieth century. His paintings, prints, drawings, and ceramics often show fiddlers, flowers, acrobats, lovers, and scenes from the little Russian-Jewish town where he was born in 1887. People and animals fly through the brilliant skies of his paintings and houses stand on their heads.

Chagall also made 12 stained-glass windows for a synagogue in Jerusalem. They are considered some of his masterpeices and have been compared to jewels in a crown.

You've probably seen stained-glass windows in churches, temples, and other public buildings. Did you ever think of the people who made them? Next time you see one of those windows take a close look. Imagine all the love and hard work that went into making it all by hand.

MAKE A STAINED GLASS WINDOW

This is one way to get the glowing effect of light through stained glass.

① START with a piece of brown paper cut to fit the window where you'll hang it.

② DRAW a frame, then make a picture or design lightly in black crayon.

The black lines <u>must</u> connect to the frame or each other.

③ COLOR in between the lines with bright colored crayons. The go back and DARKEN the black lines.

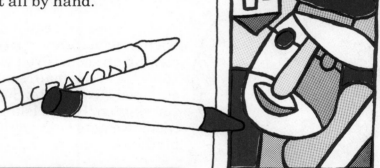

④ When your design is complete, moisten a cotton ball with mineral oil and rub lightly over the brilliantly colored shapes: The paper will become TRANSLUCENT.

⑤ This step is optional: ask an adult to help. Lay the "window" wrong side up on wax paper and IRON it. The crayon will melt and give a finished look.

Dear Diary:

July 8
Surprise!

Make today full of surprises. Surprise parties are great fun. Have you been to one lately? Here's a way to send somebody a birthday "surprise party" in the mail:

In a big envelope enclose a balloon, some confetti, a birthday candle, a flat favor (like a package of bubble gum cards or a booklet of stickers), and a card that says "SURPRISE! Happy Birthday." Sign your name or just "guess who." Use *two* first class postage stamps on the envelope and write "Please hand cancel" next to them. Mail your surprise two or three days before your friend's birthday so it's sure to get to him or her on time.

Of course you can mail fun surprises to friends even if their birthdays aren't coming up soon. If you would like to get a surprise in the mail, send a self-addressed stamped envelope to: Surprise! P.O. Box 152, Barrington, Rhode Island 02806 (Please include a note with your name and birthday.)

Dear Diary:

July 9
So Sew Day

Elias Howe loved machines. Born in Massachusetts on July 9, 1819, even as a kid, he was fascinated by the way mechanical parts moved together. When he grew up, Elias worked in a cotton machinery factory. He became interested in inventing a machine that could sew and in 1846, after five years of working on it in his spare time, Elias Howe received a patent for the first lockstitch (two-thread) sewing machine. If your family owns a sewing machine now's the day to ask for an explanation of how it works.

Untangle these threads.

These two threads are so tangled up that no one could sew with them. Guess which spool's thread is on the needle, then trace it to see if you're right. Color that thread with a colored pencil.

Dear Diary:

July 10
Whistler's Day

James Abbott McNeill Whistler (Whew, what a name!) was born in Massachusetts on July 10, 1834, but spent most of his life in London. He was a great painter and a colorful personality. He's best known for the picture called "Whistler's Mother," which is actually titled *Arrangement in Grey and Black, No. 1: The Artist's Mother*. (We should really be celebrating Long Name Day!)

Have fun with "Whistler's Mother."

Here is a cartoon of Whistler's famous *Arrangement*. Finish the picture any way you like.

Dear Diary:

July 11
Bucky's Birthday Eve

Buckminster Fuller's birthday is tomorrow (born 1895) but it seems appropriate to celebrate today —he always was ahead of his time! "Bucky," as Fuller is affectionately known all over the world, is a space age designer, but instead of rocket ships he designs ways for people to live better on earth. He's best known for his geodesic domes. You may have played on small Fuller domes in playgrounds but Bucky designed one big enough to fit over a whole city!

BUILD A GEODESIC STRUCTURE

Bucky discovered that the strongest shape is the triangle so he builds his domes with many triangles put together.

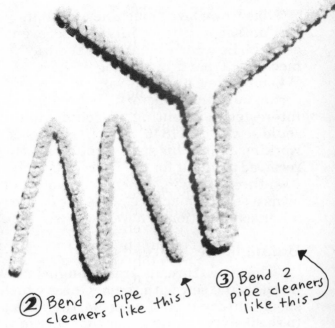

② Bend 2 pipe cleaners like this ↑   ③ Bend 2 pipe cleaners like this

① **Begin** by building a simple tetrahedron (a triangular pyramid ——→) with six drinking straws and four pipe cleaners.

④ Three straws can be put together like this (using the "M-shaped" pipe cleaner).

⑤ **Connect** 5 straws with the 4 pipe cleaners like this: to create this shape

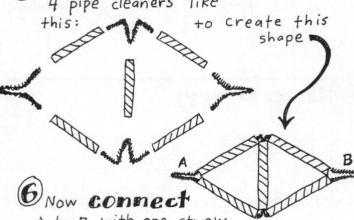

A   B

⑥ Now **connect** A to B with one straw and you've made a tetrahedron. By the same method of building (all triangles) use more straws and pipe cleaners to build complex geodesic structures.

WHAT PLANET IS THIS?

Dear Diary:

July 12
Thoreau's Birthday

Henry David Thoreau was born on July 12, 1817 in Concord, Massachusetts, and lived there most of his life. He kept a very complete journal of his thoughts and activities. When he was 28 years old he built a little one-room house by Walden Pond in Massachusetts and lived there — "a mile from any neighbor" — for over two years. He ate mainly from his own small garden and spent his time "adventuring on life." *Walden*, his most popular book, is the record of that experience.

His simple style of living touched every part of his daily life, even what he wore. He didn't believe in buying new clothes till his old ones were completely worn out. "No man ever stood the lower in my estimation for having a patch in his clothes," he said.

THOREAU
U.S. 5 cents

Dear Diary:

TRY IMAGINATIVE PATCHING

Kids are famous for wearing holes in the knees of their jeans. You can cover those holes with picture patches that are fun to make <u>and</u> wear.

① USE SCRAP FABRICS. Cut them into simple shapes to completely cover the hole or areas you want to decorate.

② THREAD a needle with embroidery thread and make a knot at the end

③ SEW the patch on using the "blanket stitch."

④ Now make the shape into a picture by adding more fabric shapes or just more stitches.

stitches →

← Buttons

July 13
The Night Watch

Tomorrow is France's greatest national holiday, Bastille Day. The festivities begin tonight as marchers carry flaming torches and Chinese lanterns on long poles through the darkened streets of France (La Retraite aux Flambeaux). Bands play patriotic songs, and spectators join in the parade.

Like America's Fourth of July, Bastille Day is celebrated with fireworks.

Make a "firecracker."

This is really a neat way to wrap a small gift. You need the cardboard tube from a toilet paper roll, wrapping paper, and string or pipe cleaners.

① WRAP a small gift, candies, or a rolled-up message in tissue paper and put them inside the tube.

② WRAP the tube in paper, leaving two extra inches at each end. TWIST the ends closed.

③ INSERT a heavy string or pipe cleaner in one end to look like the wick of the firecracker. Then TIE both ends with a string.

④ DIP the end of the wick in white glue then red glitter. It'll look like it's lit!

July 14
Bastille Day

When the French Revolution began in 1789 (only 6 years after the American Revolution ended) the Parisians launched their first attack on a prison—the Bastille—that stood, for them, as a symbol of injustice. They took the fortress by storm, freed the prisoners, carried them through the streets, and cheered them as victims of tyranny.

Bastille Day is the French "independence day." Tonight there will be feasts, fireworks, and colorful street dances in almost every part of France as the people joyously celebrate their national holiday.

Have French toast for breakfast.

(The recipe is on the next page.)

For more information about France write to: Embassy of France, 972 Fifth Ave., New York, N.Y. 10021.

Dear Diary:

Dear Diary:

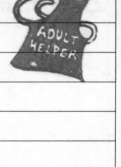

ADULT HELPER

4 of JULY - France

FRENCH TOAST

French toast can be made with any kind of bread, but several-day-old french bread cut into 3/4-inch slices is best.

① BEAT TOGETHER with a fork or whisk till well blended:

    4 eggs
    1 cup milk
    1/2 tsp. vanilla
    1/2 tsp. cinnamon

② DIP the bread in the egg mixture then BROWN the first side of the bread in a well-buttered skillet over medium heat.

③ Use a spatula to turn the bread over Cook till golden brown.

GLUE together with white glue THE FRENCH FLAG

Red↑ white↑ blue

This recipe will make about 8 slices. Stack 2 slices to make a serving. TOP with maple syrup or honey or (to make it really French) fresh fruit and sour cream.

St. Swithin's Day, if thou dost rain,
For forty days it will remain.
St. Swithin's Day, if thou be fair,
For forty days 'twill rain nae mair.

According to this traditional rhyme, today's weather will set the style for the next 40 days.

St. Swithin was the bishop of Winchester in England from the year 852 till his death in 862. It was customary to bury bishops *inside* the church in fancy tombs, but before St. Swithin died he said he wanted to be buried outside the church so the rain of heaven could fall on his grave. Over 100 years later his remains were moved into the church and a legend grew that this had displeased the soul of St. Swithin. Perhaps this is how the weather story began.

The idea that it might rain for 40 days brings to mind the popular Bible story of Noah and the Ark (Genesis 6:13). If it does rain today you may not need an ark, but you probably *will* need something to do.

BUILD AN ARK.

1. Cut down an empty milk carton like this:

A   B   Fasten with brass fasteners

2. Crease the front and back panels to make the bow and stern.

3. Make pairs of animals to ride inside (see January 14).

(This ark will really float — in rain puddles or bathtubs.) Cover it with aluminum foil to make a "space age" ark.

Dear Diary:

July 16
An Atlas At Last!

The first "world atlas," a book of maps by Claudius Ptolemy, drawn around 150 A.D. was finally printed on this date in 1482. Needless to say a lot was missing since ten years later, Columbus discovered America.

Make a map of your neighborhood.

Draw the streets, bikeways, paths, and special places near where you live. Make a "key" to identify the symbols you use. If you like, start with these.

Dear Diary:

July 17
Amazing Days'
Olympic Games

Every four years the Olympics are held—there are summer games and winter games, each played in a different country, but always in the same spirit of friendship. Here's a crossword to test your knowledge of the Olympics . . . just for fun.

Across

2. Popular athletic competition performed on bars, etc.
4. Founder of the modern Olympics, Baron Pierre de ____.
5. If two runners finish a race at the same time, they ____.
6. A race between teams; each runner runs only part of the course.

Answers appear at the back of the book.

Down

1. The Olympics are the greatest ____ sports event in the world. (Hint: The athletes don't get paid.)
2. The country where the ancient Olympics were held, as early as 776 B.C. Also the first modern Olympics were held there in 1896.
3. The Olympics are held in both winter and

____.

4. The rings of the Olympic flag represent the earth's five major

____.

The official flag of the Olympic Games shows five interlocking rings on a white background. The rings represent the five major continents, and at least one of the colors appears in the flag of every country on earth. Can you find out what the five colors are and in what order they come?

This Olympic torchbearer has lost his way. Help him reach the games.

Dear Diary:

July 18 is National Day in Spain. It is the day the Spanish Civil War began in 1936. In the evening there will be many festivities including dancing in the streets to Spanish music and the familiar click-click of castanets.

Make castanets.

"CLICK" "CLICK" "

These famous rhythm instruments, often made of wood or ivory, always accompany Spanish flamenco dancers.

① FIND two small pieces of wood (lumber scraps or building blocks) shaped like this → You must be able to hold them both with one hand.

② WRAP a rubber band around one end so it holds them together tightly.

③ PUT a toothpick (or something about that size) between the blocks ½ inch from the rubber band:

④ You've made castanets. Make two sets and play one with each hand.

"CLICK"

Dear Diary:

"CLICK"

"CLICK"

July 19

First Women's Rights Convention, 1848

The first women's rights convention in America was held on July 19, 1848, in Seneca Falls, New York. It was organized by Lucretia Mott, Elizabeth Cady Stanton, and others. At that meeting a declaration was drawn up and signed by 100 women and men who believed that women were equal with men and should have all the rights of full citizenship, including the right to vote. Many other meetings followed and now, over 130 years after that first convention, women and men still continue to work for the full equality of women.

These are a few of the many women who've led the way: Lucy Stone, Carrie Chapman Catt, Julia Ward Howe, Lucretia Mott, Elizabeth Cady Stanton, Elizabeth Blackwell, Abigail Scott Duniway, Alice Paul, Betty Friedan, and Gloria Steinem. See how many of their *last* names you find in this word-search.

```
A  C  F  S  O  U  B  J  S  B
B  E  I  S  T  O  N  E  A  J
D  H  M  T  Z  A  Q  Z  I  Q
F  R  I  E  D  A  N  H  P  W
D  U  N  I  W  A  Y  T  M  B
P  W  E  N  W  F  T  P  O  F
H  O  W  E  E  T  T  A  T  N
C  L  U  M  A  S  Y  U  T  K
B  L  A  C  K  W  E  L  L  L
```

Dear Diary:

July 20

Moon Day

On this date in 1969 earthlings first landed on the moon. U.S. astronauts Neil Armstrong and Edwin Aldrin, Jr. were the first people to walk on its surface. They brought back firsthand reports, photos, and moon rocks when they returned to earth on July 24. What a trip!

Since ancient times people have been fascinated by the moon and have dreamed of traveling there.

Be a moonwatcher.

1. Look in an almanac or today's newspaper for the phases of the moon, the dates of the new moon, first quarter, full moon, and last quarter.
2. Look in the back of *Amazing Days* and punch out the four moon-phase stickers. Stick them on the correct dates in your diary. They'll remind you to look at the moon as it goes through its 29½-day cycle.

(Did you ever realize that the words "month" and "Monday" come from "moon?")

Dear Diary:

Amazing Daily

HEAT WAVE CONTINUES

Summer is proving to be the hottest season of the year, exactly as predicted by *Amazing Daily's* astute weather forecaster, Ms. April Showers. Back in May, Showers claimed: "Summer is going to be hot, hotter than spring! Temperatures are almost sure to be the highest of the year." Today, Showers made her autumn forecast: "Fall promises to be cooler. Many leaves on trees will probably change color and fall off, and frost on the pumpkin should be expected." But for now—*hot* is the word.

Fan Fad Draws New Fans

Fantastic Folding Fan Fanatics (also known as the 4-F's) reported a large increase in membership earlier this week. The formerly small club of folding fan collectors is headed by Fanny Finestine of Fannin, Florida. "Fans have always been in my family," says Finestine. "My father collected feather fans, the kind that don't fold. It was my mother who first found folding fans, and I sort of followed suit. Once we practically had a family feud over a flamingo feather fan Father found. (He said it was the final straw when he found Mother dusting furniture with it.) Fans are fun. I guess the reason so many people have joined us lately is all this heat though. Fans are fine for keeping cool too."

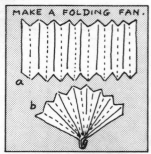

Geysers Erupt On Lawns All Over America

Amazing Daily sent reporters to investigate rumors of geysers springing up on lawns earlier this summer. They now confirm their early suspicions that these water bursts are not geysers but lawn sprinklers operated by Green Grass Growers of America, and kids trying to keep their cool.

Summer Sports
by Sam Smack

Every sport has its own shoes—tennis shoes, track shoes, bowling shoes, bingo shoes (bingo shoes??!), and so on; but what sport requires NO shoes? Well, sports fans, it's a brand-new sport called the barefoot relay, and here's how to play (any number can play):

Each player needs two containers (bowls, boxes, etc.) and five marbles.

The idea is to move all the marbles from one container to the other using only your bare feet.

On your marbles, get set, GO! First player to do it wins. Marblous!

Dear Diary:

July 22
Calder's Birthday

Alexander Calder, born July 22, 1898, was an artist who loved movement. His first major artwork was a miniature circus for which he made toy animals, wire-sculpture acrobats, and other "performers" that really moved. For years Calder gave shows of his tiny circus, moving the performers through their many acts by hand.

In 1932 Calder began his most famous work: abstract sculptures that moved. Another artist, Marcel Duchamp, named them "mobiles." Calder's mobiles are made of sheet-metal shapes and wires carefully connected so the slightest air current causes the whole thing to move. People have been so fascinated by the lovely "dance" of these shapes in the air that Calder has become one of the most popular twentieth-century sculptors.

Make a Mobile

C

Use stiff wire or light wooden sticks.

Make shapes of stiff paper or cardboard.

B

Use thread to hang shapes and connect wires or sticks.
(Careful that the threads don't tangle.)

EXPERIMENT:
ADD MORE SECTIONS.
TRY DIFFERENT SHAPES.

A

The most important aspect of a mobile is balance.

If it is well-balanced it will move in the slightest breeze.

Start by making and balancing the bottom section (A). Then go on to B and C.

Dear Diary

July 23
Ice Cream Cone Invented, 1904

On this glorious date in 1904 the ice cream cone was invented, quite by accident! At a world's fair, the Louisiana Purchase Exposition, in St. Louis, Missouri, two concessions were set up side by side: one sold ice cream, the other sugar waffles. The ice cream vendor ran out of dishes (his ice cream must have been really yummy!) so the waffle vendor began to roll his waffles in the shape of a cone so folks wouldn't have to eat the ice cream with their fingers. The idea was a hit, and the rest is history.

Make a summer snowman.

- Put two scoops of ice cream on a cone.
- Quickly make the snowman's face and buttons with raisins. Use a chocolate kiss, a cookie, or a fresh berry for a hat.

Dear Diary:

July 24
Leo Begins

People born between July 24 and August 22 are born under the sign of Leo, the lion. According to astrologers they are guided by the sun, and, like the lion and the sun, they are powerful personalities. They are born leaders who want to do things their own way. Their main fault is that they can be *too* proud.

Leo people love the active, outdoor life—especially this time of year because they enjoy sunshine. They are cheerful, generous people with many friends.

They love bright, showy things so when you make birthday cards for your Leo friends make them colorful and fancy. Here's one idea:

Fold a long paper into 3 parts.

In the center of the sun is the Leo symbol.

Use crayons or markers to make the sun and rainbow colorful. The blue part can be cut away - the card will still stand up.

Dear Diary:

July 25
Day of the Puzzling Rebus

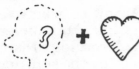 1,000,000 - N + ♥

The rebus above tells the name of a famous person who was born on this date in 1897. Hint: she was the first woman to fly all the way across the Atlantic Ocean alone (1932). Five years later she attempted to fly around the world. Her plane disappeared somewhere over the Pacific Ocean and no trace was ever found. Puzzling!

Here are some more rebuses (word-and-picture puzzles) for you to figure out:

Try making up your own rebuses. Write a rebus message in your diary space.

Dear Diary:

July 26
G.B.S. Day

George Bernard Shaw, born July 26, 1856, was a wonderfully funny, intelligent man — and also one of the most important writers of this century. He won the Nobel Prize for literature in 1925. The plays he wrote are still produced and include *Pygmalion* (later made into the musical *My Fair Lady*), *Major Barbara*, *Saint Joan*, and *Androcles and the Lion*.

G.B.S. (as he was known) had his own ideas about everything: he wanted to simplify the alphabet, socialize governments, and abolish Christmas (wha!?!?). He'd laugh at being included in *Amazing Days* because he didn't even celebrate his own birthday — although he did eat birthday cake and ice cream and almost anything sugary — he had a real sweet tooth! But he ate no meat at all — in fact, he was one of the most famous vegetarians ever. G.B.S. once said, "The strongest animals, such as the bull, are vegetarians. Look at me. I have ten times as much good health and energy as a meat eater." And he was very healthy. He lived to be 94 years old.

Be a vegetarian for a day.

Being vegetarian just means leaving meat out of the menu. You will be able to make up protein requirements by eating nuts, cheese, and eggs.

Menu

Breakfast
half cantaloupe
granola and milk
bran muffin
fruit juice

Lunch
peanut butter and jelly sandwich
on whole wheat bread
carrot and celery sticks
favorite fruit
milk

Dinner
macaroni and cheese
favorite cooked vegetable
green salad
iced tea
dessert

Wolfgang Amadeus Mozart was one of the most amazing children ever! Born in 1756, he started playing the harpsichord (an instrument much like a piano) when he was 3 years old, composed minuets at 5, toured Europe between the ages of 6 and 15 playing harpsichord, violin, and organ for kings and queens, composed symphonies at 8, and an opera at 12 — and that was just the beginning! When he died at the age of only 35, Mozart had composed over 600 musical works — some of the most beautiful music ever written!

Today is Mozart's "half birthday;" his birthday is January 27 — today is exactly 6 months later.

When is your half birthday?

Find your birthday month below. The month next to it is your half birthday month:

January .... July
February .... August
March .... September
April .... October
May .... November
June .... December

Dear Diary:

Dear Diary:

If you were 9 years old on your last birthday, you'll be 9½ on your half birthday. Have a mini-celebration.

July 28
Mona Lisa's Mustache Day

What kind of artist would paint a mustache on the *Mona Lisa*?! Actually a very important artist. Marcel Duchamp, who was more interested in ideas than pictures did just that. He probably felt that people praised old paintings too much and didn't pay enough attention to new artists and new ideas. So in the early 1900's (he was born on July 28, 1887) Duchamp bought a small reproduction of Leonardo's *Mona Lisa* and drew a mustache and goatee on it. Many people who saw it were shocked and thought Duchamp had done something terrible. All he had really done was to challenge their old ideas.

Celebrate Duchamp's birthday by wearing a false mustache. (If the *Mona Lisa* could, you can too.)

Copy the mustache below or make up your own. Draw it on stiff paper and cut it out. Make it comfortable. (The most comfortable false mustache is one drawn right on your face with makeup.)

Draw mustaches on pictures of people in old magazines. It's fun to really change how they look. (Only draw on pictures that belong to *you*.)

Dear Diary:

July 29
Archy's Day

Once there was a very famous newspaper columnist who was a cockroach! He was really the fanciful creation of a noted writer named Don Marquis, born on this date in 1878. According to Marquis, Archy the cockroach typed his column by jumping on the keys of the typewriter; because it was so much work (and he couldn't work the shift key) he never used capital letters or punctuation.

People loved to read Archy's column in the New York *Sun*. His "insect's view of life" was fresh and funny and often wise. Archy (and his friend Mehitabel the cat) became so popular that his columns were put together into a best-selling book, *The Lives and Times of Archy and Mehitabel*.

Here's one of Archy's stories.

i heard a
couple of fleas
talking the other
day says one come
to lunch with
me i can lead you
to a pedigreed
dog says the
other one
i do not care
what a dog s
pedigree may be
safety first
is my motto what
i want to know
is whether he
has got a
muzzle on
millionaires and
bums taste
about alike to me

July 30
Procession of the Sorceresses

The Procession of the Sorceresses is a mystery. Hardly anyone has seen it, or even heard of it. But somewhere in the world today (or tonight) a parade of female magicians is on the march. Who knows? It might even come right down your street.

Be ready to join the procession...
(MAKE A SORCERER'S HAT.)

① FOLD a newspaper page like this:

 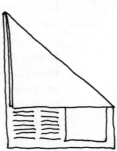  

② Now OPEN it up and form a cone. TAPE it together.

③ PAINT it with black or purple tempera paint. Paste on paper moons, stars, and planets (or draw them with white glue and sprinkle on glitter).

Imagine being an insect, and write in your diary from that point of view.

Dear Diary:

Dear Diary:

July 31
Tennis, Anyone?

Tennis, one of America's favorite sports, was invented by Walter Wingfield of England and brought to this country by Mary Ewing Outerbridge in 1874. (The first tennis rackets, balls, and net she brought into the United States were seized by customs officials who thought they were weapons.)

See how much you know about tennis.
Fill in these names where you think they belong:
Arthur Ashe, Bjorn Borg, Jimmy Connors, Evonne Goolagong, Billie Jean King, Bobby Riggs.

_____ This Australian player has a birthday today!

and
_____
_____ These two played each other in a match called The Battle of the Sexes in 1973. The female player won.

_____ He was the first black to be voted Number One player in America.

_____ This player was born in Sweden.

_____ America's top male player in the late 1970s.

Dear Diary:

August 1
Lammas Day

Wheat, oats, rice, corn, barley, millet, and rye are the seeds or fruit of certain cultivated grasses. Hundreds of years ago in the British Isles when the grain was harvested the farmers celebrated. On the first day of August wheat was ground and made into loaves of bread, then offered to God as a sign of thanks. This ceremony was called Hlaf-mass (Loaf-mass), and later became known as Lammas Day.

Young shepherds looked forward to this festival as a day of fun and excitement. For weeks ahead they built "Lammas towers" of stones and mud and grass. Sometimes the towers were twice as tall as the shepherds themselves. On August 1, they rose early and breakfasted on bread and cheese. The rest of the day was spent trying to find and knock down towers others had built—while at the same time protecting their own.

Nowadays few people grind their own wheat for bread or even know when the grain is harvested, so Lammas Day is only remembered as a festival out of the past. But grains are still a basic part of what we eat.

Dear Diary:

what number is also a great game?

TEN IS, of course

August 2
Friendship Day

Make a GRAND GRANOLA!
(Granola is a delicious whole grain cereal.)

① IN A LARGE BOWL COMBINE:

2 cups uncooked oatmeal
1 cup wheat germ
2 cups total, any combination of the following:
sesame or shelled sunflower seeds,
crushed cashews or walnuts,
slivered almonds, flaked
barley, buckwheat,
or shredded
coconut.

② In another bowl mix together:
¼ cup honey
¼ cup vegetable oil

③ POUR the honey mixture over the grains, nuts, and seeds. STIR till everything is evenly coated.

④ SPREAD the mixture about ½-to 1-inch deep in baking pans.

⑤ BAKE at 325° for about 45 minutes. Every 10 minutes or so stir the granola so it all gets evenly browned.

ADULT HELPER

⑥ After you take it out of the oven, ADD 1 cup of dried fruit:
raisins, chopped apricots, dates, or apples

When it cools it gets crunchy.
EAT it as a snack - by the handful - or on yogurt or ice cream, OR with milk as a breakfast cereal.

IT'S GRANDOLA!

Back in 1919, Joyce C. Hall (the man who founded Hallmark Cards) had the idea for Friendship Day. There were all kinds of other special days, he thought, so why not one for friendship? He suggested that on the first Sunday of August, folks should make a special effort to remember their friends: call on the telephone, visit, write a letter, send a card or flowers— anything to say "Glad you're my friend." Lots of friendly folks thought it was a good idea, and in 1935 Congress agreed, making Friendship Day official.

♥ Make out of season valentines (see February 5). Sign them "guess who" and deliver them secretly.

⊗ Make up a code with your best friend. Substitute a symbol for each letter of the alphabet. If only you and your friend know the code you can send each other messages that nobody else can read. Make it up here:

Dear Diary:

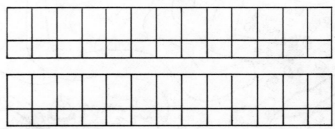

Valentines in August?!

August 3
Columbus Sailed from Spain, 1492

*In fourteen-hundred-and-ninety-two,
Columbus sailed the ocean blue ...*

... and he set sail on August 3 from Palos, Spain.

Help Columbus find his way to America.

Christopher Columbus's little fleet of ships—the *Niña*, the *Pinta*, and the *Santa Maria*—hoped to reach China or India by sailing around the world. Instead they found a new world—America.

Do you remember the date Columbus actually sighted land in the new world? That date is celebrated in America as Columbus Day.

NORTH AMERICA

ATLANTIC OCEAN

Palos (start)

Watlings Island (Finish)

CUBA

AFRICA

This is Columbus's coat of arms. Design a coat of arms for yourself! ← Draw it here.

Dear Diary:

August 4
Your Lucky Day

When you blow out all the candles on your birthday cake for good luck and a wish-come-true you're observing traditions that are very, very old. They began as superstitions but have become a lot like games.

Gather some good luck today.

Here are some traditional ways to do it:
• Find a clover patch. Sit down and look carefully through the leaves. Be patient. When you find a four-leafed clover press it in *Amazing Days* and keep it always.

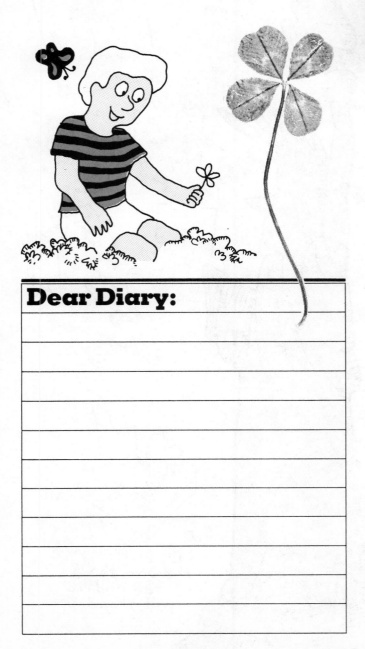

• Find a penny (or any coin). Wear it in your left shoe. Never spend it. A coin with the year of your birth on it is the best luck of all.

• Find a button, you'll make a new friend.

• Sneeze! If you sneeze several times in a row, that's even luckier:
One for a wish,
Two for a letter,
Three for a kiss,
Four for something better.

Spiders are very lucky. If you see one spinning a web you'll soon get something new to wear. Crickets and ladybugs are lucky too.

• Find a horseshoe or wear a horseshoe-shaped pin. Here's how to make the pin:

① CUT this shape out of stiff paper →

② PUNCH **SEVEN** holes in it with a pin point. (seven is a lucky number.)

③ Wear it with a safety pin. Let the horseshoe point UP so it "holds the luck."

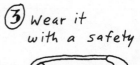

GOOD · · LUCK

• Find out what day of the week you were born; that's your lucky day. Write it here:

_____

Dear Diary:

August 5
Cornerstone of the Statue of Liberty Laid, 1884

On this date in 1884 the cornerstone was laid for the pedestal of what would become the world's most famous monument, the Statue of Liberty. "Miss Liberty" was a gift to America from the French people, designed by the sculptor, Auguste Bartholdi, who had the idea as early as 1856. The iron "skeleton" that allows the giant sculpture to stand 151 feet tall (from the tip of her torch to her toe) was designed by Gustave Eiffel, the engineer who built the famous Eiffel Tower in Paris. "Miss Liberty" was dedicated on October 28, 1886. Each year over a million people visit the well-known lady standing on her island in New York harbor.

A monument is a public artwork—usually sculpture—that stands for a memory or an idea. "Miss Liberty" began as a monument to the alliance between France and the United States during the American Revolution, but has come to stand for freedom throughout the world. Wherever you live there's almost certainly a monument to *something*. Visit a monument you know of today (or soon). Find out what it stands for.

Dear Diary:

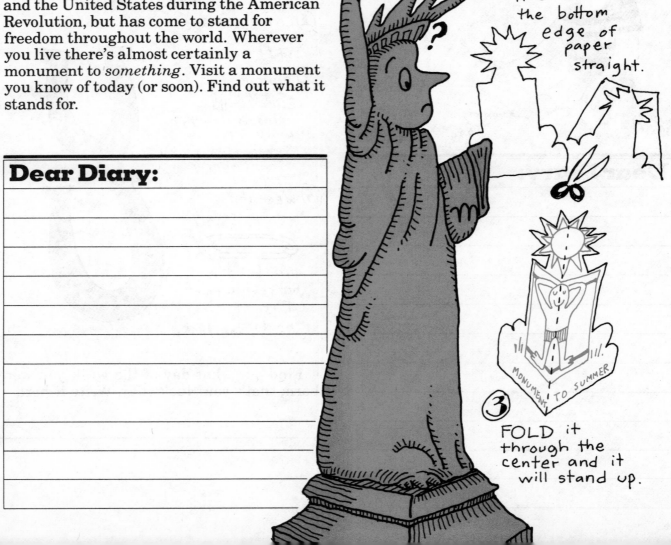

Design your own Monument.

It could be in memory of someone famous, or just something you like. (There's a monument to "Popeye" in Crystal City, Texas.)

① DRAW your monument on stiff paper.

MONUMENT TO SUMMER

② CUT it out but leave the bottom edge of paper straight.

MONUMENT TO SUMMER

③ FOLD it through the center and it will stand up.

August 6
Scott Nearing's Birthday

Scott and Helen Nearing live in a stone house that Helen built in Harborside, Maine. They grow almost all their food in a large garden in the summer and in a sun-heated greenhouse in the winter. They chop the firewood that heats the house and grow a cash crop of blueberries to pay for the few things they buy. They also find time to play music, visit with guests from around the world, and write books like their well-known *Living the Good Life*. They're known as homesteaders.

Scott was born on August 6, 1883, which makes him almost 100 years old today. He's done lots of things in his long life—taught economics, written over 100 books, and lived off the land for over 40 years.

Scott and Helen do things differently from a lot of people (oh, you noticed?).

On Christmas, Thanksgiving, and other days that Americans tend to overeat, the Nearings fast (eat nothing) to show their concern for people in the world who don't have *enough* to eat. In what year will you be 100 years old? _____ Imagine what your life will be like then and write about it in your diary.

Dear Diary:

Dear Diary:

August 7
Upside-Down Day

Try looking at the world through your legs. The sky looks like a great blue ocean far below, and the earth and trees turn into a mass of chunky green clouds. Lie on your bed with your head bent slightly back. Look at the ceiling and imagine that it's really the floor. Your house will suddenly look quite different—it's all in the way you look at things!

Try writing upside-down. Hold a mirror vertically on your piece of paper and look into it as you write. It will take time to get the knack of it. Later, try drawing upside-down.

These faces can be looked at from up or down. Try filling in the blank heads with your own upside-down faces.

The food-of-the-day is naturally (ta-da!) pineapple upside-down cake.

August 8
Star Light, Star Night

Night

Stars over snow
    And in the west a planet
Swinging below a star—
    Look for a lovely thing and you
      will find it,
It is not far—
    It never will be far.

Sara Teasdale, born August 8, 1884, looked and found many lovely things and put them into her poems. She especially loved stars and knew the names of many of them. (Did you know many stars have names?)

The Falling Star

I saw a star slide down the sky,
Blinding the north as it went by,
Too burning and too quick to hold,
Too lovely to be bought or sold,
Good only to make wishes on
And then forever to be gone.

There's an old tradition that says falling stars and the first star of evening are good for wishing. Tonight, about twilight, look for the first star. When you see it say, "Star light, star bright, first star I've seen tonight, wish I may, wish I might, have the wish I wish tonight." Then make a wish. (Don't tell anybody what it is or it won't come true.)

Have a starlight picnic to celebrate Sara Teasdale's birthday. Pack a supper to eat outside while gazing at the August sky. Or just have a snack on your terrace or patio. Look for the pictures the stars make (constellations) just the way people did thousands of years ago.

And speaking of thousands of years ago . . . did you know that when you look at the stars you're looking into the past? Some stars are so far away their light takes millions of years to reach our earth.

Dear Diary:

August 9
Jesse Owens' Olympic Victory

The Olympic Games are held every four years in a different country, and the whole world watches as great amateur athletes perform. On this date in 1936 in Berlin, Germany, Jesse Owens, a young black runner from Cleveland, Ohio, won his fourth Olympic gold medal. He was the undoubted champion of the games, breaking Olympic records nine times and equaling them twice. Only a year before Owens had set three world track records—sprinting, hurdling, and jumping—and tied another in a space of 75 minutes! No wonder Jesse Owens is considered one of the finest athletes of all time!

The BACKWARDS Race

The THREE-LEGGED Race

HOLD YOUR OWN OLYMPICS.

Get some friends together to **RUN** these fun races.

① The backwards race is just that — RUN BACKWARDS! Be sure to look over your shoulder to see where you're going. (A tap dancer, Bill "Bojangles" Robinson, set a world's record of 8.2 seconds for the 75-yard backwards dash.)

② The three-legged race is run by pairs of people with their legs tied together. Use strips of soft cloth, tied firmly—not tightly.

The KNEE-BOBBLE Race

The BALLOON BOUNCE Race

③ The knee-bobble race is run holding a balloon, beanbag, or some such thing between the knees. The runner can't touch it with his/her hands after the race begins, and if it drops he/she has to return to the starting line and begin again.

④ In the balloon bounce race each runner must bounce a balloon all the way to the finish line.

Make "gold medals" for the winners of your "Olympics."

Ribbon →

cardboard covered with gold foil paper →

Dear Diary:

August 10
Ecuador's National Holiday

Today is Independence Day in a country on the western coast of South America. The equator, which divides the earth into northern and southern hemispheres, runs right through the country giving it the Spanish name Ecuador.

To see how the equator divides our planet in half pretend an orange is the earth. Slice it in half. The top half of the orange is like the Northern Hemisphere where North America is. The bottom half is like the Southern Hemisphere where most of South America is. But when you sliced "the earth" in two you cut right through Ecuador.

Now slice up a banana (Ecuador's most important export) and an apple or other fruit. Put them in a bowl. Peel and section the orange and add it to the bowl. Toss in some raisins and you've made a yummy fruit salad. That's delicious geography!

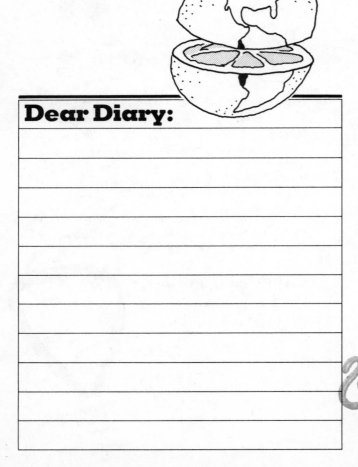

Dear Diary:

August 11
Popcorn Festival

Usually popcorn is what you munch while watching movies, but in Van Buren, Indiana, popcorn is the star of the show! Van Buren claims to be the popcorn center of the world because so much of the stuff is grown and packed in and around town, so every year during the second weekend of August the folks there hold a festival. There's a parade with marching bands and floats, a Popcorn Queen, and . . . guess what sells for only five cents a bag for the whole weekend! But you don't have to be in Van Buren to join the fun.

If you don't have a popper USE a large saucepan (2 quarts or bigger) with a tight-fitting lid.

1. POUR in enough cooking oil to cover the bottom.

2. PUT the pot over medium-high heat and ADD three "test-kernels."

3. When they POP, ADD enough popcorn just to COVER the bottom.

4. USE two potholders: With one hand, HOLD the lid on tight, with the other HOLD the pot handle and shake.

(The shaking helps POP all the corn and keeps it from burning.)

So that's how it's done!

ADULT HELPER

⑤ As soon as the popping stops POUR it into a bowl and ENJOY a great snack.

ADD salt or your favorite seasonings, butter, lemon juice, Parmesan cheese, or peanuts.

TRY floating popcorn on soup. That's what the American settlers did when the Indians first showed them how to POP it!

I LOVE POPCORN

How many bugs can you find camouflaged (hidden) in this picture?

Certain insects really do look exactly like leaves, thorns, or sticks. In fact, lots of animals protect themselves with camouflage.

Abbott Thayer, an American painter born on this date in 1849, wrote (with his son) the first important study of concealing color and pattern in the animal kingdom, which became known as Thayer's Law. Military use of camouflage to disguise soldiers, forts, and weapons was based on Thayer's study.

Dear Diary:

Dear Diary:

PEACE. I'm a tree.

"Number Thirteen"

Alfred Hitchcock, born August 13, 1899, is probably the best known of all movie directors. *Number Thirteen* was the first movie Hitchcock directed, back in 1921. Since then he has completed over 60 of them. (In almost every one "Hitch" makes a brief appearance. It's fun to try to spot him when you see one of his movies on TV.) He's considered the master of suspense films, and his name has practically come to mean "scary."

Here are titles of some of his many movies: *The Secret Agent, Rich and Strange, Murder, Blackmail, The Lodger, Suspicion, Spellbound, Notorious, Rope, Stage Fright, Strangers on a Train, I Confess, Dial M For Murder, To Catch a Thief, The Wrong Man, The Birds, Frenzy, Family Plot.*

Hide the titles in sentences to complete this story:

THE MAN WHO KNEW TOO MUCH

"*The Lady Vanishes*," said *Rebecca*. "Beyond a *Shadow of a Doubt*, she was behind that *Torn Curtain*, then, *Bon Voyage*, she was gone! Her name was *Marnie* and before she disappeared she said *The Trouble with Harry* was . . .

Dear Diary:

What WAS the trouble with Harry?

Fresh-From-The-Garden Day

If you or anyone in your family raised a vegetable garden this year, a lot of the produce is probably ripe and ready for the picking. Have a fresh-from-the-garden celebration—a meal of all fresh foods. Make a centerpiece of fresh flowers, or make a vegetable totem pole.

carrot hat

Radish faces with bean features

celery arms

onion face, carrot peel mouth

carved potato

You don't need a vegetable garden to make this totem pole, just the vegetables. Carve faces and/or use straight pins to attach raisins, peas, or beans for features. Put the "heads" together with toothpicks.

Dear Diary:

August 15
Lady Day

August 15 is celebrated by Roman Catholics as the Feast of the Blessed Virgin Mary, sometimes simply called Lady Day. In Poland it is called the Feast of Our Lady of Herbs, and to celebrate people gather great bouquets of sweet-smelling herbs and flowers and take them to churches where they adorn the statues of Mary. Imagine how wonderful the churches in Poland smell today!

You're probably most familiar with the herbs used in the kitchen: dill in pickles, oregano and basil in Italian dishes, parsley in salads, and mint and camomile in tea. If you have a garden there are probably some herbs there too. Ask the gardener in your family to show you which plants are herbs, or rub the leaves of various plants to see which ones are fragrant.

If you have mint in your garden, you're extra lucky. It can be used in tea, salads, or just washed and eaten by itself. Candies are made from peppermint and spearmint.

Mint is a perennial, which means you don't have to plant seeds each spring, it will just come up again year after year. And it's very easy to grow it indoors for the winter. Here's how:

① Start **TODAY!** CUT 2 or 3 stems of mint about 8-12 inches from the top.

② REMOVE the bottom 6 leaves on each stem. Put the stems into a bottle of water.

③ PUT the bottle in indirect sunlight and keep it filled with water until the stems produce ROOTS — about 2-3 weeks.

④ PLANT stems in a medium-sized pot in potting soil. Water it well.

⑤ KEEP your mint on a sunny windowsill and enjoy its sweet smell and taste all winter. Each time the soil dries out WATER again thoroughly.

Now for some REAL peppermint

Dear Diary:

August 16
Eve of the Gold Rush

Gold! That word sent men and women hurrying into frontier adventures after George Carmack and Skookum Jim discovered the precious metal in Bonanza Creek in the Klondike in 1896. People in Dawson City (in the Yukon Territory very near Alaska) still celebrate August 17 as Discovery Day. This gold rush, called the "Klondike Stampede," really got under way almost a year later when a steamship carrying a load of gold from the region docked in Seattle, Washington. Word spread quickly—*gold!*—and over 30,000 people from all over (some from as far as Japan and Australia) rushed to the Klondike to "strike it rich."

For more information about the Yukon and its famous gold rush, write to: Klondike Visitor's Association, Dawson City, Yukon Territory, Canada.

Dear Diary:

STRIKE IT RICH with Gobbledygold

These chewy nuggets are good as gold and taste even better!

① CREAM together 3 T. butter at room temperature and 3 T. honey in a mixing bowl

② ADD a sliced banana to the creamed mixture and beat till well blended. *mash it in.*

③ In another bowl mix together:
  ½ cup whole wheat flour
  ½ cup uncooked oatmeal
  ½ tsp. baking soda
  ½ tsp. salt
  ¼ tsp. ginger

④ ADD the dry ingredients into the creamed mixture. STIR.

⑤ ADD ½ cup broken pecans or walnuts and ½ cup GOLDEN raisins. Stir till well blended.

⑥ DROP the batter by teaspoonsful onto a lightly oiled cookie sheet about an inch apart. ADULT HELPER.

⑦ BAKE in a 375° oven for about 20 minutes, until well browned. Remove the nuggets from the cookie sheet and let them cool for a minute or two before gobbling them down. Who'd have thought your oven was such a GOLD MINE?

August 17
Balloon Crossing

Even though balloons were being flown over a hundred years before airplanes were invented, the first successful crossing of the Atlantic Ocean in a balloon took place many years *after* Lucky Lindy's historic airplane flight (see February 4). Between 1873 and 1978 balloonists made 13 tries resulting in 13 failures. Finally, Ben Abruzzo, Maxie Anderson, and Larry Newman set out to cross the Atlantic in a magnificent balloon called *Double Eagle II*. They took off from Maine on August 11, 1978, and touched down near Paris, France, on August 17, becoming the aeronautic heroes of the year!

TRY YOUR OWN "BALLOON CROSSING." Here's a way you can race toy balloons across a room or outdoors.

① PUT the end of a long string through a drinking straw.

② STRETCH the string across a room, between two trees, or anywhere you can securely fasten the two ends of the string.

③ BLOW UP a big balloon till it's almost full of air. Hold the end closed.

④ PUT a piece of tape over the straw and gently attach it to the balloon.

⑤ LET GO of the end and ZOOM.

Dear Diary:

(For races put two strings exactly side by side about 18-inches apart.

August 18
Nash Eve

The Panther

The panther is like a leopard,
Except it hasn't been peppered,
Should you behold a panther crouch,
Prepare to say Ouch.
Better yet, if called by a panther,
Don't anther.

Ogden Nash, born August 19, 1902, wrote some of the funniest poems in the English language. Like "The Panther," most of Nash's verses are written in couplets, two lines together that rhyme:

The Fly

The Lord in His wisdom made the fly
And then forgot to tell us why.

Try writing some funny verses to celebrate Nash Eve. Here's one more by Ogden Nash for inspiration:

Celery

Celery, raw,
Develops the jaw,
But celery stewed,
Is more quietly chewed.

Dear Diary:

August 19
National Aviation Day

When Wilbur and Orville Wright were very young they made and sold kites to earn spending money. They were fascinated by toys that could fly and by machines. When they were older they built, sold, and repaired bicycles for a living. Then they put their knowledge of kites and machines together and began to work on the creation of a machine that would allow *people* to fly. They first invented successful gliders (like big kites) then they built an "aeroplane" they called the Flyer. It had double wings (wood frames covered with cotton), propellers, and a small gasoline-powered engine. On December 17, 1903, at Kitty Hawk, North Carolina, Orville and his Flyer flew! That was the first time a machine carrying a man had remained airborne through its own power. (The flying time was only 12 seconds—imagine!)

December 17 is celebrated as Wright Brothers Day because of the historic flight. Today is National Aviation Day because Orville Wright was born on this date in 1871.

Fold a great paper airplane.

① Fold an 8½-x 11-inch piece of paper in half. Open it up again.

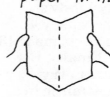

② Fold two corners UP like this:

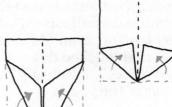

③ Fold again like this:

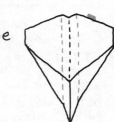

④ Fold both wings DOWN about ½-inch from the center crease:

⑤ Fold wing tips UP about 1-inch from the ends:

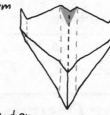

⑥ To give the plane a tail reverse the center crease at the back 1-inch of plane (colored in picture 5). FOLD UP

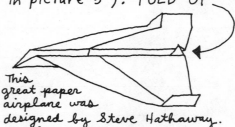

This great paper airplane was designed by Steve Hathaway. Thanks, Steve!

Not until 1977 did a person invent a plane that could fly on human power alone. Dr. Paul MacCready designed the Gossamer Condor, which, powered by the pedaling of one man, has flown across the English Channel.

Dear Diary:

Print your own headline and write your own story about this amazing day. Add snapshots, drawings, and cartoons too.

Dear Diary:

August 21
Ozma's Birthday

Today is the birthday of Ozma, the princess who rules Oz. Members of the International Wizard of Oz Club celebrate Ozma's birthday with a special cake and "Ozcream." (According to Fred Meyer, the club's distinguished secretary, "Ozcream" is simply vanilla ice cream with an "Ozzified" name.)

Did you know there are more than 40 books in the Oz series? *The Wonderful Wizard of Oz* was the very first.

Help Dorothy and her friends find their way to the Emerald City.

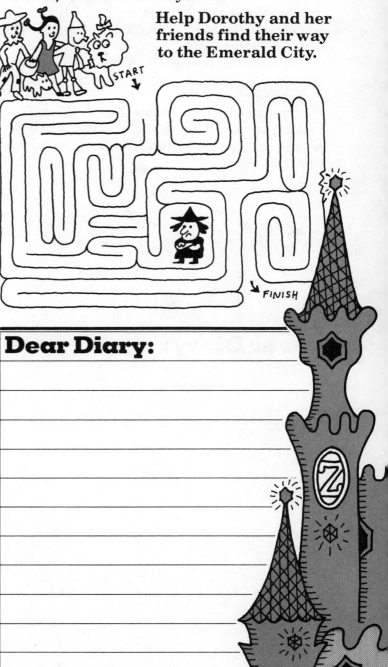

Dear Diary:

August 22
Virgo Begins

People born between August 22 and September 23 are born under the sign of Virgo, the virgin. According to astrologers, they are intelligent, imaginative people who are good at figuring things out. They love to learn new things and have amazing memories for keeping information close at hand. They are orderly and tidy, but one of their worst faults can be caring *too* much for details—being "picky" and overly critical of others. Virgo people are very careful and are especially good at skilled crafts and other detailed work.

List all the people you know born under the sign of Virgo. Which ones seem to fit the description?

This is what the constellation "Virgo" looks like. Imagine, if you can, how ancient people saw a woman in these stars and draw her there.

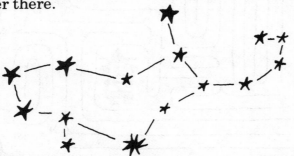

August 23
Yo-yo Day

On this date in 1975, superb yo-yoer, Tony Flor, did 7,351 consecutive loop-the-loops with a yo-yo.

If you have a yen to yo-yo:

1. Find two large matching heavy buttons (they should be at least an inch across).

2. Sew them together back and forth through the holes with a toothpick in between as a spacer. When the buttons are sewn securely, remove the toothpick and wrap more thread around the middle threads till a strong shank is formed. Sew through the shank and clip off the ends of the thread.

3. Now tie one end of a yard-long piece of string around the shank.
4. Wind the string around the shank and make a loop at the end to slip onto your middle finger.

Dear Diary:

Dear Diary:

Roy G. Biv Day

Roy G. Biv is a very colorful name, but it doesn't belong to one particular person. It's sort of like a code name. Here's a hint: "G" stands for green. Get it?

Okay, one more hint: "I" stands for indigo, a very deep blue.

R_____
O_____
Y_____
Green
B_____
Indigo
V_____

You guessed it! The letters stand for the colors of the rainbow in their natural order.

Is today sunny? If so, turn on the garden hose and make a fine spray using your thumb or a nozzle. See the rainbow? Look at the order of the colors from top to bottom.

(If you don't have a garden hose use a glass prism to make a rainbow. Or put a small mirror vertically into a pan of water and face it toward the sun—the rainbow will appear on the bottom of the pan.)

Color this rainbow with colored pencils, fine-line markers, or crayons.

Color this rainbow with colored pencils, fine-line markers or crayons.

Arrange the clothes in your closet in rainbow order. How about the books on your bookshelf? Write in your diary using a different color pen or pencil for each letter or word.

ROYGBIV

Purple doesn't start with "V."

O, come on, Violet! You're bound to figure out THIS one!!

Dear Diary:

U.F.O. Day

Flash! What was that? All of a sudden the two people see it—a tremendous airship studded with blue lights passing quietly overhead—and then it's gone.

Twenty minutes later four more people, this time scientists from Texas Tech, sight strange blue lights moving in the sky. Photos are taken.

Sound like a good science fiction story? Maybe so, but this one's true. The place—Lubbock, Texas. The date—August 25, 1951. No one will ever be sure what the six Texans saw or where it came from. It remains a U.F.O.—Unidentified Flying Object.

Play U.F.O., a drawing game for two or three players.

You need one die ( ) and a pencil and paper for each player.

Take turns rolling the die. When any player rolls a 1 ( ) he or she may draw the first part of his or her U.F.O. and so on progressively through 6 ( ).

The drawing can only be put together in this order. First player to finish the drawing wins.

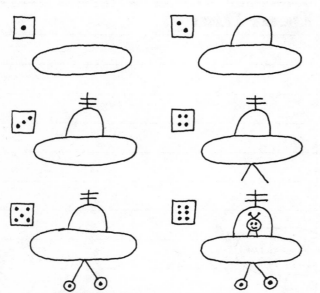

There's just one catch: once your drawing has progressed to the third stage you may not roll a 3 ( ) again. If you do, you have to start your drawing over.

Dear Diary:

August 26
Easy Essay Day

Well, it's almost back-to-school time and you *know* the first day back you're bound to write a paragraph about your summer. Be one step ahead: fill in the blanks of this silly essay just for the fun of it!

What I did on my summer vacation

My _____ and I got tired of _____ all summer, so we decided to _____ and go to _____ . We in our _____ and took off for _____ .

The first day we saw a(n) _____ by the side of the _____ . We stopped to _____ , but it _____ . That night we stayed in a(n) _____ .

The next day we visited _____ who tried to _____ , but we got out of there in a(n) _____ .

Finally we got to _____ where we were greeted by _____ . _____ showed us _____ and took us to _____ . We stayed out till _____ o'clock in the _____ . We _____ well that night!

When we got home, we _____ .

August 27
First All-Metal Clarinet Patented, 1889

The "Clarionet" patented on this date in 1889 was manufactured by Charles Gerard Conn of Elkhart, Indiana. Before Conn's instrument all clarinets were made of wood.

There are thousands of different musical instruments in the world. Some are very old like the drum, and some are new like the Moog synthesizer—a kind of musical computer.

Make a drinking straw clarinet.

A clarinet has a "reed" that vibrates when the musician blows on it; a "reed" is the musical secret of this instrument too.

1. Flatten about ½- to 1-inch of an ordinary drinking straw.

2. Using scissors, cut a point in that end.

3. Put that end into your mouth and blow. The "reed" will vibrate and make one clear musical note.

4. Try cutting the straw different lengths to different notes.

Dear Diary:

Dear Diary:

August 28
Monster Mystery Day

Scientists are still hunting for a mysterious monster believed to live in Loch Ness (loch is Scottish for lake), a deep, murky lake in northern Scotland. Hundreds of people claim to have seen the Loch Ness monster (nicknamed "Nessie"), but only a few have taken photos, most of which are unclear. However, on this date in 1968 a team of scientists from the University of Birmingham (in England) using sonar *did* detect several very large objects moving under water much faster than any fish known to live in the loch. Sea monster? Giant slug? Witnesses describe a creature much like a plesiosaur, a dinosaur that lived in the seas around Scotland 70 million years ago. Some scientists say it's definitely possible that one or more of the creatures are still around. They recall that up until 1938 a certain kind of prehistoric fish (coelacanth) was thought to have been extinct for millions of years; then a fisherman caught one—*alive*!

MAKE A NESSIE PUPPET.
- MAKE your monster out of stiff paper
- Accordion-FOLD the center of its body so it can squinch up and stretch o-u-t.
- ATTACH 2 sticks with tape to the back to hold and move your puppet.

Dear Diary:

August 29
Chop Suey Concoction Day

For the most part people in China do *not* eat chop suey. In fact, it was first concocted in New York City! In 1896 Chinese ambassador Li-Hung Chang came to America to visit President Grover Cleveland. On August 29 his chef (Li-Hung Chang traveled with 31 servants including three cooks and a barber) put the dish together to appeal to both Americans and Chinese. It was a smash hit, and people have been enjoying chop suey (with or without chopsticks) ever since.

Have a Chinese supper.

See if your mom or dad knows how to "stir-fry" chop suey. If not you can buy it in a can at the Chinese food section of your grocery. You might want to get chow mein noodles, Chinese tea, and fortune cookies for the event also.
- Cook brown or white rice according to the instructions on the package.
- Heat up the can of chop suey. Season with soy sauce.
- Serve over rice. Then put a handful of chow mein noodles on top. (You can call it "chop mein" or "chow suey.")
- Serve hot Chinese tea with the meal, and fortune cookies for dessert.

Dear Diary:

August 30
Frankenstein Night

Over 160 years have passed since Mary Shelley, born August 30, 1797, wrote the novel, but *Frankenstein* continues to send chills up the spines of readers and moviegoers alike.

Amazing facts about "Frankie":

• Mary Shelley was married to Percy Bysshe Shelley, a great English poet. They spent the summer of 1816 in Switzerland with another famous poet, Lord Byron. They told ghost stories every night and Byron suggested they each write a tale of terror. Mary's story became the world-famous *Frankenstein*.

• "Frankenstein" is not really the name of the monster but of the scientist who put him together from parts of dead bodies he stole from graveyards. The monster's name was Adam (still, everybody usually calls him Frankenstein).

• In Mary Shelley's original novel the monster speaks perfect, beautiful *French*!

• The first movie version of *Frankenstein* was made by Thomas Edison (see February 11) in 1910.

• The most famous actor to play the monster was Boris Karloff (see November 23) in 1931. The makeup and costume he wore for the part took three hours to put on every day!

Here's a spooky way to change your face without using any makeup—just a flashlight. Tonight, after dark, turn off all the lights and sit in front of a mirror. Turn on the flashlight and shine it up, just in front of your face. You won't believe how weird you look! Some people say if you stare at your face this way for a long time (five minutes or longer) it will change before your eyes to look like the face of someone who lived *and died* long ago.

Dear Diary:

August 31
Almost Football Season

With August drawing to a close lots of football fans and players are looking forward to their favorite time of year. If you play football you may have already started practicing. Soon fans will crowd the bleachers, cheerleaders will jump and shout, and players will carry that funny-shaped ball down a hundred-yard field to make touchdowns. When football games begin everyone knows fall will soon be here.

The first professional football game was held on September 3, 1895, in Latrobe, Pennsylvania, although non-professional football goes back much further, having its roots in soccer and rugby.

WANTED: A PIGSKIN

Dear Diary:

How many different pictures can you make from the football shapes above?

September 1
Tarzan Day

Q. Who was the original "swinger?"
A. Tarzan.

Almost everyone knows Tarzan. Edgar Rice Burroughs (born September 1, 1875) wrote the first of 24 Tarzan books in 1912, and they have been made into movies, TV shows, and comic strips. But according to *Tarzan Alive*, a book by Jose Farmer published in 1972, Tarzan is a real person still living somewhere in Africa!

Q: Why doesn't Tarzan use swinging vines any longer?
A: If they were any longer he'd hit the ground.

Q: When Tarzan wears only his loincloth, what animal does he resemble most?
A: A little bear.

Q: What animal keeps Tarzan's extra clothes?
A: The elephant—in his trunk.

Q: Why can't the leopard hide from Tarzan?
A: Because it's always spotted.

Q: What animal never tells Tarzan the truth?
A: The one that is always lion.

Q: What is Tarzan's favorite card game?
A: Crazy apes.

Q: What animal *won't* Tarzan play cards with?
A: The cheetah.

Q: What animal didn't come to Tarzan and Jane's wedding?
A: The missing lynx.

Q: Who's round and purple and swings through the jungle?
A: Tarzan of the grapes.

AH - AHAHAHA - AHA - AHA!

SWING TODAY

Note: If you don't have easy access to jungle vines, a swingset will do fine!

September 2
Labor Day Celebration

The first Monday of September is Labor Day, a happy end-of-summer holiday honoring American workers. It was founded in 1882 by Peter J. McGuire, a carpenter who began work at the age of 11. At first the day was mainly celebrated by the members of labor unions; today, all Americans—no matter what their occupation—celebrate Labor Day by not working!

Today's a good time to think about what work you'd like to do as an adult. Write about it in your diary space.

You shouldn't have to work *too* hard to answer these occupation riddles.

Q: Who mows the grass of a baseball field?
A: A diamond cutter.

Q: Who makes people smile, then shoots them?
A: A photographer.

Q: Whose job keeps her on her toes?
A: A ballerina.

Q: Who gets paid for loafing?
A: A baker. (He or she also makes a lot of dough!)

Q: Who gets paid to talk about old times?
A: A history teacher.

Dear Diary:

Dear Diary:

LABOR DAY

LABOR IS LIFE

U.S. POSTAGE 3¢

Amazing Daily

September 3 *All The News That's Fit To Tickle*

KING PROCLAIMS TODAY SEPTEMBER 14

London, 1752—If you lived in 1752 you would have woken up this morning thinking it was September 3, but you would have been wrong. In that year, King George II proclaimed today September 14, 1752. This confusing action was part of Great Britain and the American Colonies' adoption of the Gregorian calendar which was more accurate than the Julian calendar the people then had been using (despite this loss of eleven days).

Julian Calendar Inaccurate

The Julian calendar had been in use since 46 B.C. when it was established by Julius Caesar. Bit by bit the calendar proved to be an inaccurate way of dividing the year because it gradually moved ahead of the seasons until it had become a whole eleven days off. If the people had stuck with the Julian calendar the autumn equinox would have come on September 12 that year; by skipping eleven days it came on September 23 as it should. With the year back on the right track, the calendar should not have to be changed again.

Calendar Change Sparks Riots

Crowds were rioting in streets throughout Great Britain and America on September 3, 1752 protesting the eleven missing days of September. People who rented their homes were upset by having to pay a month's rent for only 19 days of living. Others were simply confused by a calendar in which "Friday the second" was followed by "Saturday the fourteenth." Perhaps most upset were kids with birthdays on one of the missing days. It was rumored that these kids banded together to demand their parties. Their battle cry: "Down with the calendar. We want cake!"

September 4
Manhattan Discovery Day

On this date in 1609 the English explorer Henry Hudson (exploring for the Dutch) discovered the island Native Americans called Man-a-hat-ta, "Island of the Hills." It's now called Manhattan. With an area of only 31 square miles (80 square kilometers) it is New York City's smallest borough, but one of the most important cultural and business centers in the world.

People everywhere are familiar with New York's famous sights—Broadway theaters, Madison Square Garden, the United Nations headquarters, the Empire State Building, and more.

Dear Diary:

Dear Diary:

Find your way through this Manhattan map-maze from Central Park to the Brooklyn Bridge.

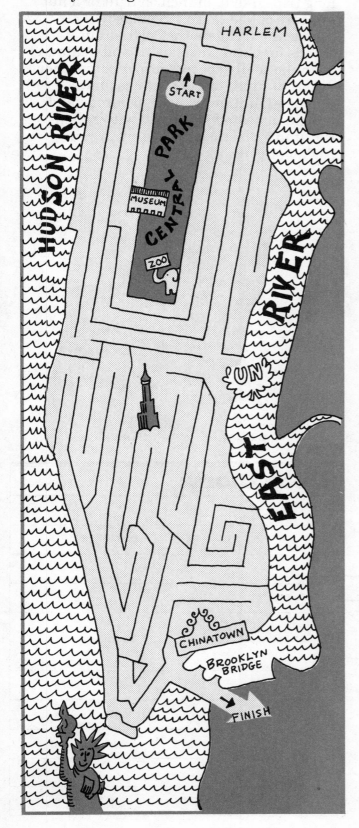

Amazing Daily

September 5   *All The News That's Fit To Tickle*

PROCRASTINATORS CELEBRATE BE LATE FOR SOMETHING DAY

Philadelphia—Members of the Procrastinators Club of America set this date aside to promote their favorite pastime. "Procrastinate Now" is their motto.

"People who rush around and never relax and get all worried about being on time are people who die early. Then they are referred to as the late Mr. So-and-So. Why not be late while you're alive!" says Les Waas, president of PCA since 1956. (The club has not gotten around to holding its 1957 elections.)

The PCA makes a habit of putting things off. They sometimes hold a Christmas shopping seminar on December 26, usually wait to celebrate the New Year till at least June (to see if the year's worth it), and though National Procrastination Week is officially the first week of March, PCA members put it off till at least the second week. Don't worry if you don't get around to celebrating BE LATE FOR SOMETHING DAY today—you can do it later.

Procrastinators Plan Snail Race

Sacramento, California—The Escargot Chapter of the PCA is planning a National Snail Race for sometime in the late future. Snails will be placed inside a marked circle; last snail to leave the circle will be declared the winner.

Club Membership Amounts to Milions

Members of the PCA probably number in the millions, reports President Waas. Most of them, however, have not joined yet. Requests for membership information may be sent to: Procrastinators Club of America, 1405 Locust Street, Philadelphia, Pennsylvania 19102.

Dear Diary:

September 6
Bicycle Celebration

Members of the Boston Bicycle Club got up extra early on the morning of September 6, 1882. At 4:38 A.M. they began America's first 100-mile bike trip sponsored by a club. It wasn't a race. The seven people who rode the whole 102 miles from Worcester, Massachusetts, to Boston stopped often for food, refreshments, and repairs. They finished their ride about 9:30 P.M., and you can bet they all slept well *that* night!

There are about a hundred different ways to have a bicycle celebration: Go for a ride, give your bike a bath and a lube-job, have a race, play bike-basketball, draw a picture of your bike (much harder than it sounds), join a bike club (call the Y.M.C.A. or your city recreation department for information), or plan a bike trip. If you know an adult who likes to bike, you might be able to interest him or her in leading a five-mile jaunt.

Gorp for the road.

Take along a snack. Bikers who take long trips like to munch on fruit or a nut mixture called "gorp." (Sounds like something from another planet but it stands for Good Old Raisins and Peanuts!) To make really special gorp mix together different kinds of nuts (raw cashews, almonds, sunflower seeds, peanuts, and unsalted toasted soybeans) with raisins. Put it in a plastic bag to carry in your pocket or your bike bag.

Draw a picture of YOUR bike here 🡒

Dear Diary:

September 7
Grandma's Day

Anybody can paint who wants to," said Grandma Moses. "Like all kinds of work, the more you do, the better you do."

Grandma Moses was born on September 7, 1860 and died December 13, 1961. Of course she wasn't called "Grandma" when she was born but Anna Mary Robertson. She married Thomas Moses and worked hard as a farm wife for many years, but always wanted to find time to paint. She was 76 years old when she finally began painting scenes from her youth in upstate New York. Within five years Grandma Moses was famous for her paintings and her charming personality. At 90 she was proclaimed Grandmother of the Nation by various clubs. And at 100 she danced a jig to celebrate. She painted 25 pictures *after* her hundredth birthday!

National Grandparents Day falls very near and sometimes on Grandma Moses's birthday. It's the first Sunday after Labor Day, by presidential proclamation.

Now is a good time to pay your grandparents a visit, if possible. Ask one of them or someone in your family to help fill in this "family tree."

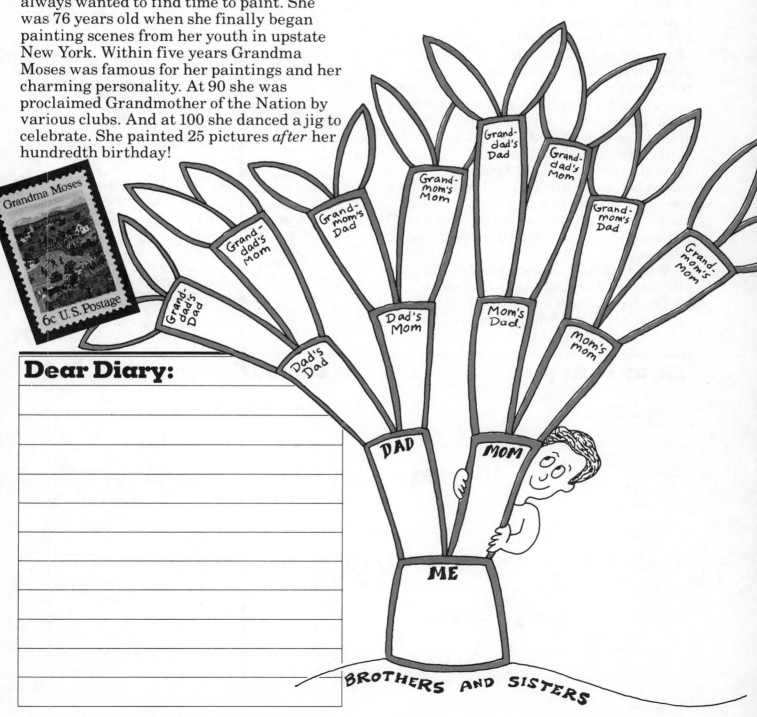

Grandma Moses

6c U.S. Postage

Dear Diary:

September 8
Crazy Eight

Celebrate September 8 with a rousing game of crazy eights! You can play with two to five other players.

1. Shuffle and deal five cards to each player (unless there are only two of you, then you get seven each).

2. Put the rest of the deck (called the "stock") in the center of the table. Turn the top card face-up and put it next to the stock.

3. In turn, each player must put a card from his/her hand on the face-up pile. It must match the top card on the pile in suit (♦ ♥ ♣ ♠) or rank (2,3,4, . . . J,Q,K,A). For example, if the ♦ 3 is the top card face-up, the player may put any ♦ or any 3 on top of it. If the player has no ♦ and no 3, he/she must draw cards from *stock* until he/she gets one or the other to play . . . *unless the player has an 8.*

4. Eights are wild! That means any 8 can be placed on any card. (But good players use them mainly to win, not just to avoid drawing cards from the stock.) When any 8 is played the player gets to choose what suit follows.

5. When stock is all gone the face-up pile is turned over to make new stock.

6. The first player to get rid of all the cards in his or her hand is the winner. Crazy!

Dear Diary:

September 9
California's Admission Day

Happy Birthday, California! On this date in 1850 "the Golden State" was admitted to the Union.

Grow a California tree. (Not a redwood; your ceilings aren't high enough.)

① Buy a California avocado at the grocery store. It looks like a big green egg. (Tell your friends a flying saucer dropped it in your back yard - maybe it'll hatch a Martian baby ?!?)

Florida   California

② Slice it in half, being careful not to hurt the big pit inside. Remove the pit. (Eat the avocado in a green salad or on a sandwich with lettuce, tomato, and mayo.

③ Soak the pit in water for a few minutes, then peel the thin brown skin off.

④ Stick three toothpicks around the middle and set it in a glass of water. Put it in a dark place.

⑤ Change the water every few days, and eventually a root and stem will poke out. (Be patient. It may take a month or so.)

⑥ When it has leaves, plant it in a pot of soil. It will grow into a tree.

Dear Diary:

September 10
Rosh Hashanah Celebration

Jewish people all over the world celebrate their new year in the fall : A period of 10 days called the high holy days, the most important days in the Jewish calendar.

According to tradition there is a *Book of Life* in heaven in which each person's fate is recorded for the coming year. That's why on Rosh Hashanah people send greeting cards that say, "May you be inscribed for a good year!"

On the first morning of the new year Jews go to the synagogue where the shofar, a ram's horn, is blown like a trumpet—a symbol of unity for the Jewish people. Throughout the high holy days they seek to make up for any wrongs done in the past year and to prepare for a coming year of holiness. Yom Kippur is the tenth and holiest day of the year, a day of prayer and fasting.

The high holy days come at a different time each year, reckoned by the Jewish calendar which is over 5,000 years old. Look on the last page of this book to see when Rosh Hashanah comes this year.

Have a Rosh Hashanah treat.

At the first meal of the new year there is always a jar of honey on the table. The family dips slices of apple and pieces of hallah (white bread, usually twisted in a braid) in it in hopes of assuring "a sweet year."

Slice an apple into quarters. Remove the core, then slice each quarter two or three more times. Sprinkle the apple with a little lemon juice to keep it from turning brown. Dip each slice into honey and enjoy!

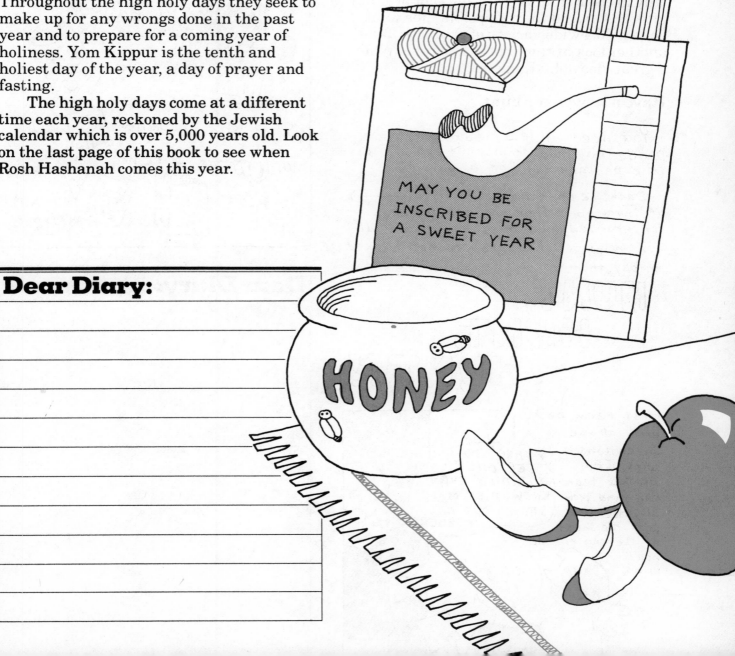

MAY YOU BE INSCRIBED FOR A SWEET YEAR

HONEY

Dear Diary:

September 11
Tribute to the Unknown Inventor

When you brushed your teeth this morning you probably squeezed toothpaste out of a soft metal tube that collapses as it empties. A very clever invention if you think about it! Simple, yes, but somebody had to invent it. John Rand was that somebody, and he had it patented on this date in 1841.

The collapsible tube was invented to hold oil paint. It changed the course of art because it made paint portable—artists could easily take their paints outside and paint landscapes as they looked at them. (Before, they had drawn outside but painted only in their studios. Paintings got brighter after 1841.) And the collapsible tube went on to hold a wide variety of products. Take another look at that toothpaste tube. What a great idea John Rand had!

Have a scavenger hunt.

You need at least four players. Divide into two or more teams. (This is especially fun for a party.)

Each team takes this list ⟶ of inventions that are easily taken for granted and tries to collect all the things listed. You're not allowed to buy them—

HUNT, HUNT, HUNT!!

First team back with all the inventions wins. If neither team can find them all, the one with the most at the end of one hour wins.

SCAVENGER HUNT

1. paper clip
2. Ball-Point pen
3. Whistle
4. ZOWIE bottle top
5. candle
6. toy balloon
7. photo
8. TIN CAN
9. Rubber stamp
10. Screw
11. Paper bag
12. TEA BAG

ARE YOU SERIOUS? I DIDN'T EVEN KNOW THEY **MADE** STAMPS OUT OF RUBBER!

Dear Diary:

September 12
Yam Festival

Early in September the Ashanti people of Ghana, Africa, hold their Yam Festival, an important harvest celebration. During the festival drum music, dancing, and even marriages take place, and young women step into adult society. Of course, it's also a time for eating yams.

MAKE CANDIED YAMS.

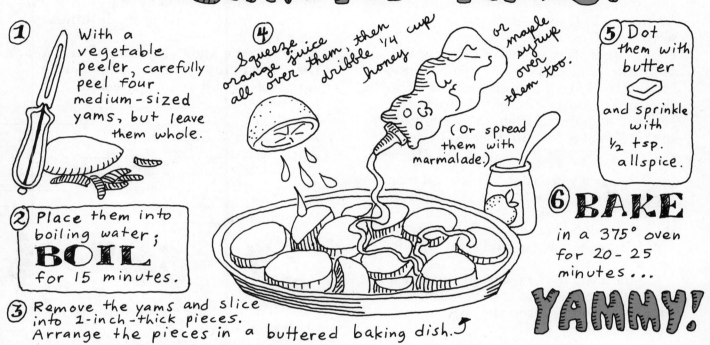

① With a vegetable peeler, carefully peel four medium-sized yams, but leave them whole.

② Place them into boiling water; **BOIL** for 15 minutes.

③ Remove the yams and slice into 1-inch-thick pieces. Arrange the pieces in a buttered baking dish.

④ Squeeze orange juice all over them, then dribble ¼ cup honey or maple syrup over them too. (Or spread them with marmalade.)

⑤ Dot them with butter and sprinkle with ½ tsp. allspice.

⑥ **BAKE** in a 375° oven for 20-25 minutes... **YAMMY!**

ADULT HELPER

Dear Diary:

In October folks in Opelousas, Louisiana, have a yam festival too. It's called the Yambilee, and most of its activities (like the crowning of King Willyam and Queen Marigold) are held in the city's Yamatorium. Everybody has a "yam good time." For more information write: Louisiana Tourist Development Committee, Box 44291, Baton Rouge, Louisiana 70804.

September 13
Robert Indiana's Birthday

Commemorative stamps always dress up envelopes and in 1973 there was an especially nice design. Originally a painting by Robert Indiana, an American artist born on this day in 1928, this stamp from his painting used the letters of the word "love."

Indiana often uses words in his paintings, and "LOVE" may be his most famous work. By pushing the four letters of the word together he created interesting shapes and painted them in several colors so there's not a definite background.

Make a **WORD** *into* **ART**

Choose a word that has special meaning for you. Write the letters of the word on scratch paper, making them touch in different ways. Make some large, some small, some sideways, and some upside down.

When you make a design you like a lot, draw it with markers or crayons on a larger piece of paper. Color in the spaces in different colors.

Dear Diary:

September 14
Calendar Day

September 14, 1752, was the day the Gregorian Calendar (the one we use today) was adopted by Great Britain and the American colonies. Look back to September 3's *Amazing Daily* for more information.

Here's an amazing fact: Until the calendar change in 1752, March 25 was called New Year's Day. For example, March 24, 1750, was followed by March 25, 1751. The Gregorian Calendar made January 1 New Year's.

Everyone knows the date of New Year's Day. How many of the calendar's other extra special days can you recall?

February 14 _____
March 17 _____
March 21 _____
April 1 _____
May 1 _____
July 4 _____
October 31 _____
December 25 _____

Hints:

(Of course, the answers are all in *Amazing Days*.)

Dear Diary:

Can you guess the food of the day?

Dates.

September 15
Get Ready for Native American Day

Native American Day, observed in most states on the fourth Friday of September, honors our land's first citizens. Native Americans have lived in this hemisphere for thousands of years, long before Columbus and other Europeans arrived in the "New World" and mistakenly called its people Indians. (Columbus thought he had arrived in India.)

One traditional art is beadwork—tiny glass beads woven together in intricate patterns with great care. Some of the beads in the design on this page are colored to create Native American symbols. Use thin markers or colored pencils to add more designs of your own. (If you decide to try real Indian beadwork, you'll find supplies and instructions at most hobby shops.)

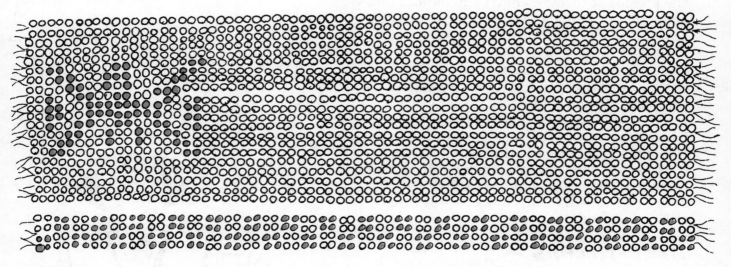

Most people remember the stories of how the Indians helped the Pilgrims, shared their Thanksgiving, and taught them and other early settlers many important ways of farming and survival. Today the Native American gifts and language have become so much a part of American life that it's easy to forget where they came from: over half the states of the U.S. have Native American names, not to mention hundreds of towns, rivers, lakes, and mountains. Maize (corn), popcorn, succotash, squash, and peanuts are only a few of the foods they introduced to the European settlers. People from around the world come to see Indian ceremonies and dances and beautiful displays of Native American arts and crafts.

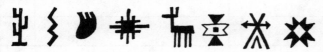

Draw your bead design on a poster announcing the date of Native American Day to put up at school, in your public library or town hall, or at home.

Dear Diary:

September 16
Mexican Independence Day

Mexican people are celebrating their Festival of Independence (Fiestas Patrias) today. Last night at 11:00 that country's president, standing on the balcony of the National Palace in Mexico City, repeated the *Grito de Delores*, or Call to Freedom, which began the fight for independence from Spanish rule in 1810. Then the crowds who had gathered to see the president threw confetti and danced and shouted as rockets and fireworks lit up the sky.

Today there will be more music, dancing, fireworks, and parades. Towns have a carnival spirit, alive with games, food, and all sorts of festivity. Many city streets look like they're decorated for Christmas, hung with strings of lights in red, white, and green—the national colors.

In small shops people enjoy tortillas, flat cornmeal pancakes that are eaten alone—steamed, fried, or baked—or filled with other foods.

white

green

red

MAKE NACHOS – A FAVORITE MEXICAN SNACK

① ARRANGE tortilla chips, broken taco pieces, or dip-sized corn chips on a cookie sheet.

② SLICE a hunk of sharp cheddar cheese into very thin pieces. Put one slice on each chip.

③ CUT UP a jalapeño pepper (from the Mexican food section of your grocery) into pieces no bigger than the end of your little finger. Remove the seeds. Put one piece of pepper on each slice of cheese. (Don't overdo it — they're hot!)

④ BROIL the nachos till the cheese gets bubbly and golden - only 2 two to four minutes. Then eat them hot out of the oven - and, boy, ARE THEY HOT !!!

ADULT HELPER

Dear Diary:

September 17
Citizenship Day

In the year 2001 when you steer your spaceship to Planet X and are greeted by a crowd of little green creatures who want to know "Where do you come from?" what will you answer? Probably you'll say, "From the planet Earth."

All human beings are citizens of Earth as well as of their individual nations, states, cities, or towns. But only now, in the space age, are people beginning to think of themselves as planetary citizens.

Fill in your citizenship card. Make a copy of it to carry in your wallet.

```
Name _____
Address _____
Citizen of (town or city) _____
(Country)_____(planet)_____
```

If you'd like to register as a "citizen of the world," write to this address for information: Planetary Citizens, 777 U.N. Plaza, New York, N.Y. 10017.

Note: Citizenship Day is celebrated each year on September 17, the date on which the U.S. Constitution was signed in 1787.

Dear Diary:

September 18
Alone Day

Have a party . . . but don't invite any of your friends; in fact, don't invite anybody! Have a party all by yourself to celebrate Alone Day. (Well, *maybe* invite your dog or cat.)
• Pack a snack in a paper bag and head to your favorite hideaway for a private picnic.
• Take time to enjoy your own thoughts: daydream, draw or paint, read, write in your diary.
• Take a long look in the mirror. (Wow, how can one person be *so* good-looking!)
• Sing a solo in the shower.

Play solitaire.
Here's one way: Take the four jacks out of a deck of cards. Shuffle the rest, then deal them out into eight piles, face up (six cards in each). Pick up pairs of *like* cards—two kings, two sixes, and so on—that are at the top of any two piles. You can only pick up a pair, not a trio, so if three cards match only use two. If one pile runs out you can pick the top card of another pile and put it in the blank space. Pair up all the cards: You win! If not, then shuffle and try again.

Dear Diary:

Today is the birthday of Greta Garbo, a great movie actress whose most famous line was said to be, "I want to be alone."

Mickey Mouse's Birthday

Steamboat Willie, the first animated cartoon with sound, was first shown on this date in 1928. It premiered at the Colony Theater in New York City, and starred none other than Mickey Mouse! Happy Birthday, Mick! Walt Disney himself—Mickey's creator—provided the voice for his beloved character. Have you ever noticed that Mickey is drawn with a series of circles? That makes him very easy to draw in different positions.

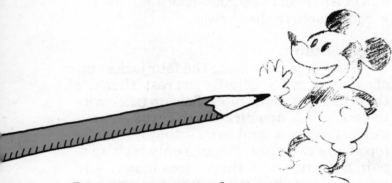

Invent a cartoon character.

Use simple shapes (circles, squares, triangles) to create a human, animal, or space creature. Draw him or her several times in different positions. Then, make up a whole comic strip.

Dear Diary:

A Telegram for You

Telegrams usually bring big news—often very happy greetings: "MGM WANTS YOU FOR PART IN REMAKE OF WIZARD OF OZ" or "YOU WON SWEEPSTAKES STOP PRIZE ARRIVES TODAY."

The telegram below came for you this morning. In 15 words or less, fill in the message you would *most* like to read.

WESTERN ONION
TELEGRAPH COMPANY

Date: September 20 ...XBLL·OV·E
Message:

Dear Diary:

Amazing Daily

September 21   *All The News That's Fit To Tickle*

FREEDOM OF PRESS NOT BIG IN 1690

Boston, 1690—The very first newspaper of any kind in this country was "Publick Occurences," published only once—September 25, 1690. Boston authorities found the paper offensive and prevented further editions.

Daily News Is Good News

Philadelphia, 1784—The Pennsylvania Packet and Daily Advertiser went on sale today to become the first daily newspaper published in America. The big question remains—is there enough news to fill up a paper every day?

Kids Edit Own Newspaper

_____
(your town)

Brilliant newspaper editor

_____
(your name)

today began the publication of a new paper called

_____

The first edition contained neighborhood news and was hand-written, cleverly using carbon paper to make several copies. Blank spaces were left, and filled with rubber stamp pictures, drawings, and stickers. The editor plans to borrow a typewriter to print future editions, with a projected circulation of eight copies.

Your Birthday

Born today, you are beautiful, popular, have a winning personality and a dynamite smile, and are a sucker for flattery. Happy birthday anyway.

Newspapers Contain More Than News

Look through today's newspaper. Many contain a variety of different sections. Clip out the ones that are most interesting to you and glue or paper clip them on this page. Choose from:

Amusements	People
Coins	Sports
Comics	Stamps
Crossword puzzle	TV
Editorials	Travel
Movies	Weather

September 22
Pen Pal Day

How would you like to have a friend in another country—someone to write to and get letters from and maybe even visit someday? If you'd like to correspond with someone of your own age and interests the International Friendship League will match you with a pen pal. The league matches each request individually with young people in any of 130 countries. To get a registration form, send a self-addressed stamped envelope to: Pen Pals, 22 Batterymarch St., Boston, Massachusetts 02109.

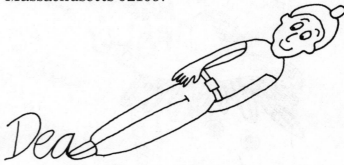

Note: Today is the birthday of the Earl of Chesterfield (1694-1773) who is remembered for his charming and witty letters to his son. They are still read and considered models of the art of letter writing.

Dear Diary:

Dear Diary:

September 23
Autumn Begins

Autumn officially begins when the sun "crosses" the equator from north to south, which usually happens on September 23. (You can find out the exact time from the newspaper.) Day and night are each almost exactly 12 hours long on the first day of autumn.

For people in the Southern Hemisphere (below the equator —Chile, Argentina, Peru, Bolivia, most of Brazil, Angola, Tanzania, and Australia) today is the first day of spring. Their seasons are exactly opposite ours. Christmas comes in the summer!

Make a "Harvest Dummy" to greet the season.

Many New Englanders put a floppy scarecrow on the front porch or in the yard to decorate for fall. it's a tradition. This funny man or woman greets visitors, waves to passing cars, and says, (without words) **HAPPY FALL!**

1. GATHER together some old clothes in bright fall colors.
2. BUTTON up the shirt, ZIPPER up the pants, and stuff them with crumpled newspaper.
3. STUFF gloves, socks, and don't forget shoes! Use safety pins to CONNECT gloves to sleeves, pants to shirt, etc,
4. Use a paper bag, mask, or pillow for a head. DRAW a face with permanent markers. An old mop makes a handsome wig.

Should he or she sit in a chair or stand, tied to a pole or tree in the yard? Wherever, this cheerful character will look even more like fall if accompanied by a pumpkin and some mums.

Hiya, Jack!

Dear Diary:

September 24
Libra Begins

People born between September 24 and October 22 are born under the sign of Libra, the scales. According to astrologers they are warm, friendly people who smile often. They don't like conflict and will go out of their way to stop quarrels and solve problems. Because they listen to both sides of a question, Libra people often have trouble making up their minds. (Sometimes they can be real procrastinators!) They love music, amusements, and all kinds of excitement.

The scales represent balance and symmetry, qualities that Libra people are always striving for.

Make BALANCE SCALE cut-out cards for all your Libra friends.
1. FOLD a piece of paper in half.
2. CUT half of a picture or design out of both sides at once. When you open it up the fold will be the center so be sure to leave enough of the folded edge uncut so that the two sides stay together.
   Fold →
3. OPEN it up and color the whole design with crayons or markers. Don't forget to write "Happy Birthday" somewhere on it.

September 25
Balboa Discovers The Pacific, 1513

Columbus crossed the Atlantic ocean to discover the new world. So did all the European explorers who came after him. None of them knew about an ocean on the other side of the American continent, to the west.

Vasco Nuñez De Balboa was a Spanish explorer who came to America in 1501. Native Americans told him about the ocean to the west, and in 1513 they guided him to a mountain where, on September 25, he became the first European to see the Pacific from the Pacific's eastern shore.

Balboa didn't name the ocean. A Portuguese explorer, Ferdinand Magellan, called it "pacific," meaning peaceful, when he sailed its calm waters in 1520.

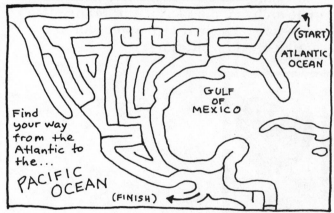

Find your way from the Atlantic to the... PACIFIC OCEAN

(START) ATLANTIC OCEAN
GULF OF MEXICO
(FINISH)

Dear Diary:

Dear Diary:

September 26
Johnny Appleseed's Birthday

Wearing a cooking pot for a hat and a coffee sack for a vest, Johnny Appleseed tramped across early America planting apple orchards; selling, trading, and giving away his apple seeds; bringing herb medicine to people and animals who needed it; and living his happy, useful life outdoors.

Born in 1775, his real name was John Chapman and settlers who met him were delighted by his gentleness and generosity and awed by his knowledge. Through the stories the settlers told each other, Johnny Appleseed became a true American folk hero.

Apples are probably the most traditional fall food. If you live near an apple orchard, plan to visit it. Many allow visitors to pick their own apples for a small fee, and what fun it is.

Dear Diary:

BAKED APPLE TREATS

① WASH an apple very thoroughly.

② Using an apple corer or a knife (be very careful) and core the apple. Don't break through the bottom. remove the seeds

③ STUFF the apple with peanuts, cashews, almonds, or walnuts and raisins, Right to the top!!

④ Dribble honey into the middle, too.

⑤ SPRINKLE with cinnamon and allspice and top with a pat of butter.

⑥ Place your apple in a pie plate or shallow pan with a little water and BAKE in a 350° oven for about 45 minutes or till a fork goes through the skin easily.

ADULT HELPER

(That apple might have come from a tree Johnny planted <u>himself</u>! apple trees live to be well over 100 years old.)

September 27
Thomas Nast's Birthday

Cartoons often are funny and make folks laugh, but many also make serious comments about what's going on in the world. Look in today's newspaper and find the editorial page. On it there may be a political cartoon which will most likely be making a comment about some important news story. You may want to ask an adult to explain its meaning.

Thomas Nast, born on this date in 1840, was probably the most famous political cartoonist in American history. He created the cartoon symbol of the Democratic party (the donkey), and the Republican party (the elephant), and also was the first artist to draw Santa Claus as we now know him. When Nast directed his cartoons at a ring of crooked politicians who were running New York City in the 1860's, the drawings brought action: "Boss Tweed and the Tammany ring" were brought to trial and convicted of their crimes.

Many fine cartoonists have followed in Nast's footsteps, drawing pictures that help citizens think about and understand current political issues.

September 28
Cucumber Day

On this date in 1973 an Englishman named Norman Johnson sliced a cucumber into 240 slices in only 24.2 seconds. That's fast! His feat set a world's record for cucumber slicing, and was seen on an English television show called *Record Breakers*. Each inch of the cuke was sliced twenty times—what a great sandwich that must have made!

Oh, you've never heard of cuke sandwiches?

① PEEL a cucumber with a vegetable peeler.

② On a cutting board, hold on to the cuke with one hand and carefully slice off one end (about an inch). Then cut about 20 slices as thin as you can make them - slowly.

③ SPREAD two pieces of bread with butter or mayonnaise. Put on the cuke slices and add salt and pepper.

④ Now enjoy a treat the English have been eating for years.

Dear Diary:

Dear Diary:

September 29
Sundown Dance

One of the most famous Native American celebrations is the sundown dance of the Taos Indians in New Mexico. Every year on September 29 around sunset, members of this Pueblo group perform traditional dances including the eagle dance, turtle dance, horsetail dance, and others. Some are joyous social dances just for fun; others are religious celebrations.

Perform a sundown dance.

One of the simplest and most basic Native American dance steps is called "toe-heel." The whole dance step is only four counts:

1. (Toe.) Take a step with your right foot. Put your weight on only the ball of your foot.
2. (Heel.) Now lower your right heel so your whole foot is on the ground.
3. (Toe.) Take a step with your left foot, again put your weight only on the ball.
4. (Heel.) Lower your left heel. Toe-heel-toe-heel-toe-heel . . .

September 30
Autumn Tree Trimming Day

Today's the last day of September. The leaves and grasses are beginning to turn their rich fall colors, marigolds will soon be at their golden best, and the air is taking on the invigorating crispness of autumn. Here's a way to bring some of the outdoors indoors.

Trim an "autumn tree."

1. Go for a walk, and take along a bag to collect fall decorations. "Autumn ornaments" are colorful leaves, seed pods, pinecones, sweet gum balls, dried flower heads, and anything small and beautiful.
2. Find a leafless branch that fell off a tree. It should have a nice shape and some twigs.
3. Sink the bottom of the branch in a flowerpot or coffee can filled with sand or gravel. Make sure it won't fall over.
4. Tie fall-colored ribbons or yarn onto the natural things you collected. Hang them on your autumn tree.

This fall decoration can get better and better through October. Whenever you find a beautiful leaf or another autumn treasure add it to your "tree."

Dear Diary:

Dear Diary:

October 1
Deltiology Day

Today is a big day for deltiologists (postcard collectors). The very first postcard was issued by the Austrian post office on this date in 1869. A year later, also on October 1, the United Kingdom and Switzerland both issued their own postcards. People started collecting soon after and nowadays deltiology is one of the most popular hobbies in the world.

Start a postcard collection.

Save the cards people send you from their vacations or anywhere else. A shoe box is just the right size for storing them. Museums have especially nice cards to buy. If you write to chambers of commerce requesting cards from their cities and states, they'll often send several free.

Message:
MAKE POSTCARDS
Use a piece of fairly stiff paper at least this big (3½ - x 5 - inches).
On one side make a picture with felt-tip pens, crayons, paint, or rubber stamps. Or cut pictures from a magazine and put them together to make a funny scene. →
USE YOUR IMAGINATION!
On the other side draw a line down the center.

POST CARD

Write your message on the left
← and the name and address of the person you're sending it to on the right.

HI!

Dear Diary:

Send postcards for birthdays, holidays, and just saying "hi." They're cheaper, use less paper, and are often more fun than folded cards.

October 2
Gandhi's Birthday

India celebrates its independence on January 26 and again today, the birthday of Mohandas Gandhi (1869-1948) whom Indians honor as the father of their nation. Gandhi helped free India from British rule, not with guns and battles but through his own method of nonviolence. The whole world came to know Gandhi and his peaceful methods of change. (America's Martin Luther King modeled his fight for civil rights on Gandhi's creative peaceful methods.) He is remembered as *Mahatma* Gandhi, which means Great Soul.

Gandhi studied a system of exercise called yoga that's thousands of years old. Now, millions of people in America practice it too. If you know someone who does yoga, ask him or her to show you some of the exercises.

The lotus — "pretzel position."

1. Sit on the floor on a carpet or mat.
2. Cross your right foot over your left thigh comfortably.
3. Now gently bring your left foot over your right thigh. (If you can't, just tuck it under your knee; this is called the "half lotus.")

Dear Diary:

October 3
Universal Children's Day Celebration

On the first Monday of October, kids from many different countries, wearing their national costumes, gather around the Peace Bell at the United Nations headquarters in New York City to celebrate Universal Children's Day. According to the U.N. General Assembly, which established the special day in 1954, the celebration should foster "worldwide fraternity and understanding among children."

UNICEF is the United Nations Children's Fund, which promotes Universal Children's Day. In 104 countries, UNICEF helps over 900 million kids through good health care, nutrition, education, and emergency assistance when needed. On Halloween (which is also UNICEF Day) lots of kids in America raise money to help the children in poorer countries. You can get everything you need to "Trick or Treat for UNICEF" and a neat *free* Halloween poster. Write today to: U.S. Committee for UNICEF, 331 E. 38th St., New York, N.Y. 10016.

Ask for item 1001 (a UNICEF money collection carton), and item 1301 (a UNICEF Day/Halloween poster). Please say how old you are in your letter.

Dear Diary:

October 4
St. Francis of Assisi's Feast

Francesco Di Pietro De Bernardone was born about 800 years ago in the town of Assisi, in Italy. He was a joyous young man who devoted himself to God and became one of Christianity's most beloved saints. He loved all the world and cared deeply for animals as well as people. Francis once tamed a fierce, man-eating wolf so that the animal lived peacefully in the village of Gubbio and was fed by the people there who grew to love him dearly.

Because he loved animals so much, and because he sang the praises of nature, little statues of St. Francis are often placed in gardens, and sometimes in bird feeders. He is the patron saint of animals.

Feed the birds.

St. Francis would probably like his feast to be a banquet for the birds. Put out bread crumbs, seeds, rice, oats, unsalted popcorn, coconut, or raisins, You can just toss the food on the ground, or make a simple bird feeder.

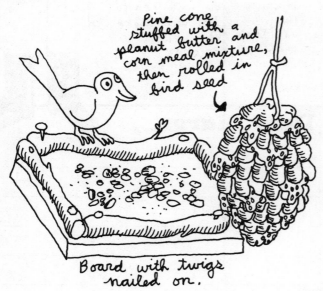

Pine cone stuffed with a peanut butter and corn meal mixture, then rolled in bird seed

Board with twigs nailed on.

If you decide to feed the birds every day be sure to keep it up all through the winter, because they will come to depend on the food you put out. But it's fine to just give them a treat every now and then.

Put the food out fairly near a window so you can watch the birds that come to the feast. Make a list in your diary of the kinds you see.

Dear Diary:

October 5
World Series Celebration

The first radio broadcast of the World Series was aired on this date in 1921. Since then, radio and TV coverage of the series has become an American tradition. In October, baseball fans get together to listen to or watch the games, eat and drink, and cheer their favorite team! (In the World Series the American League and National League pennant winners play each other for the world championship. The first team to win four series games is the big winner.)

When the Series comes round this year watch the games with your friends.

Serve ball park snacks like roasted peanuts in the shell and something cold to drink.

Decorate with pennants for each team (see April 11)

Here's a joke to play on your unsuspecting friends

This is a good time to compare and trade baseball cards.

I bet I can tell you the score of the game before it starts.

Aw, come on. No way.

Zero to zero. I said, "before it starts."

Dear Diary:

October 6
Giant Celebration

The giants in fairy tales are sometimes as tall as skyscrapers. But did you know giants really exist? They're human beings that grow to amazing heights of over seven feet. One man actually grew to 8 feet 11 inches tall. Wow!

Patrick Magee was the first giant to present himself to the public in the United States (on this date in 1825).

BE A GIANT.

① FIND a sturdy stool or chair to stand on.

② PUT a big pair of boots in front of the legs of the stool.

③ PUT ON the longest overcoat your mom or dad has. STUFF a pair of gloves and safety-pin them inside the sleeves →

④ STAND on the stool. The coat and boots cover it up so you look really tall. A big hat will make you look even taller. Now call someone to come see...

Dear Diary:

Little Orphant Annie Day

L ittle Orphant Annie is great fun to read at night, especially in October. Its author, James Whitcomb Riley, was born on this date in 1849.

Little Orphant Annie

Little Orphant Annie's come to our house to
stay,
An' wash the cups and saucers up, an' brush
the crumbs away,
An' shoo the chickens off the porch, an' dust
the hearth, an' sweep,
An' make the fire, an' bake the bread, an'
earn her board-an'-keep;
An' all us other children, when the supper
things is done,
We set around the kitchen fire an' has the
mostest fun
A-list'nin' to the witch tales 'at Annie tells
about,
An' the Gobble-uns 'at gits you
Ef you
Don't
Watch
Out!

Onc't they was a little boy wouldn't say his
prayers, —
So when he went to bed at night, away
upstairs,
His Mammy heerd him holler, an' his Daddy
heerd him bawl,
An' when they turn't the kivvers down, he
wasn't there at all!
An' they seeked him in the rafter room, an'
cubbyhole, an' press,
An' seeked him up the chimbly flue, an'
ever'wheres, I guess;
But all they ever found was thist his pants
an' roundabout: —
An' the Gobble-uns 'll git you
Ef you
Don't
Watch
Out!

An' one time a little girl 'ud allus laugh an'
grin,
An' make fun of ever'one, an' all her blood
an' kin;
An' onc't, when they was "company," an' ole
folks was there,
She mocked 'em an' shocked 'em, an' said
she didn't care!

An' thist as she kicked her heels, an' turn't to
run an' hide,
They was two great big Black Things
a-standin' by her side,
An' they snatched her through the ceilin'
'fore she knowed what she's about!
An' the Gobble-uns 'll git you
Ef you
Don't
Watch
Out!

An' little Orphant Annie says, when the
blaze is blue,
An' the lamp-wick sputters, an' the wind
goes woo-oo!
An' you hear the crickets quit, an' the moon
is gray,
An' the lightnin' bugs in dew is all
squenched away, —
You better mind yer parents, and yer
teachers fond an' dear.
An' churish them 'at loves you, an' dry the
orphant's tear.
An' he'p the pore an' needy one 'at clusters
all about.
Er the Gobble-uns 'll git you
Ef you
Don't
Watch
Out!

Dear Diary:

October 8
Seker Bayrami

About this time of year kids in Turkey celebrate Seker Bayrami, the candy holiday. Turkey is famous for two kinds of candy: halvah, sold in many delicatessens and health food shops in America, and Turkish delight. Most Turkish candies are made from honey, almonds, and sesame seeds.

Easy sesame brittle.
1. Butter an 8x8-inch baking pan or a 9-inch pie plate.
2. Put 1 cup raw sesame seeds in a heavy skillet and stir over medium heat till they're brown. Pour them in a bowl till later.
3. In the skillet melt ⅓ cup butter.
4. Stir in ¼-cup honey let the mixture cook over medium heat for about 3 minutes.
5. Now pour the sesame seeds back in and stir for about 3 more minutes (till it turns golden and seems thick).
6. Spread the mixture in the buttered pan while hot. Let it cool for about a minute then cut it into squares with a buttered knife. Now let it cool completely. Remove the squares with a knife and put them on waxed paper. They're delicious, but don't eat too many all at once — they're also very rich!

Dear Diary:

October 9
Leif Ericson Day

Many people believe that Leif Ericson, a Norse explorer, visited North America 500 years before Columbus. No one knows exactly where he landed or what he explored for he began no permanent settlements, but Icelanders and Americans both celebrate Leif Ericson Day in his honor.

Do you ever wish there were still uncharted places for *you* to explore? There are! When you are older you may explore outer space, the depths of the vast oceans, or even jungles and frontiers still unknown to civilization. An explorer must remember two things especially: Look closely at every detail, and remember, there's always more to find out!

Ericson may have sailed a vessel much like this viking ship. Find your way through the uncharted seas of this maze.

START

FINISH

Dear Diary:

October 10
Opera Day

Opera is a kind of play in which the actors sing. It's usually very grand entertainment with gorgeous sets and costumes held in fancy opera houses. The singers have amazing voices, but best of all operas usually tell action-packed stories. The Italian composer, Giuseppe Verdi, born on October 10, 1813, wrote 25 operas, many of which are among the most often performed operas of our day.

PUT ON A PUPPET OPERA!

THIS Big-mouth Puppet → is sure to be the ⭐ of the show!

Dear Diary:

① CUT OUT about a 3-inch circle of cardboard. (Trace around a glass or can.) Bend it in half.

② PUT your hand inside an old sock and GRASP the cardboard circle, so it looks like a mouth...

③ GLUE. PUT white glue all around the edge of the circle; PUT it into place in the sock, FOLD it closed carefully, and put a heavy book on top.

④ when dry, stuff tissue paper, cotton, or cloth in the head of the puppet to make a forehead and chin. ← stuff

⑤ SEW or GLUE ON eyes, nose, yarn hair, and arms. Felt-tip pens are great for adding details.

This puppet is a great opera singer because his or her mouth opens so easily... and gets so WIDE! Almost any story can become an opera; just have the puppets SING instead of talk.

October 11

Eleanor Roosevelt's Birthday

Eleanor Roosevelt, born in 1884, was painfully shy but when she grew up she came to be known and loved everywhere. In 1905 she married Franklin D. Roosevelt, who was elected President of the U.S. four times. As First Lady, Eleanor traveled throughout America to see what needed doing. She visited schools, hospitals, work places, and even went down into a coal mine to inspect conditions there. She spoke out for minority rights and helped the government really get things done to help the people of America.

In 1945 when the United Nations was founded, Eleanor represented the United States as a U.N. delegate. She helped write the Universal Declaration of Human Rights, adopted by the U.N. in 1948 (see December 10). When Eleanor Roosevelt died in 1962 the world lost one of its leading citizens.

Can you read this?

Try writing your name as a rebus (word and picture puzzle). If you don't remember how to do it see July 25.

Dear Diary:

October 12

Columbus Day

Q: Do you know what bus crossed the ocean?
A: You guessed it: Colum*bus*!

He finally reached America (Watling Island in the Bahamas) on this date in 1492. Columbus thought he had arrived in India, and he never did realize the true importance of his discovery: Columbus's voyage led to European exploration of the Americas.

Make a Columbus Day treat for your family.

1. Slice a canteloupe or honeydew melon into quarters.
2. Scoop out the seeds.
3. Draw this cross on 1x1-inch and 2x2-inch paper squares. Attach them with tape to drinking straws or wooden skewers.
4. Push the straws or skewers into the melon slices so they look like the sails of the *Niña*, *Pinta*, and *Santa Maria*.

Make one ship for each member of your family. A yummy breakfast or dessert!

Dear Diary:

October 13
Baker's Dozen Day

For some reason, 13 is considered an unlucky number by superstitious people. They think 13 people should never sit down together at one table. They also think if the thirteenth day of a month falls on a Friday it will be such an awful day there's no reason to get out of bed. But there's at least one place 13 is a *lucky* number — in a bakery or kitchen when cookies are being made! Thirteen is a "baker's dozen." That means 12 plus one more for good luck!

MAKE THREE BAKER'S DOZENS of **Gingerbread** cookies.
(This should make today lucky even if it's Friday.)

① **PREHEAT** oven to **375°**.

② With a fork or whisk, **BEAT** together ⅓ cup softened butter and ⅔ cup molasses till fluffy.

Mmmm.

③ **BEAT IN** one egg thoroughly.

④ **MIX TOGETHER**

2½ cups whole wheat flour

1 tsp. baking soda

1 tsp. salt

2 tsp. cinnamon

1½ tsp. ginger

⑤ **ADD** dry ingredients to the wet. **BEAT** just enough to mix the dough well. Put it into the refrigerator for at least an hour and a half.

⑥ Using a floured rolling pin, **ROLL** the dough out to ⅛-inch thick on a well-floured counter.

⑦ **USE** cookie cutters or a glass to make the cookie shapes. **PLACE** them on a buttered cookie sheet almost touching.

⑧ **BAKE** for 5 minutes (till brown on bottom and firm). Remove them from the pan to cool.

Dear Diary:

ADULT HELPER

Decorate with raisins and cream cheese icing (may 18).

October 14
Get Ready for Jack Frost

First frost" is the first time the temperature dips below 32°F (0°C) in the fall. It's important to bring in houseplants and pick any flowers for the house before first frost, for they're likely to be killed by freezing temperatures. Also many vegetables should be harvested before then.

When frost does come it often makes beautiful patterns of ice on the windowpanes. Folks say that Jack Frost has been at work with his paintbrush. Jack is also given credit for the beautiful colors of trees this time of year.

GO ON A TREE-SURE HUNT.

Which of these trees can you find by looking at their leaves?

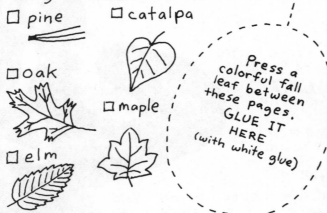

☐ pine

☐ catalpa

☐ oak

☐ maple

☐ elm

Press a colorful fall leaf between these pages. GLUE IT HERE (with white glue)

Dear Diary:

October 15
National Poetry Day

Today was chosen as National Poetry Day because it's the birthday of the ancient Roman poet, Vergil, born in 70 B.C. His epic poem, the *Aeneid*, has been a source of inspiration to poets of all ages. It tells the story of a hero who survived the Trojan War (remember the Trojan Horse?) and sailed west to Italy to the city of Rome. His adventures are very exciting and beautifully told. (There are several fine translations of the *Aeneid* especially for kids.)

Celebrate National Poetry Day by writing a poem.

Make your poem an eerie Halloween rhyme. Just conjure up some bewitching pictures in your mind and write down what they're like. If you want your poem to rhyme (it doesn't have to), here's a special Halloween rhyming dictionary that might help:

bat
fat
cat
rat
witch's hat
sat

goon
moon
loon

corn
horn
mourn
thorn
torn

bite
bright
candlelight
flight
fright
height
midnight
moonlight
night

October 16
Webster's Birthday

itch
stitch
witch
ditch

ghost
host
most
post

dreary
eerie
leery
weary

fairy
hairy
scary
Mary

alone
bone
flown
groan
gravestone
unknown
moan

foul
fowl
growl
howl
owl
prowl
scowl
yowl

Noah Webster, born on this date in 1758, put together the first American dictionary of the English language. Celebrate his birthday by ribbing your friends with these riddles:

Q: Where does afternoon come before morning?
A: In the dictionary.

Q: How is a dictionary like a birthday cake?
A: It has *butter, cream*, and *flour* in it.

Q: What can you find in the dictionary, yet it's still lost?
A: *Lost*.

Q: How is a dictionary like a mailbox?
A: It has lots of letters in it.

Q: Why does the letter *U* feel left out?
A: It's the only vowel that's not in *t-h-e d-i-c-t-i-o-n-a-r-y*.

Q: What word is spelled wrong even in the dictionary?
A: *Wrong*.

Q: When does the cart always come before the horse?
A: In the dictionary.

Dear Diary:

Dear Diary:

October 17
A Salute To Schools

A.S. Neill, born on this date in England in 1883, was a teacher with an extra dose of imagination. He had the idea to start a school where kids and grownups had equal say, where kids had the choice of classes they took, and where the most important goal was the happiness of each person at the school. He called it Summerhill, and it's still going after 50 years.

Neill's ideas of freedom for children helped change lots of schools all over the world into better places for kids.

What's good about *your* school? What's bad? Imagine what the perfect school would be like and write about it.

Draw a picture of your school here. 5

Dear Diary:

October 18
Start Making Your Costume Today

Only two weeks till Halloween, October 31! It's time to start planning and making your costume.

Look through all the old clothes your family has around. Too big for you? All the better; you can stuff the extra spaces with pillows and look completely different. Just add a mask. Maybe one article of clothing will give you an idea for a whole costume. Outer space creature? Witch? Monster? Weirdo?

THE OLD-PILLOWCASE BIG-HEAD COSTUME TRICK!

① CUT slits in an old pillowcase for your head and arms ← like this.

② PAINT or sew a very big face on the pillowcase. You'll be wearing the pillowcase over your body.

③ MAKE a mask large enough to wear over your whole head that looks like a hat (see Oct. 22).

④ TO WEAR it, pad yourself well to stuff the pillowcase and give the impression of a giant head on a tiny body.

Dear Diary:

October 19
Be-a-Bigfoot Day

How long is your foot?____inches. A Bigfoot's foot is anywhere from 14 to 20 inches long!

Lots of people claim to have seen Bigfoot (also known by its native American name, Sasquatch) in British Columbia and the northwestern United States. According to their descriptions it is a large half-human, half-apelike creature covered with black fur. On October 20, 1967, Roger Patterson photographed what he says was a female Bigfoot near Bluff Creek in California. Though blurry, it's the best picture of a Bigfoot yet!

Be a Bigfoot.
1. Get two brown paper grocery bags.
2. Put your feet inside and stuff the bags with newspaper.
3. Pull the top of each bag close around your leg, and wrap it with masking tape.
4. Paint red toenails, at the bottom of the bags.

Believe it or not these Big Feet are light and comfortable to wear. They could be the start of a great costume . . . or just a funny stunt!

October 20
Clown-around Day

If you're a circus lover, celebrate today! The Barnum Circus, later to become the Ringling Brothers and Barnum & Bailey Circus, opened on this date in 1873. Even then it was called "The Greatest Show on Earth."

Clown around today!

Every clown invents his or her own face makeup and costume, so get to work.

At this time of year near Halloween, most dime stores have clown makeup. You need clown white greasepaint (or white cold cream), and stick makeup in red and black. Lipstick and eyebrow pencil will do fine.

Start by covering your whole face with white. Be careful not to get any in your eyes. Now look at your "blank face" and imagine what your clown face should look like.

With red, draw a mouth below your real mouth but touching it. With black, draw exaggerated eyebrows on your forehead above your real eyebrows. Add any decorations that add to your clown's expression. (Don't forget a fantastic nose!)

After you've finished your face, put on some baggy clothes and a silly hat and have fun!

Dear Diary:

Dear Diary:

Amazing Daily

October 21   *All The News That's Fit To Tickle*

NUCLEAR NOODLE EXPLODES

Anti-nuclear groups are saying "I told you so" after the nuclear noodle tragedy at Nine-Mile Noodle, Nebraska. "We warned them," said Nanny Nonukes in an exclusive interview today. "There's just no need for cooking noodles with nuclear power. They can be well-done easily on conventional ranges, hot plates, and new solar cookers." When the giant noodle plant blew, last night, one half of the state was covered with nasty noodle fallout. "We'll be cleaning up for quite a while," said one National Noodle Guardsman. "You can bet the people of this state will be eating no noodles for quite a while. Imagine living under that kind of pressure!" He further explained that Nebraskans should be scraping the noodles off their own roofs to avoid any more cave-ins. It seems nuclear noodles are quite heavy.

Notable Noodles In History
by Mac A. Roni

History is filled with people who really used their noodles. Today's notable noodle is Alfred Nobel, born on October 21, 1833. Nobel invented dynamite which made him very rich. Unfortunately some people soon found out that the explosive was effective for blowing other people up in wars. Poor Nobel became sick and guilt-ridden as he saw the death and injury his creation caused, and with his money he set up a fund to award prizes to people who made important contributions to the good of humanity.

The Nobel Prizes are given each year on December 10, Human Rights Day, in physics chemistry, physiology or medicine, literature, and peace.

Dear Diary:

Sarah Bernhardt's Mask-Making Day

Sarah Bernhardt, whose real name was Rosine Bernard, was born on this date in 1844, and is remembered as one of the greatest actresses who ever lived. Her audiences were spellbound by her presence on the stage and the beauty of her voice. There must have been real magic in her performances for people still talk about "the divine Sarah."

These masks symbolize the theater. The smiling mask stands for comedy, and the sad mask for tragedy. Masks are usually worn for fun nowadays, for Halloween, Mardi Gras, and costume parties. But masks were originally used in religious ceremonies and dramas. By wearing a mask an actor could easily become a different being—human or animal. The reason people started wearing masks on Halloween was to fool the real witches and goblins who they believed were out that night. Folks figured if they looked scary themselves, they'd be left alone.

Dear Diary:

Make a paper bag mask.

①USE a brown paper grocery bag big enough to fit over your head.

②SCRATCH it with your fingernails where your eyes are to mark where the eye-holes go. Then TAKE OFF the bag and CUT OUT the holes with scissors. The eye-holes don't have to be the eyes of the mask. Make them nostrils, spots, or freckles.

③Out of colored paper CUT eyes, nose, mouth, ears, hair, and decorations. MAKE them big and bright. PUT them on with white glue.

④ADD details with white glue.

yogurt cup covered with foil

Aluminum foil is good for dressing up astronauts and outer space creatures

hole in mask covered with colored cellophane

Cotton makes fun eyebrows, mustaches, and animal fuzzies.

crepe paper fringe in layers makes good hair or fur

People born between October 23 and November 21 are born under the sign of Scorpio, the scorpion. According to astrologers they are fascinating and secretive people. They are often outstanding leaders. They feel strongly about things and can change moods at the drop of a hat. Watch out for a Scorpio person's temper! But when they dedicate themselves to a worthy goal they are almost sure to reach it, thanks to a strong will and aggressive nature. If something gets in their way they just try harder.

Make a paper scorpion.

This scorpion can be a card for your Scorpio friends (write "Happy Birthday" on its underside) or a creepy Halloween decoration.

Cut this shape out of stiff paper:

Bend the legs down so it stands up.

Bend the tail up and over like this:

Dear Diary:

October 24
United Nations Day

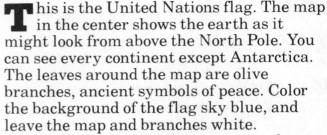

This is the United Nations flag. The map in the center shows the earth as it might look from above the North Pole. You can see every continent except Antarctica. The leaves around the map are olive branches, ancient symbols of peace. Color the background of the flag sky blue, and leave the map and branches white.

The United Nations was organized at the close of World War II as a way of preventing another world war. Today, 150 nations (representing almost 4 billion people) work together in the U.N. to preserve peace and benefit humankind. U.N. Day is celebrated in almost every country in the world.

The United Nations headquarters are in New York City. Inside the beautiful General Assembly building is a post office that sells U.N. stamps. They're like the postage stamps of countries, except they can only be used on mail sent from the U.N. headquarters in New York or Geneva, Switzerland. People from all over collect U.N. stamps because they're so unusual. For information about collecting U.N. stamps write to: United Nations Postal Administration, P.O. Box 5900, Grand Central Station, New York, N.Y. 10017.

Dear Diary:

October 25
Picasso's Birthday

Pablo Picasso, one of the world's most famous artists, loved children's artwork. Like other artists of the twentieth century he admired the freshness of their paintings—the bright colors and bold shapes. Picasso used the things he learned from children in his own art, too. He made drawings, paintings, ceramics, sculpture, and prints throughout his long life (1881-1973).

With his friend Georges Braque, Picasso invented a new kind of artwork. They cut out bits of paper and scraps of material and pasted them together to create pictures. Then they added a few painted lines to complete the idea. The French called it collage, which means paste-up.

Make a collage.

In putting together a collage imagine you are painting a picture. Collect scraps of paper (look in the wastebasket), food labels, old magazines, pieces of fabric, bits of string, ANYTHING that can be pasted on paper.

Put them together on paper in different ways. PLAY! This part's the most fun.

After you've made a picture or design you like, glue down one piece at a time with white glue or rubber cement— bottom pieces first! Add more to your collage with paint. That's what Picasso did!

October 26
Witches' Brew Day

Fillet of a fenny snake,
In the cauldron boil and bake;
Eye of newt, and toe of frog,
Wool of bat, and tongue of dog,
Adder's fork, and blind-worm's sting,
Lizard's leg, and owlet's wing;
For a charm of powerful trouble,
Like a hell-broth boil and bubble.
Double, double toil and trouble;
Fire burn, and cauldron bubble. *

Doesn't that just make your mouth water? Oh . . . well, it would if you were a witch. Here's a recipe you'll like more:

1. FILL a tall glass with ice cubes. (Freeze raisins and cloves in the cubes and tell everybody it's "eye of newt, and toe of frog.")
2. POUR cranberry juice in to half-fill the glass.
3. Very slowly POUR in orange juice. Leave about 1½-inches at the top.
4. Now slowly pour in Ginger ale to the top.
5. ADD a straw. The drink will stay in layers. By moving your straw up and down you can sip three drinks from one glass.

Dear Diary:

Dear Dia[ry:]

*From Macbeth by Shakespeare.

October 27
Good Bear Day

Today is the birthday of President Theodore ("Teddy") Roosevelt, born in 1858. In 1902, while the president was in Mississippi, a bear cub wandered into his camp. Teddy was a hunter, but he refused to shoot the young animal, of course. A popular cartoonist drew this picture to tell the story.

The cartoon gave Morris Michtom, a candy seller and toymaker in Brooklyn, a good idea. He and his wife made a stuffed toy bear to sell. They put a sign on it that said "Teddy's Bear."

The rest is history! Almost everyone wanted one. Mr. Michtom founded the Ideal Toy Company to make all the bears folks ordered, and over the years teddy bears became a cherished part of childhood all over the world.

If you have a teddy bear give him a place of honor today, and maybe a fresh ribbon around his neck for the occasion — it's sort of *his* birthday!

Dear Diary:

You can make this jointed teddy out of stiff paper for a toy, puppet, or birthday favor. Use brass fasteners where the *X*'s are.

There's a club of adults that celebrate this day. They're called The Good Bears of the World, P.O. Box 8236, Honolulu, Hawaii 96815.

October 28

Fingerprint Day

Smart burglars started wearing gloves in 1904 after the St. Louis Police Department became the first to fingerprint all persons arrested on serious charges. (They adopted the system on October 28.)

Fingerprint art.

There are no other fingerprints exactly like *yours* in the whole world. Use them to make pictures:

Print your fingers on stationery, cards, wrapping paper, or anywhere—on this page, for instance.

Use a stamp pad or paper towel soaked with tempera.

Make the prints into drawings by adding lines with pens or pencils.

October 29

Bones and Gravestones Day

In New England many old gravestones are so interesting that people make crayon rubbings of them to hang on their walls. Here's a way you can make a rubbing of the *whole graveyard*:

1. Find a long piece of white paper and a black crayon without its paper wrapper.

2. Use the side of the crayon to make rubbings of the bottoms of several friends' sneakers. (Not the whole bottom—about this much  so it looks like the shape of an old gravestone.)

3. On each shoe-rubbing write a weird name.

4. After you have several "gravestones" add the ground, spooks, skeletons, and whatever else will make your picture creepy and fun. You can title it "Bless Their Soles."

Note: John Keats, a famous English poet whose birthday is today, didn't want his name written on his gravestone. Instead the stone reads: "Here lies one whose name was writ in water."

Dear Diary:

Dear Diary:

October 30
Jack-o'-Lantern Day

Once there was a mean, stingy, and dishonest old man named Jack. In his whole life he never did anything good for anybody. When a beggar asked him for a coin or something to eat, Jack cursed him. When somebody needed a place to spend the night, Jack slammed the door.

Finally Jack died. He was too mean to get into heaven, but the devil (who didn't like Jack's tricks) wouldn't let him into hell either. According to this old Irish story, Jack still wanders the earth looking for a place to stay. He carries a lantern carved from a large turnip and lit by a lump of coal the devil gave him. So on Halloween, the Irish carried turnip lanterns hoping to frighten away evil spirits.

When they came to America they discovered that pumpkins made even better Jack-o'-Lanterns than turnips did. And as for Jack, his mean stingy old heart must have softened over the years of wandering the earth, for nowadays he has an important place in homes all over America on Halloween night . . . and usually he's smiling!

When you carve your Jack-o'-Lantern today give him a really original face (he doesn't have to have triangle eyes). Practice making up faces on the blank pumpkins below:

When you scoop the seeds out of your pumpkin, save them to eat. First put them in a bowl of fresh water and pull the seeds from the stringy pulp. Now spread them out on a baking pan or cookie sheet. Sprinkle them with corn oil and salt, and bake in a 350 degrees oven for about 15 to 20 minutes, till golden. This makes a really good Halloween snack.

Dear Diary:

October 31
Halloween

Halloween is one of the oldest holidays we celebrate, dating back to ancient times. In many cultures it has been thought of as a night when ghosts and witches roamed the earth, and folklorists say it is the last of the fairies' three great festivals. (May Eve—April 30 and Midsummer's Eve—June 23 are the first two.) The Irish brought the popular customs of Halloween to America in the 1840's. Since then it has developed into a night of marvelous imagination when few people are surprised by strange creatures roaming the streets and frightful pumpkin faces glowing in windows everywhere.

Before going out tonight, take care of a few matters.

Halloween checklist.

☐ Make sure your costume is on right side out. According to an old tale, if it's inside out you're likely to meet a witch at midnight.

☐ Carry a clove of garlic in your pocket, just in case any vampires get *too* friendly!

☐ Carry a noisemaker. (Spooks *hate* loud noises.)

☐ Wear something light colored and watch out for cars. Automobiles are still the most dangerous thing on the street.

☐ Don't forget your UNICEF collection carton. Halloween is also National UNICEF Day.

☐ Have a Happy Halloween!

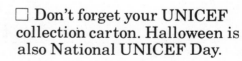

Dear Diary:

November 1
All Saints' Day

Today is All Saints' Day, which commemorates all the saints who don't have their own feast days set aside. It used to be called All Hallows and the night before, Hallows Even(ing) (which got shortened to Halloween).

Sing "When the Saints Go Marching In."

Almost everyone knows the tune of this jazz classic, made famous by black bands in New Orleans.

When the Saints Go Marching In

Oh, when the Saints go marching in,
Oh, when the Saints go marching in,
Lord, I want to be in that number
When the Saints go marching in.

And when the new world is revealed,
And when the new world is revealed,
Lord, how I want to be in that number
When the new world is revealed.

And when they gather round the throne,
And when they gather round the throne,
Lord, how I want to be in that number
When they gather round the throne.

Dear Diary:

November 2
Day of the Dead

In Mexico today colorful toy vendors are selling skeleton puppets and skull masks, men are wearing dancing skeleton tie pins, and bakeries are filled with breads and pastries shaped like skulls and decorated with flowers.

It's the Day of the Dead, when many people believe the souls of their loved ones return to earth for a visit. Beautiful tables of food and marigolds are prepared for them, and people also take picnics to the family graves where there's lots of feasting and merriment. It may sound strange, but it's a very happy holiday! (In the United States November 2 is called All Souls' Day.)

Make a dancing skeleton.

① CUT the body shape out of shirt cardboard. Color in around the bones with black ink.
② PUSH a thumbtack through the cardboard where the paper clips attach.
③ The paper-clip arms will hold on to your shirt pocket.

One more tradition: After supper tonight, Mexican families will enjoy steaming mugs of hot chocolate. Why not you too?

Dear Diary:

November 3
Take a Sandwich to Lunch Day

Sandwiches have come a long way, since their humble beginning in 1762. As the story goes, John Montagu, the fourth Earl of Sandwich (1718-1792, birthday today), loved gambling more than eating. Once he stayed at a card table for 24 hours straight. When he finally got hungry he ordered a piece of meat between two slices of bread to save the time of using a fork. No mustard, even! As a joke, his title, Sandwich, was given to food served between bread, and the name stuck.

Build the Earl of Sandwiches.

This monumental meal surely deserves the title. Study the building plans carefully before starting construction. (Beware: It won't fit in a sandwich bag!)

PROPOSED
EARL OF
SANDWICH
ELEVATION   ½ SCALE

← BREAD ⑫

← MAYO ⑪

← LETTUCE ⑩

← RAISINS CHOPPED NUTS ⑨

← CREAM CHEESE ⑧

← BREAD ⑦

← HONEY ⑥

← APPLE SLICES ⑤

← SHREDDED CARROTS ④

← BANANA SLICES ③

← PEANUT BUTTER ②

← BREAD ①

NOTE: BUILD FROM BOTTOM UP

Dear Diary:

November 4
Rodin's Birthday

Next to Michelangelo, Auguste Rodin (born November 4, 1840 in Paris) is probably the world's best-known sculptor. You've probably seen pictures or small reproductions of *The Thinker*, his most famous statue. Many people were shocked by the rough texture of Rodin's sculpture, but he expressed strong emotion through his powerful forms and rugged or delicate surfaces. You can see many of his works in American museums.

PLAY STATUES
THIS GAME IS GREAT FUN WITH MORE THAN FOUR PLAYERS.

① On a large outdoor play area mark a starting line. All the players except IT stand behind the line to begin. IT stands about 50-feet away with his or her back to the other players.

② As IT counts out loud quickly to 10, everybody else runs or walks toward him/her.

③ When IT reaches 10 he/she turns around quickly. Everyone else must "freeze" like a statue. If IT sees anyone move - even a little - that person must go back to the starting line.

④ IT turns around and counts to 10 again.

⑤ Finally someone will tag IT before He/she gets to 10. IT turns around and chases everyone, trying to tag any player. The starting line is base.

⑥ The person IT tags becomes the new IT.

Dear Diary:

November 5
Guy Fawkes Day

Bake "parkin" for afternoon tea or dessert.

 Parkin is a traditional Guy Fawkes Day cake that's so moist you can eat it as a pudding.

1. Preheat the oven to 350 degrees.

2. In a double boiler over hot water, heat ⅔ cup molasses or cane sugar and ½ cup butter till the butter melts.

3. In a bowl, mix together:
   - 1 cup white or whole wheat flour
   - ⅔ cup rolled oats
   - 1 T. sugar
   - ½ tsp. ginger
   - ¼ tsp. ground cloves
   - ½ tsp. salt
   - ½ tsp. baking soda

4. Grate a little lemon rind into the dry ingredients.

5. Mix the melted butter mixture and ⅔ cup milk into the dry ingredients a little bit at a time. It makes a thin batter.

6. Pour into an 8-inch-square or 9-inch-round buttered pan and bake for about 35 minutes.

7. For a really great dessert, top each serving with whipped cream. Jolly good!

Dear Diary:

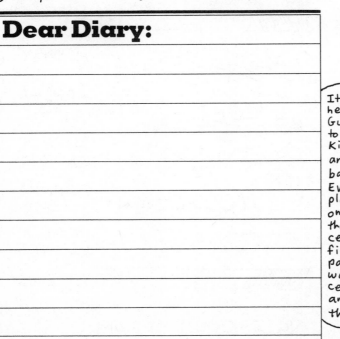

It says here that Guy Fawkes tried to blow up the King of England and Parliament back in 1605. Ever since the plot was discovered on November 5, the English have celebrated with fireworks and parties. Why would they celebrate such an awful thing?!?

Any excuse for fun!

November 6
Basketball Day

The very first basketball was a soccer ball and the hoops were peach baskets. A Canadian rugby and lacrosse player, James Naismith, invented the game of basketball in 1891 because of the need for an active game that could be played indoors in winter. Since its peach basket days, basketball has become one of America's favorite sports—indoors and out. Almost every school has a basketball hoop (and lots of playgrounds and home garages do too).

Today is James Naismith's birthday, born in 1861. Celebrate with basketball. Practice shooting and dribbling, or get up a game.

If you don't have a basketball, wad up some scrap paper from the wastepaper basket and try shooting it back in the basket from across the room.

Or play "basketcard" with a friend. From about six feet away, try sailing playing cards into a basket or box—it's harder than it sounds.

Dear Diary:

November 7
Revolution Day

Today is a national holiday of the largest country in the world, the Union of Soviet Socialist Republics (U.S.S.R.). It is called Revolution Day, the anniversary of Russia's revolution of 1917. In every major Soviet city—especially Moscow, the capital—the streets are decorated with colored lights and people are gathered to watch long military parades. Many kids hold bright balloons.

Write in Russian.

This code is based on the Russian alphabet, similar to our alphabet in many ways. Some letters are the same, some are completely different, some are mixed up, and two repeat—when you use "C" or "H" just as English uses them remember to draw a line underneath. For example,

CHOСКИНГ!
(SHOCKING!)

А	Б	C	Д	Е	Ф	Г	Н	И	Ј	К	Л	М
A	B	C	D	E	F	G	H	I	J	K	L	M

Н	О	П	Q	Р	С	Т	У	В	W	Х	Y	З
N	O	P	Q	R	S	T	U	V	W	X	Y	Z

Dear Diary:

November 8
Inkblot Day

This inkblot is rather like the ones used in a famous psychological test devised by Hermann Rorschach (pronounced "ROAR-shock"), born on this day in 1884, in Switzerland. Rorschach was always fascinated by the patterns inkblots made and the different pictures different people saw in them. Even as a young man his nickname was "Kleck," German for inkblot. When he grew up he studied personality and mental health through his inkblot test.

Make blot pictures.

① FOLD a piece of paper in half, and OPEN it up again.
② DROP some wet paint (watercolor or tempera) any old way on the inside of the paper. CLOSE it like a book and press lightly with your hand.
③ OPEN to see your creation. What's there ???

Dear Diary:

November 9
Remember Smokey Day

Smokey Bear is the only animal in America with his own zip code (20252). He has gotten as many as 13,000 letters in one week. Smokey is an American black bear, the living symbol of forest fire prevention and he lives in the National Zoo in Washington, D.C., but he's not the very *first* Smokey.

The first Smokey was found as a cub clinging to a charred tree after a New Mexico forest fire in 1950. His burned paws were treated, but he limped all his life. He later lived in the National Zoo with his mate, Goldie, till November 9, 1976, when he died peacefully in his sleep.

The new Smokey, young and active, does his job well: posing for posters and ads for the U.S. Forest Service that remind folks, "Only *you* can prevent forest fires!"

Q: Who's Smokey?
A: A rare bear.

Q: How can you help him do his job?
A: Mention prevention.

Q: Who takes care of the real Smokey?
A: The zoo crew.

Q: What are the woods after a fire?
A: The sorest forest.

Dear Diary:

November 10
Vachel Lindsay's Birthday

Imagine walking across the United States! Vachel Lindsay, born November 10, 1879, in Springfield, Illinois, was one of America's amazing characters — a kind of modern Johnny Appleseed who walked all over the country planting, not seeds, but poems. He read his poems aloud, traded them for meals and lodging, and enchanted thousands of people with his jazzlike rhythms. He roamed the country for more than 20 years giving his poems away; he once said, "There is more poetry in the distribution of verse than in the writing of it."

This poem is a man's answer to his grandchildren's question, "What is the moon?"

The moon? It is a griffin's egg,
Hatching to-morrow night.
And how the little boys will watch
With shouting and delight
To see him break the shell and stretch
And creep across the sky.
The boys will laugh. The little girls,
I fear, may hide and cry.
Yet gentle will the griffin be,
Most decorous and fat,
And walk up to the Milky Way
And lap it like a cat.

November 11
Veterans' Day

Veterans' Day honors people who have been in the armed forces, and honors the memory of those who died in wars.

November 11 was chosen for Veterans' Day because World War I ended at 11 A.M. this date in 1918. Many Americans will observe two minutes of silence at 11:00 this morning, a tradition since 1918.

Do you know any veterans? Family members, teachers, or older friends who may have served in the armed forces? Ask them to sign their names in your diary and tell you a little about their experience.

Dear Diary:

Dear Diary:

Celebrate Lindsay's birthday by giving his poem away. Copy it to send to a friend, or read it aloud to someone who'll enjoy it.

November 12

_____ Day

Dear Diary:

November 13
Treasure Hunt

Don't tell anybody, ye landlubber, but Robert Louis Stevenson (1850-1894) buried his own treasure in bookshelves all over the world. Dig up a copy of _Treasure Island_ and ye'll see what I mean. Meanwhile, it's his birthday, so put on your eyepatch and celebrate, ye dog, or I'll have ye walk the plank.

Have a treasure hunt for a friend with a November birthday. The treasure might be a bag of homemade cookies (see August 16) or any surprise.

You'll need about 5 or 6 slips of paper for the treasure hunter. Each clue leads the hunter to the next and finally to the treasure. For example:

The FIRST clue is in your hand. Find the SECOND in the sand.

The second clue might be hidden in a sandbox or an indoor cactus garden. Jolly, Roger!

Dear Diary:

November 14
Around-the-World Celebration

Around the World in Eighty Days, that famous book by Jules Verne is still popular, but in 1889 it was a new, exciting best-seller. A 22-year-old reporter who called herself Nellie Bly (but whose real name was Elizabeth Cochrane) had a great idea: Why not try to go around the world in *less* than 80 days?! Verne's book was only a story, but she would do it for real!

So on November 14, 1889, Nellie Bly set out from New York City. Remember, there were no airplanes or cars then; she traveled by ship, train, ricksha, and burro, and returned to New York in only 72 days, 6 hours, 10 minutes, and 11 seconds (with a monkey from Hong Kong on her shoulder!).

By the end of her journey almost everyone in America knew of the daring Nellie Bly. Even Jules Verne sent a telegram from France saying "Hurrah! Hurrah!"

Go around the world with Nellie Bly.

All you need is one die (one of a pair of dice), and a small marker. Play alone or with a friend.

Start by putting your marker on New York. Cast the die and move ahead according to the number that comes up. On a piece of paper keep track of each number you throw. The total amount represents the number of days in your journey. Can you get back to New York in less than 80 days?

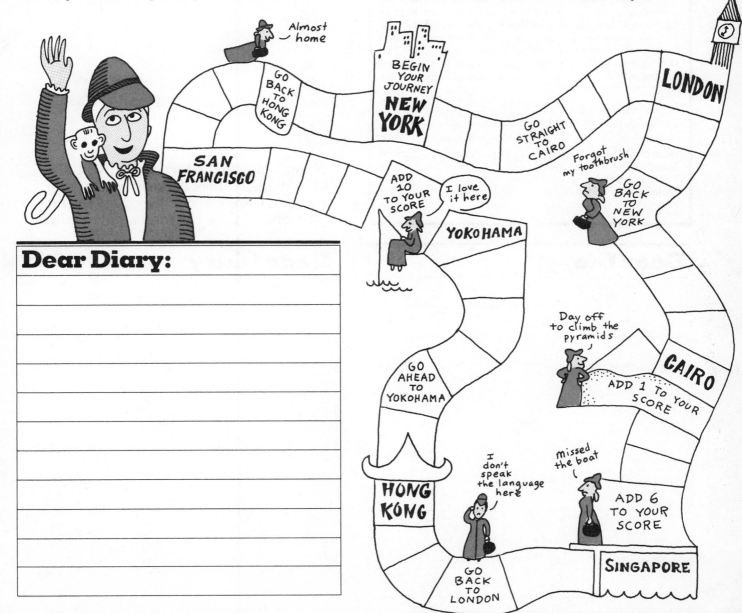

Dear Diary:

Amazing Daily

November 15   *All The News That's Fit To Tickle*

HOLIDAY PROTEST ENDS EARLY

Japan—Two-, four-, and six-year-olds here protested the traditional celebration of Shishi-Go-San this morning. They claimed the holiday discriminates against them in favor of three-, five-, and seven-year-olds. Parents admitted this was true. Shishi-Go-San means seven-five-three and honors children of those ages with a second birthday party. But, the parents pointed out, the six-year-old of this year is the seven-year-old of next. This argument seemed to satisfy many of the protesters who voted to end their hunger strike in time for breakfast.

November 15 Proclaimed Almost-Everything Day

South China, Maine—Members of AFAY (April Fools All Year) today proclaimed November 15 Almost-Everything Day.

O. B. O'Brien, spokesperson for the group, said, "January 17 is National Nothing Day, so November 15 takes care of the other extreme."

Pike Spies Peak

Colorado, 1806—Lieutenant Zebulon Pike discovered an extremely high peak in the Rocky Mountains today, says *Amazing Daily* reporter, A. Little Byrd. "Though he could tell he was on the right mountain, it seems Pike lost his way and turned back before reaching the top. He never did have a good sense of direction." In spite of that, it is believed the peak will be named for its discoverer. "Zebulon's Zenith" seems the obvious choice.

Today's Tongue Twister

Perky Papa Pike picked out Pike's Peak for a picnic. Poor pokey Papa Pike returned from Pike's Peak pooped.

November 16
Hand Day

Celebrate your hands!
- Get a manicure.
- Paint your fingernails.
- Play handball.
- Shake hands with everyone you see.
- Wave good-bye.
- Play pattycake.
- Wear rings on every finger, even your thumbs.
- Make rings.
- Walk on your hands.
- Dance on your hands to *Hand*el's Water Music.
- Learn hand signs.
- Have your palm read.
- Trace around your hand and turn it into a picture:

Note: Today is the birthday of W. C. Handy (1873-1958), a black American composer and band leader remembered as "the father of the blues." Give the man a hand, folks!

Dear Diary:

Dear Diary:

Try your hand at these punny picture puzzles:

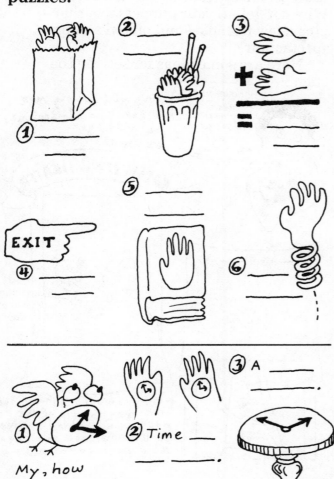

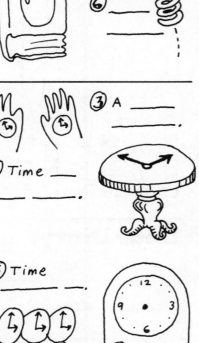

Q. What time is it when the clock says 25 o'clock?
A. Time to get the clock fixed.

Eli Terry patented his design for the first American-made clock on this date in 1794; *and*, tomorrow is the anniversary of the United States' adoption of *standard time* in 1883. Before *standard time* people set their watches and clocks by the sun—when it was directly overhead the time was 12 noon. This meant that people living only 15 miles apart often set their watches differently. With the adoption of *standard time* the U.S. was divided into four time zones, and timekeeping became much simpler.

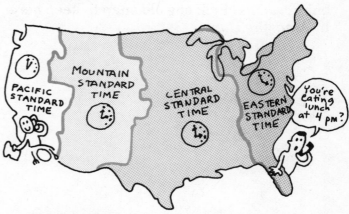

Dear Diary:

Answers appear at the back of the book.

November 18
Old Snapshots Day

Nowadays there are cameras that take pictures and develop them in front of your eyes in minutes, but before Louis Daguerre (born on this date in 1789) the only photographic process took six to eight *hours*! In the 1830's Daguerre, a French painter and inventor, perfected the *daguerreotype* — Dog what?! Dog-AIR-o-type — a photograph on a copper plate that required only 20 to 30 minutes. Many daguerreotypes were made from then on, especially portraits.

Look through the family photo album with your folks — they'll love showing you their old pics. They may even own a daguerreotype of a great-great-grandparent. Look at the ones of you as a baby . . . *cute*! Pick one old snap to keep here in *Amazing Days*.

November 19
Bring On the Puppets

The world's most famous puppet has a special day coming up on November 24. Why not get all your puppets together — plus a few friends — and put on a puppet spectacular!

Here are some ideas for setting the stage.

Hand puppets can perform anywhere. Your arm can even be a stage

Try performing over a fence, a clothesline, or a hedge — or in the . . .

OPEN DOOR THEATER

Cloth pinned across doorway

◄ For marionettes, hang the cloth from the top of the door. Stand behind a screen so the audience only sees the puppet - not you!

Dear Diary:

Dear Diary:

November 20
Dreamland Journey

What did you dream last night? If you can't remember, draw your favorite dream or worst nightmare ever.

Dear Diary:

November 21
Get Ready for Thanksgiving

On this date in 1620 the pilgrims aboard the *Mayflower* signed their famous document, the Mayflower Compact, their first plan of self-determined government in their new land. They hadn't even thought about a thanks-giving at that time; they were just getting ready to settle in Plymouth, Massachusetts. Almost a year later when the crops had been harvested, the pilgrims and their Native American friends held the famous first Thanksgiving. Nowadays it always comes on the fourth Thursday of November.

Make place cards (to dress up the table and let everyone know where to sit).

1. For each card FOLD one small piece of stiff paper in half.
2. On another paper, draw and color different vegetables. CUT them out and glue to the cards

3. See if you can use vegetables that begin with the same letter as each person's name. Print the names in color.

Dear Diary:

November 22
Sagittarius Begins

People born between November 22 and December 22 are born under the sign of Sagittarius, the archer. According to astrologers, they are cheerful, happy people always "on the go." They love to work, and are good at concentrating on a task. Like a good archer, they're likely to hit any target they aim for. Sagittarius people are outgoing and love to be surrounded by their friends, but they don't like to be told what to do. They think for themselves! Don't be surprised when a Sagittarius friend throws a party on the spur of the moment or sees something expensive and buys it without considering the price—they're very impulsive! And they're great friends, *if* you can keep up with them.

GIVE A GAG GIFT.

Make the old arrow-through-the-head-trick for your Sagittarius friends. They usually love dumb jokes.

1. Twist the ends of 3 or 4 pipe cleaners together to make one long wire.
2. Bend it over your head like a hairband. Bend up the two ends.
3. Cover each end with a drinking straw. Put white glue inside so they'll stay.
4. Glue a paper arrowhead to one end and feathers to the other.

Dear Diary:

November 23
Boris Karloff's Birthday

The most famous horror-movie actor of all was born on this date in 1887. Boris Karloff scared the pants off moviegoers everywhere as the monster in *Frankenstein* (1931) and as The Mummy (1932).

Try these monstrous riddles on your fiends . . . er, friends.

Q: What monster flies kites?
A: Benjamin Franklinstein.

Q: Why was the invisible man crazy?
A: You know the old saying: Out of sight, out of mind.

Q: Why did the monster think Dr. Frankenstein was so funny?
A: The doctor kept him in stitches.

Q: What kind of test does Dracula always do well on?
A: A blood test.

Q: What monster is easiest to clean?
A: A wash-and-wear-wolf.

Q: Why did the other monsters think the mummy was conceited?
A: He was all wrapped up in himself.

Make up more monster riddles of your own (groan).

Dear Diary:

November 24
Pinocchio Day

The Adventures of Pinocchio was written by Carlo Lorenzini (he called himself Carlo Collodi) born in Italy on this date in 1826. In the book, Pinocchio is a mischievous marionette carved from an amazing piece of wood that laughs and cries. After a bookful of harrowing adventures Pinocchio becomes a real boy.

You can make a marionette from scraps and string. To start out, get together a cardboard tube from a toilet paper roll, a large needle and strong thread or string, a paper cup, spools, beads, or other "stringables."

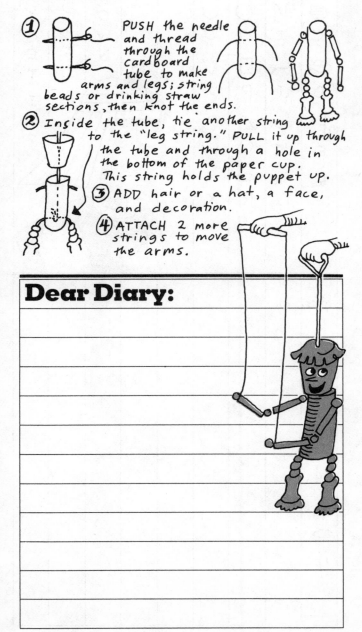

① PUSH the needle and thread through the cardboard tube to make arms and legs; string beads or drinking straw sections, then knot the ends.

② Inside the tube, tie another string to the "leg string." PULL it up through the tube and through a hole in the bottom of the paper cup. This string holds the puppet up.

③ ADD hair or a hat, a face, and decoration.

④ ATTACH 2 more strings to move the arms.

November 25
Antarctica Jump Day

On this date in 1956 one brave and bundled-up person perpetrated the first successful parachute jump in Antarctica. Now *why* anybody wanted to jump into the coldest continent on earth we haven't figured out. Maybe he wanted to visit Santa and got his poles mixed up; or maybe he wanted to find a penguin for a pet. Whatever the reason, celebrate the frozen feat (he *must* have had frozen feet!) with a special punch concoction.

Parachutist's penguin punch.

This is the perfect drink to carry in your thermos to Antarctica or other cold climates—like the playground at this time of year.
1. Put 2 cups of fresh apple cider in a saucepan.
2. Add a cinnamon stick and 3 or 4 whole cloves (or the same spices ground up) and a little nutmeg.
3. Heat over a medium flame till steaming.

This super-warmer-upper is ever popular served with pastries, pumpkin pie, popovers, popcorn, peanuts, pretzels, or pecan pancakes.

Dear Diary:

Dear Diary:

King Tut was just nine years old when he became Pharaoh of Egypt. When he died, he was only 18. His body was mummified and laid to rest in a tomb which, once hidden under the Egyptian sand, was not reopened for more than 3,000 years. On November 26, 1922, Howard Carter, a British archaeologist, entered King Tutankhamun's tomb. The doors to the shrine that held the mummy moved as easily on their hinges as if they'd been closed yesterday.

The discovery of King Tut's tomb was one of the most important archaeological events ever: twentieth-century people were able to look into a pharaoh's tomb and Egypt's ancient culture as if they have returned in a time machine. Carter and a crew of archaeologists worked 10 years to carefully remove the priceless contents of the tomb. In the late 1970's the Treasures of Tutankhamun were displayed in six museums in the United States and viewed by millions of Americans.

Write in hieroglyphics.

The ancient Egyptians wrote with pictures that sometimes stood for whole words and sometimes for sounds. This substitution code is loosely based on that system of writing.

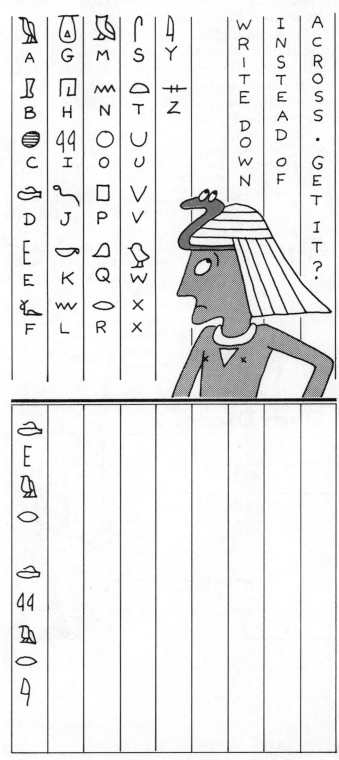

The ticket stub from the exhibit shows King Tut's cartouche — a picture of his name.

November 27
Onion Festival

If people are crying in the streets of Berne, Switzerland, on the fourth Monday of November, it's not because anything sad has happened; it's just that there are onions piled high along the street to celebrate the Onion Festival, one of that country's most wonderful autumn market days. Funny-costumed people with big onion head masks (made of paper and cloth) march through the streets, much like the marchers in America's Thanksgiving parades.

1. Peel 1 or 2 small yellow onions per person.
2. Slice them into ½-inch rings. No crying, now; run them under cold water as soon as they're sliced.
3. Separate the rings and put them in a bowl. Pour buttermilk over them. Let them soak in the buttermilk at least 1 hour (3 or 4 hours is even better).
4. Discard the buttermilk.
5. In a clean brown paper grocery bag put ¼ cup flour seasoned with salt and pepper for every 2 onions.
6. Drop the onion rings in the bag, close the top tight and shake.
7. When the onions are well coated with flour, ask your adult assistant to drop them into hot oil and cook till golden brown. Drain on more grocery bags. An onion feast!

Dear Diary:

November 28
First Skywriting in America, 1922

Look! Up in the sky! It looks like . . . It is! Letters! . . . And they spell . . ." Captain Cyril Turner of the Royal Air Force amazed New York City on this date in 1922 by writing in the sky. To find out America's first skywritten message find your way through this rather cloudy maze:

Only one message will be spelled out if you find your way to the END.

Dear Diary:

Louisa May Alcott Day

Little Women is the story of a family of four girls growing up during the Civil War. It was an easy book for Louisa May Alcott to write (it took only three months) because it was the story of her family. She changed the names of her sisters and herself (in the book she is Jo), but *Little Women* is pretty much a true story. Over 100 years have passed since she wrote it, but kids today still love to read about Meg, Jo, Beth, and Amy.

Louisa May Alcott was born on November 29, 1832. Her family had very little money. When her birthday came around, her friends came over not for cake and ice cream but for thin slices of bread and apple. She lived in Concord, Massachusetts, most of her life, but during the Civil War she worked as a nurse in Washington, D.C. The popularity of *Little Women* and the books that followed it (*Little Men*, for one) made Louisa May Alcott a successful author, able to provide for the family she so loved.

Put a snapshot or drawing of your whole family on this page. Write something about your family in your diary.

Louisa May Alcott

Dear Diary:

Mark Twain Was a Fake Name Day

Q: How's it possible Mark Twain was born on this date in 1835 but he wasn't born Mark Twain?

A: "Mark Twain" was a pseudonym (fake name) that Samuel Langhorne Clemens used when he wrote books like *Tom Sawyer*, *Huckleberry Finn*, and *The Prince and the Pauper*, and funny stories like "The Celebrated Jumping Frog of Calaveras County."

Q: How's it possible Mark Twain was born in both Florida and Missouri?

A: He was born in Florida, Missouri (Florida really is a city in Missouri).

At least nine other people in *Amazing Days* also had pseudonyms. These pseudonyms and real names are mixed up; guess who's who:

Real Names	Pseudonyms
Benjamin Franklin	archy the cockroach
Greta Gustaffson	Sarah Bernhardt
Ehrich Weiss	Carlo Collodi
Elizabeth Cochrane	Greta Garbo
Don Marquis	Poor Richard
Frances Gumm	Judy Garland
Charles Lutwidge Dodgson	Harry Houdini
Rosine Bernard	Nellie Bly
Carlo Lorenzini	Lewis Carroll

Dear Diary:

Answers appear at the back of the book.

December 1
Advent Celebration

December is finally here, and with it the season of Advent when Christians around the world look forward to the coming of Christmas. (Advent means "coming.")

A tradition in some European countries that is getting popular in America is the Advent calendar, which makes special notice of each day till Christmas. Sometimes it's a beautiful picture with tiny doors cut into it, and each door has numbers from 1 to 24 printed on it. On each day of December another door is opened to reveal a surprise picture or verse. Almost always behind door 24 (Christmas Eve) there's a picture of Mary, Joseph, and the Baby Jesus. The calendar is a nice way to mark off the days till Christmas.

Make an Advent calendar.

This Advent calendar is easy to make. Cut out a large Christmas tree shape out of paper for your wall or door.

Today and each day of December add one paper ornament with tape or tacks to the tree. By Christmas Eve it will be completely decorated.

You'll find a drawing in your diary space each day till Christmas Eve (surprise!). If you wish, use that picture as an idea for your daily ornament.

Recycle old Christmas cards.

Did you save the cards you received last December? They can easily become great cards for you to *send* this year. Carefully cut off the front of each card along the fold. (Throw away the part of the card that had the message and signature.) On the back of the picture write POST CARD and draw a line down the center.

Dear Diary:

December 2
Dot Day

Get out your magnifying glass and look at the Sunday funnies, a color magazine photo, or a color TV picture. Do you see the tiny dots? They are pure color—that is: red, yellow, blue (the primary colors), and black on a background of white. When you're not looking through the magnifying glass your eyes blend the colors in your mind.

Long before color TV the French artist George Seurat (born December 2, 1859) had the idea of making paintings this way. He used tiny dots of color to make large, brilliant pictures. Seurat became very famous and started other artists thinking of new ways to use color and paint.

Use felt-tip pens to add color to this picture. Use tiny dots of red, blue, and yellow.

Have some fun making Christmas or Chanukah cards with colored dots.

Dear Diary:

December 3
Portrait Power!

Gilbert Stuart painted almost a thousand portraits—pictures of people! But you probably know one in particular: reproductions of his "unfinished head of George Washington," painted in 1796, hang in schools and public buildings all over America.

Stuart was born in Rhode Island on December 3, 1755, and became America's favorite portrait painter by the time he was 35 years old.

A portrait can be a drawing, painting, or photograph of one or more people. Think about making a portrait of yourself or a family member as a Christmas or Chanukah present. Such a personal gift will really be appreciated.

Dear Diary:

December 4
Chanukah Celebration

Beginning on the twenty-fifth day of the Hebrew month Kislev (sometime in December) Jewish people celebrate Chanukah, which lasts eight days. It's called the Festival of Lights because of the tradition of lighting the candles of a special menorah. This tradition reminds families of a miracle that happened over 2,000 years ago when a group of Jews won a fight for religious freedom, and a holy lamp burned bright for eight days on what seemed to be not enough oil for even one day.

One new candle is lit each evening of Chanukah until the menorah is full and glowing on the eighth night. Also small gifts are exchanged each night, songs are sung, and games are played. Chanukah is a very happy time!

Here is a menorah:

One candle is already drawn in it; that's the Shamash candle used to light all the others.

Look on the last page of this book to see when Chanukah begins this year. On the first night draw one candle in the menorah and color its burning flame.

Draw another the next night, and continue with one each evening till the menorah is full.

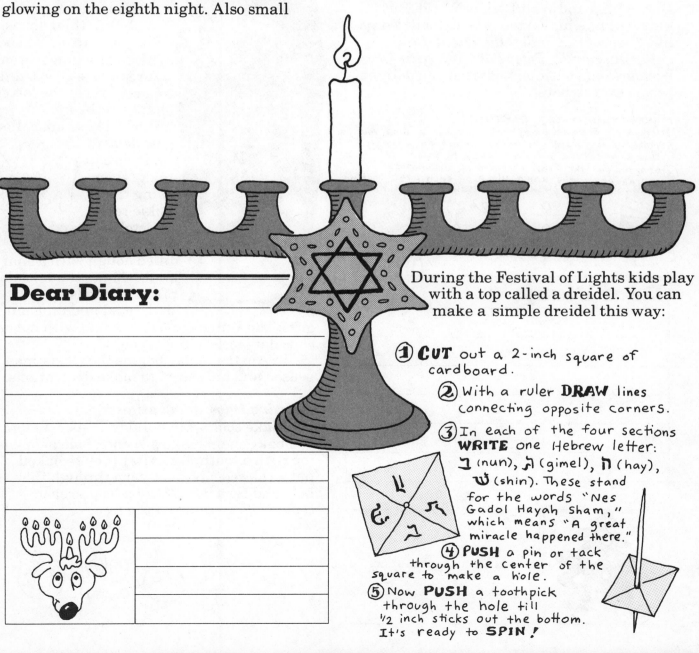

Dear Diary:

During the Festival of Lights kids play with a top called a dreidel. You can make a simple dreidel this way:

① **CUT** out a 2-inch square of cardboard.

② With a ruler **DRAW** lines connecting opposite corners.

③ In each of the four sections **WRITE** one Hebrew letter: נ (nun), ג (gimel), ה (hay), שׁ (shin). These stand for the words "Nes Gadol Hayah Sham," which means "A great miracle happened there."

④ **PUSH** a pin or tack through the center of the square to make a hole.

⑤ Now **PUSH** a toothpick through the hole till ½ inch sticks out the bottom. It's ready to **SPIN !**

December 5
Walt Disney's Birthday

Walt Disney (1901-1966) is probably the most important person in the history of animated cartoons (animated means "moving"). He perfected natural movement of cartoon characters, made the first cartoon with sound (*Steamboat Willie* with Mickey Mouse), and the first feature-length cartoon (*Snow White and the Seven Dwarfs*). The Academy of Motion Pictures Arts and Sciences was so excited about *Snow White*, they gave Walt eight Oscars—one big one and seven little ones.

Walt Disney is remembered for all kinds of movies and TV shows, as well as Disneyland and Walt Disney World. But kids still like his cartoons best of all! Films like *Pinocchio, Cinderella, Dumbo, Fantasia, Bambi, Peter Pan*, and *Alice in Wonderland* continue to amaze and delight people everywhere.

MAKE AN ANIMATED CARTOON.
1. USE an old paperback book that has a wide margin.
2. MAKE UP a simple stick figure - human, animal, space creature - anyone easy to draw.
3. Starting at the front of the book draw the character in the same place on each page making him or her move slightly with each new picture.
4. EXPERIMENT with funny movements.
5. FLIP the pages to watch your character ///MOVE!!!

Dear Diary:

December 6
St. Nicholas Day

St. Nicholas was a real person, born about 1600 years ago in what is now Turkey. Because of his many acts of kindness to children he became their special saint. Say "Saint Nicholas" 10 times real fast and you'll find out how St. Nick came to be called Santa Claus.

In some European countries St. Nick brings small gifts to kids on his own feast day, December 6, not Christmas. In Holland and France children awoke this morning to find dried fruits, nuts, and small toys left in their shoes. (Wrapped up, let's hope!) There were gingerbread figures of the good saint and cookies in the letter shapes of the kids' initials. These are called *letterbanket*, and you can make them using the cookie recipe on October 13 and cutting your initials out of the rolled dough with a sharp knife. (Make the initials of your friends for a delightful and unusual gift.) The Dutch eat *letterbanket* with hot chocolate on St. Nick's Day.

In Austria today begins the Christmas season and kids start to make decorations.

***Amazing Days* decoration ideas.**
• Make cookies in holiday shapes. Before you bake them make a ¼-inch hole near the top with a toothpick. After they're baked put a colored ribbon or yarn through the hole and tie a bow. Make a loop so each cookie can be hung on the tree.

December 7
Ratification Day

• Make a clove apple (pomander), a decoration to delight the nose. You need a box of whole cloves and a small apple. Starting around the stem, press the cloves into the apple right next to each other. Cover the whole apple with cloves. Then tie a ribbon around it so you can hang it.

• The clove apple will smell better every day. Hang it on the tree or wrap it in tissue and put it under the tree as a gift. After Christmas keep it in a drawer or closet to keep clothes smelling sweet.

• A favorite Scandinavian decoration is paper-cut chains. They are made just like paper dolls, but can be any shape at all. Fold a long piece of paper accordion-style 5 or 6 times. Cut a shape, being careful not to cut the sections apart. Open it up and stand it on the windowsill, mantel, or anywhere.

Delaware was the first state to ratify the U.S. Constitution, on this date in 1787. That makes today extra special: It's Ratification Day in Delaware.

Do you remember the names of the other 12 original 13 states? Unscramble the state names below to find out.

Stashamestucs _____

Hawh Repsnime _____

Oder Landish _____

Tencutinocc _____

Roy Kewn _____

Sew Jenery _____

Nansalpenivy _____

Dralmany _____

Givarini _____

Thorn Lacaroni _____

Ouch Tasonrail _____

Egoigra _____

Dear Diary:

Dear Diary:

Answers appear at the back of the book.

December 8
More Chanukah Fun

During the eight days of Chanukah, Jewish people enjoy special foods and fun.

Potato latkes (pancakes) are a popular Chanukah food. Try these for supper with applesauce and sour cream.

① **WASH** 2 or 3 potatoes very well. **GRATE** them coarsely.

Let the grated potatoes sit for 10 minutes then **DRAIN** off the liquid.

② **GRATE** in one small onion.

③ **STIR** in with a fork:

1 egg
2 T. flour
½ tsp. salt
¼ tsp. baking powder
dash of pepper

④ Use a tablespoon to put batter in a frying pan with ¼-inch hot oil. **FRY** each pancake till it's brown on the bottom, then **TURN** it over and fry the other side. **EAT** them hot!

ADULT HELPER

Dear Diary:

December 9
First Christmas Seals For Sale, 1907

The first Christmas seals were offered for sale on this date in 1907. They were the idea and design of Emily Perkins Bissell of Wilmington, Delaware. Christmas seals have become a tradition, and the money made from their sale helps fight lung diseases like asthma and tuberculosis (TB), as well as air pollution.

• SOUTH CAROLINA 1975

Christmas seals have become more beautiful than ever in the past few years, mainly because they've been designed by *kids*! If you are in the third grade or under, you can submit a painting for use on next year's Christmas seals. Ask your art teacher at school for details, or call your local chapter of the American Lung Association.

Look at this year's Christmas seals—your family probably got them in the mail. Pick out your favorites and stick them on this page. Use others on Christmas cards and packages.

Make your own seals by cutting out small pictures from old cards or magazines. Glue them on with a little bit of white glue or rubber cement.

Dear Diary:

Glue Christmas Seals on stiff paper for fun tree decorations.

December 10
Emily Dickinson's Birthday

I'm nobody. Who are you?
Are you nobody too?
Then there's a pair of us.
Don't tell - they'd banish us, you know.

How dreary to be somebody,
How public - like a frog -
To tell your name the livelong June
To an admiring bog.

The nobody who wrote that poem was one of America's finest poets, born on this date in 1830. Emily Dickinson lived her whole life in her father's house in Amherst, Massachusetts. She wrote more than 1,700 poems before she died in 1886.

Dear Diary:

Give a poem for Christmas or Chanukah.

1. Think of the person you're going to give it to and choose a favorite poem that he or she will like.
2. In the center of a clean white sheet of paper neatly letter the poem (it can be written by you or someone else). Now, with pens or colored pencils draw a fancy border around the edge of the paper.
3. Roll it up and tie a ribbon around the middle to give it away.

Before books were printed, they were handwritten in this way and are called illuminated manuscripts.

Note: The Universal Declaration of Human Rights was adopted by the United Nations on this date in 1948. This very important document declares that every human being (even the "nobodies") shares basic rights with all people. The U.N. celebrates December 10 as Human Rights Day.

Amazing Daily

BIJOU TRIES ELECTRICITY, 1882

Boston, 1882—The Bijou Theater here is planning to light up its present opera tonight. If the Bijou succeeds in its plans, it will become the first theater in American history lighted by electricity. Six hundred and fifty lamps have been installed, and the event is being billed as "light opera at its best."

Promoters of this brilliant event recall that the first electric lights were lit on Broadway in New York city two years ago on December 20. "Ours will be the first theater lit *inside* by electricity. Maybe someday many theaters will have electric lights. You never know."

Portland, Oregon, 1975—Fifteen thousand lights glow on a 99½-foot-tall fir tree decorating Lloyd Center here. Record-keepers claim it is the tallest cut Christmas tree ever. Other giant trees decorate the White House lawn in Washington, D.C., and Rockefeller Center in New York every year.

UFO Identified

Scientists are reminding people of last year's numerous UFO sightings on Christmas Eve in hopes they can be avoided this year. At least 200 callers jammed phone lines last year to report "a bright red light in the sky trailed by a strange airship making jingle sounds." Positive identification was made of the red light belonging to Rudolph Reindeer guiding the legendary flying sleigh of S. Claus. "The sky always seems full of weird things on December 24," says Dr. Ursula F. Owens. "I remember a few years back when a bunch of shepherds watching their flocks by night reported communicating with winged aliens bending near the earth to touch their harps of gold. We never did clearly identify that sighting, but we are fairly sure it was just swamp gas."

Halley's Comet Due Soon

Halley's Comet is due to return within sight of the earth in 1985 or 1986, astronomers predict. It was last seen in 1911. Some people believe this comet or ones like it may have been the "star in the east" that foretold the first Christmas to the "wise men."

Aurora Borealis First Recorded

The famous Aurora Borealis, or Northern Lights, was first recorded in America on this date in 1719. The spectacular rays of color that appear like a huge curtain or pattern of smoke in the northern sky can sometimes be seen all over North America. This amazing sight is now known to be caused by electrified particles from the sun striking gases in the earth's air, causing them to glow and vibrate.

Dear Diary:

December 12
Guadalupe Day

Today, the Feast of Our Lady of Guadalupe, patron saint of Mexico, is that country's most joyous holiday. People from every part of Mexico travel to the shrine at Guadalupe where there are puppet shows, parties, fireworks, and the brilliantly colored decorations that are part of every Mexican fiesta.

Kids are excited because in only four days the piñata will be hung up and the village Christmas processions (posadas) and parties will begin. Often a piñata is broken every night between December 16 and 24, but in some families one is broken only on Christmas Eve.

A piñata is a container—usually made of pottery—filled with sweets and small toys, and decorated with papier-mâché and tissue paper fringe. It is made in many designs—animals, people, stars, and toys. During the Christmas parties, kids are blindfolded and given a stick to try to break the piñata which is hung by a rope and swung to make it even harder to hit. When someone finally breaks it, there's a scramble for the goodies that spill to the floor.

Dear Diary:

MAKE A PIÑATA

You need two medium-sized paper bags, rope, colored tissue or crepe paper, scissors, tape, rubber cement, and "GOODIES."

1. PUT one bag inside the other. This adds strength so the piñata is a little harder to break.

2. FILL the bag with "goodies:" wrapped candies and dried fruit, nuts in the shell, little unbreakable toys, balloons, fortunes, and confetti (LOTS OF CONFETTI!)

3. FOLD the top of the bag down and staple or tape it closed around the end of a rope at least eight feet long.

4. Now turn the bag into an angel (or use your own ideas for decoration). Tape cardboard wings and legs to the bag

5. COVER it with tissue or crepe paper fringe.

6. GLUE or STAPLE on a paper face and halo.

December 13
St. Lucia Day

This morning Swedish kids are up earlier than their parents preparing a surprise. They're fixing coffee and cat-shaped buns with raisin eyes. One of the girls of each family is getting dressed up in a white dress, and arranging on her head a crown of greenery with *real* candles. When breakfast is all set on a tray, she'll carry it to her parents' rooms, accompanied by her brothers (the boys are called baker lads) and sisters, all singing "Santa Lucia."

Imagine having breakfast in bed served by a girl with a candle crown! But it's not a complete surprise; this lovely custom is repeated each year on December 13, St. Lucia Day. Lucia means "light" and Swedish people consider this saint the bringer of the Christmas season and the longer days that follow the winter solstice (see December 22).

Surprise your family with breakfast in bed.

Plan this with only one grown-up. Very early, before anyone else is up, tiptoe to the kitchen. Make coffee with hot milk (or tea) and cinnamon toast.

Coffee Milk

Ask your grown-up accomplice to make coffee (or tea). Heat some milk to add to each cup.

Cinnamon Toast

1. Lightly toast 2 slices of bread for each person you're going to surprise.

2. If you have cookie cutters, cut the toast into fancy shapes. (Save the crusts for feeding the birds.)

3. Spread each slice with butter, and sprinkle with a little cinnamon sugar (1/4 cup sugar mixed with 2 tsp. cinnamon).

4. If you have a toaster oven set it at "top brown" and put the toast back in till it's brown and bubbly. Set a regular oven at 400 degrees and place bread under the broiler to toast.

Arrange a tray with coffee, toast, napkins, and a lighted candle. Surprise! Happy St. Lucia Day!

Dear Diary:

December 14
Forecast the Future Today

Nostradamus, a French astrologer born on this date in 1503, became so famous for his predictions of the future that kings and queens asked him to cast the horoscopes of their children. People are still studying and trying to understand his mysterious and fascinating prophesies.

Next year is just a little over two weeks away! Write *your* predictions for next year in your diary. Forecast all good things—it doesn't hurt to think positive.

This time next year you can look back and see how many of your predictions came true.

Creatures from Mars will land on January 2 and appoint me ruler of the planet earth... hee, hee...

Dear Diary:

December 15
Bill of Rights Day

The Bill of Rights—the first 10 amendments to the Constitution—was ratified on December 15, 1791. It describes *your* fundamental rights: freedom of speech, religion, press, assembly, etc. Since 1941, this date has been observed as Bill of Rights Day by presidential proclamation.

The Bill of Rights and the Constitution itself were not written until America won its independence from Britain. One of the events leading to the American Revolution was the Boston Tea Party (December 16, 1773) when a group of citizens dressed up as Indians boarded three British ships and dumped the contents of 342 chests of tea into Boston harbor to protest the unfair tea tax.

Celebrate with your own "Boston Tea Party."

Invite a few friends. Make a pot of tea. Serve hot with honey and lemon.
Buy a loaf of Boston brown bread; it comes in a can and is usually next to baked beans in the grocery store.
Remove the bread from the can, wrap it in foil, and warm in a 300 degree oven for 10-15 minutes. Cut it into ½-inch slices and spread each one with cream cheese. WAIT! DON'T THROW IT INTO THE HARBOR! Eat, drink, and enjoy the party—
YOU'VE GOT THE RIGHT!

Dear Diary:

December 16
Beethoven's Birthday

Ask anybody to name three famous classical composers— one of them is almost sure to be Beethoven! And no wonder! Ludwig van Beethoven, born in 1770 in Germany, wrote some of the most exciting and beautiful music in the world. Kids like his colorful symphonies (he wrote nine of them). His Fifth Symphony was rearranged and recorded in the late 1970's as "A Fifth of Beethoven," a disco hit!

It's hard to believe but Beethoven wrote some of his greatest music after he became totally deaf.

Turn on a classical radio station today and you're likely to hear some of Beethoven's music. One of his symphonies may be performed in concert tonight in your town—this has become a tradition in some places. Plan to enjoy some music this week: a Beethoven concert, a church choir, Christmas caroling, or a disco dance party.

The popular "Peanuts" character, Schroeder, looks forward to December 16 all year long. He's the proud wearer of a sweatshirt with Beethoven's picture on it, in honor of his hero.

Make a Beethoven sweatshirt.

1. Find a sweatshirt or light-colored jersey that won't mind being drawn on.
2. Use a pencil and ruler to draw a grid of sixteen 2-inch squares on the front of the shirt.
3. Copy this portrait lightly in pencil or chalk, one square at a time onto your grid.

4. When Beethoven looks right, go over the drawing with a permanent (oil-base) marker.

BEETHOVEN

Dear Diary:

December 17
No Time Like Snowtime

If you live where it snows, you may know the pleasant feeling of being cozy and warm indoors while a snowstorm rages outside. This is the situation John Greenleaf Whittier (1807-1892, birthday today) captured in his classic poem, "Snow-Bound."

"Shut in from all the world without,
We sat the clean-winged hearth about,
Content to let the north wind roar
In baffled rage at pane and door,
While the red logs before us beat
The frost-line back with tropic heat;
And ever, when a louder blast
Shook beam and rafter when it passed,
The merrier up its roaring draught
The great throat of the chimney laughed;
The house-dog on his paws outspread
Laid to the fire his drowsy head,
The cat's dark silhouette on the wall
A couchant tiger's seemed to fall;
And, for the winter fireside meet,
Between the andirons' straddling feet,
The mug of cider simmered slow,
The apples sputtered in a row,
And, close at hand, the basket stood
With nuts from brown October's wood.

What matter how the night behaved?
What matter how the north-wind raved?
Blow high, blow low, not all its snow
Could quench our hearth-fire's ruddy glow."

Next time it snows (if we're lucky that's tonight) have a picnic in front of the fireplace or by a big window to watch the storm. Spread a cloth on the floor, and make hot chocolate, sandwiches, and your favorite picnic foods. Popcorn looks like snow, but won't melt when you pour butter on it!

When the snowstorm's over get bundled up and go play.

Dear Diary:

Make forts. Throw snowballs at your friends

Make angels in a snowbank.

GO AHEAD. make a snowman or a snowwoman.

December 18
Wrap 'Em Up Day

Have you finished buying and making the gifts you're going to give? Christmas is little more than a week away. It's time to get the presents wrapped up, and that can be great fun!

The Dutch don't believe in simply wrapping a present; the idea is always to disguise and even hide the gift, making the opening of it like a game. A ring (or something that small) might be dropped into a sock, the pair of socks then being rolled up and stuffed into the toe of a boot that would then be put into a box and wrapped. An ink pen might be bundled in tissue paper and stuffed in a cardboard tube, then wrapped up to look like a candle. A record album or a piece of artwork might be put in the bottom of a big box with a couple of candies or something to make it rattle. A cookbook might be put inside a cookie tin with a note: "Now you can bake your own." Gifts are sometimes hidden around the house and clues placed under the Christmas tree — a holiday treasure hunt!

cardboard tube candle

Use your imagination.

The sneakiest idea of all.

Wrap up a small toy or something for your little brother or sister. Put a tag on it to say who it's for. Now put that in another box and wrap it up with a tag that says it's for your mom. Now put that in *another* box and wrap it up with a tag that says it's for your dad. If you have enough boxes it can pass through the hands of everyone in your family. April Fools' on Christmas!

You don't need store-bought wrapping paper. Use the Sunday funny papers and plain newspaper. Paint on ribbons and bows with tempera.

Dear Diary:

December 19

Bored Night

Won't Christmas *ever* get here? Well, it does seem to take its sweet time. There's an old saying: "as slow as Christmas!"

But don't be bored. Invite a friend to sleep over at your house. Spend the night playing old board games—every one you own. (If you play Monopoly you can buy "Boardwalk.") When you get bored with the boards, watch a late movie or raid the refrigerator for a midnight snack ... well, okay, a 10 o'clock snack then!

If you can't think of anything else to do, learn to draw many-pointed stars.
1. Lightly draw a circle.
2. Evenly space dots on the circle.
3. Draw lines from one dot to another, always skipping the same number of dots as you go clockwise around the circle. For example:

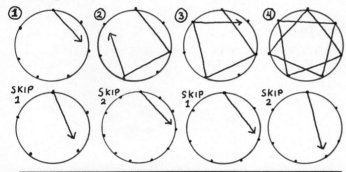

December 20

December's Fancy Pancake Morning

Begin the day with the best breakfast possible—fancy pancakes in holiday shapes, or whatever shapes *you* make them!

① In a big bowl mix together:
   1 cup whole wheat or white flour
   1 ½ tsps. baking powder
   ½ tsp. salt

② Mix in 1 cup milk (or buttermilk), 2 T. honey and 3 T. melted butter. (If the batter is too thick to pour, mix in a little more milk.

③ NOW COMES THE FUN PART!
   Using a big spoon, pour the batter onto a hot griddle or greased frying pan in fancy shapes.

   Be careful not to make them much bigger than your pancake turner. The hard part is keeping them in one piece when you turn them over.

④ Drop raisins on the wet batter for eyes, buttons, and decorations.

⑤ When the pancakes form little bubbles, lift one part to see if it's golden brown underneath. If so, turn it over carefully and brown the other side.

⑥ Serve your masterpieces with butter and maple syrup, honey, yogurt... FANCY!

Note: On this date in 1975, Brenda Lavisso flipped a pancake 8,960 times in 65 ½ minutes.

Dear Diary:

Dear Diary:

December 21
Forefathers' Day

Today is the anniversary of the Pilgrims' famous landing at Plymouth in 1620. Tonight patriotic societies around the country will hold banquets to remember the event. It's rather cold and close to Christmas for parades, but a few dedicated people in Plymouth, Massachusetts, will rise early tomorrow morning, don Pilgrim outfits, and march to Plymouth Rock to fire an old-fashioned cannon. Pilgrims, you are not forgotten!

Today is also the anniversary of the first crossword puzzle (which did *not* come over on the *Mayflower*!). It was invented by Arthur Wynne (good work, Art!) and published in the New York *World* on December 21, 1913.

Here's a crossword puzzle using the names of some pilgrims and their Native American friends. It's puzzling, but fun.

Across
2. Watercraft
4. Chief of the Wampanoag Indians: friend of the Pilgrims
5. One ____ one equals two
7. A long time
8. Not in
9. John ____ married 4 Down
10. A male child

Down
1. Pilgrims' first Indian friend
2. Plymouth Colony's most famous governor
3. Captain Miles ____
4. Priscilla ____ married 9 Across
6. Pawtuxet Indian friend of the Pilgrims

Dear Diary:

Answers appear at the back of the book.

December 22
Winter Solstice

Just about now the earth is tilted in such a way that the North Pole is as far away from the sun as it ever gets. (No wonder Santa's ready to leave home.) This is called the winter solstice. It means it's the longest night of the whole year and the shortest day for us in the Northern Hemisphere. But it also means that from now on daylight will be getting longer!

Some animals hibernate through these cold winter months, but birds spend the short daylight hours hunting for something to eat. Why not give them a treat? In northern Europe farmers tie bundles of wheat to a tall pole and set it up in the snow. As one Swede put it, "The birds must have Christmas too, you know." In America a popular tradition is decorating an outdoor "Christmas tree" for the birds.

Using a needle and thread, string unsalted popcorn, cranberries, and raisins. Use day-old popcorn so it won't break. Stuff pine cones with peanut butter and corn meal mixed together (see Oct. 4). Peel part of an apple for your tree. (Have you ever seen a bird try to peel an apple?) Stale doughnuts and bread make beautiful tree decorations... to a hungry bird.

December 23
Capricorn Begins

People born between December 23 and January 21 are born under the sign of Capricorn, the goat. According to astrologers they are deep thinkers who take life seriously. Luckily, though, they often have a witty streak that keeps their friends laughing. They are very loyal friends, but many times prefer to be alone. Capricorn people develop many interests, and love to learn.

People born in late December sometimes feel like their birthdays get ignored because of the Christmas rush. Let your Capricorn friends know you remember.

Make super-birthday cards.

Draw or cut out a picture of your favorite superhero. Let him or her carry or burst out of a birthday cake.

Make up a funny message that fits the picture.

HAVE A SUPER BIRTHDAY, MY HERO!

Note: Many people believe the wise men of the Christmas story were astrologers who studied the stars to foretell the future.

Dear Diary:

Dear Diary:

December 24
Christmas Eve

*"Twas the night before Christmas
And all through the house . . ."*
Well, what *is* going on at your house?

Many people have special traditions for Christmas Eve. Some people decorate a tree, hang up stockings, or go to a midnight church service. Some people get together for Christmas caroling; be sure to have a plate of goodies all ready in case carolers come to your door. Part of the tradition is giving a treat in return for a song. Some families read stories and poems aloud; "The Night Before Christmas" and the Christmas story as told in the Bible in the second chapter of the Gospel according to Luke are favorites.

In Mexico, tonight is called Noche Buena, and the Christ Child figure is finally placed in the beautiful nativity scene which has been set up in the home since December 16. Many kids in the U.S. mark the occasion with their own once-a-year observances: watching the sky in hopes of seeing a certain reindeer's bright red nose, and *not* being able to get to sleep!

Visiting friends is often an important part of Christmas Eve. People get together to share a bit of Christmas cheer and sometimes a cup of eggnog.

Real eggnog.

Beat one egg with 1 or 2 tsps. honey or sugar, ¼ tsp. vanilla, and a pinch of salt.

Put the egg mixture into a clean jar with ¼ cup cream and ½ cup milk.

Put the top on the jar and shake till the egg nog is frothy. A Christmas milk shake!

Put it in a cup and sprinkle a little nutmeg on top.

Dear Diary:

December 25
Christmas

PEACE ON EARTH
GOOD WILL TO ALL PEOPLE.
Merry Christmas!
Randy

On this page paste a favorite card, gift tags, and stickers, or make your own drawing to remember the day.

Dear Diary:

December 26
Boxing Day

No, today's not Muhammad Ali's birthday! (That's coming up on January 18.) The name "Boxing Day" comes from the Christmas boxes which, in England, are gifts wrapped up on December 26 especially for public servants. What a happy custom!

Think of the people who do jobs to help you and your family — mailperson, building superintendent, teachers, and anyone else. Make up a little package of Christmas cookies and homemade goodies for each one.

Put the cookies in the center of a pretty paper napkin opened up flat.

Pick up the four corners.

Tie it with a colored ribbon or yarn.

This is also a nice way to show neighbors or friends you're thinking about them. Why not add a note that says "Happy Boxing Day," (be prepared to explain it).

Dear Diary:

December 27
Kwanza

Ready to learn some Swahili? Yesterday began the Afro-American celebration of Kwanza (first fruits) which lasts seven days, each day stressing a special idea:

December 26: *umoja* (unity)

December 27: *kujichagulia* (self-determination)

December 28: *ujima* (group effort)

December 29: *ujamaa* (group economics)

December 30: *kuumba* (creativity)

December 31: *nia* (purpose)

January 1: *imani* (faith)

Kwanza was started in 1966 by Maulana Ron Karenga. That makes it a young holiday, but one that already has beautiful family traditions. These include the lighting of one candle in a *kinara* (candleholder) each day as the day's special idea is explored, discussed, and enjoyed. On the last day, celebrating families open *zawadi* (small gifts) they've made for each other, and share a *karamu* (feast).

Dear Diary:

HABARI GANI? (What's Happening?)

December 28
Get Ready for New Year's Eve

January was named after Janus, the Roman god of beginnings and endings. In Roman mythology Janus had two faces—one to look back to the old and one to look forward to the new. His image was often carved or painted on doors and gates to watch over comings and goings.

Make a New Year's door decoration.

① **FOLD** a piece of drawing paper in half.

② **DRAW** a person's profile looking toward the edge of the paper... AWAY from the fold.

③ Carefully **CUT OUT** the profile through both layers of paper.

④ Open it up. **ADD** eyes, ears, hair, and decoration with paint, markers or crayons.

⑤ **HANG** Janus above or on a door. If you can find real mistletoe, hang a sprig of it beneath him.

(Janus would make a fun New Year's card too.)

JANUS

Dear Diary:

December 29
The World's Largest Day

Why is today the world's largest? Well, Texas joined the Union on this date in 1845 making this Texas Admission Day, and Texans say EVERYTHING'S BIGGER IN TEXAS!

For example:

• Pecos Bill, tall-tale hero, is said to have been born in Texas.

• King Ranch, the largest cattle ranch in the U.S.—almost as big as the whole state of Rhode Island—is in Texas.

• The Dallas/Fort Worth Airport is the largest in the world.

• Houston hosted the world's largest dance in 1969; over 16,000 people attended.

• The world's largest beer cans are in San Antonio—huge storage tanks painted to look like cans of Lone Star beer.

• Also, in many small towns (yes, Texas does have *small* towns) you can see bigger-than-life-size monuments to the world's largest peanut, strawberry, watermelon, shrimp, and jackrabbit.

Texas was the U.S.'s biggest state until Alaska joined the Union in 1959. Test your knowledge of these other world's records:

World's largest animal: ☐ elephant or ☐ blue whale?

World's largest country (land area): ☐ U.S.S.R. or ☐ China?

World's tallest building: ☐ Sears Tower, Chicago, or ☐ Empire State Building, New York?

World's largest ocean: ☐ Atlantic or ☐ Pacific?

Our solar system's largest planet: ☐ Jupiter or ☐ Mercury?

World's largest freshwater lake: ☐ Lake Superior or ☐ Lake Michigan?

World's highest mountain: ☐ Mount Everest or ☐ Pike's Peak?

Dear Diary:

Answers appear at the back of the book.

December 30
Loose Ends Day

This year is almost over. A part of many different peoples' New Year's traditions is to finish up things started in the old year so they can begin new things in the new year.

Finish up *Amazing Days*.

• Spend today going back and tying up the loose ends of days and projects you didn't quite complete.

• Work out the puzzles you never did and draw or color on any page you want to. Add more stickers too.

• Paste in all the things you've been saving but haven't gotten around to. Make this diary into a scrapbook.

• Mark your very favorite days.

• When you've got the old year in ship-shape you can change the name of this day to *Tied Up* Loose Ends Day.

Dear Diary:

December 31
New Year's Eve

The great cycle of the year is about to begin again. The Dutch, and people of certain other nationalities, believe it's good luck to eat something in the form of a ring tonight to represent the completion of the circle of the year—a doughnut is just the thing!

So, best of luck in the coming year . . . and remember, *every* day is worth celebrating!

Dear Diary:

Credits

Answers

January 8

"Blue Suede Shoes"
"Hound Dog"
"Don't Be Cruel"
"Heartbreak Hotel"
"Jailhouse Rock"
"All Shook Up"
"Return To Sender"
"Love Me Tender"

January 12

```
P A G H Y Z H G L M N I J K N A P D C
C U F I X A B F K J O P M L D O Q E F
I B S J W V C E D I H Q R L T S R E E
N C E S L E E P I N G B E A U T Y Y B Z
D D L K I U D B C E F S S Z V Y X K A R
E M S R T N E A Z Y I U T Y W V W E Z Q
R O P Q H G F O G X W H G F Y H I Y K Q
E L I T T L E T O M T H U M B G J I S P
L N O P I Q N T U T V U V E Z F E N O
A M L K J E R S Q R S T W D C A D K N
T H E R I D I C U L O U S W I S H E S
L I T T L E R E D R I D I N G H O O D
I J A K O P D C B A Z Y X A B B C L M
N P M L C H A R L E S P E R R A U L T
```

February 1

```
M E X Y Z A B C D E F G H S J K
O A N O P Q R S T L V W X U Z A P
H C R D E F G H L J K L M A O E P
A R S T U V W I Y Z A B C N U K F
N H I J I L E N O P Q R S B I Q S
D X Y Z A N C D E F G H I A Y O C
A N O P S R L T U V W X Y N Q G O
S D E A G H I U K L M N O T R W T
G T U V W X Y Z T B C D E H N M T
A J K L M N O P Q H S T U O M W C N
N Z A B C D E F G H E V W N Y M S E
D P Q R S T U V W X Y R A S J A
H E L E N K E L L E R X A N Y R
I S A D O R A D U N C A N Y I N
L M N O P Q R S T U V W X Y N G
B W A L T W H I T M A N V O P
```

February 8

1. Astronomy
2. Cycling
3. Cooking
4. Indian Lore
5. Hiking
6. Weather
7. Radio
8. Camping
9. Lifesaving

February 15

Another word for "the vote" is *suffrage*. There are books about Susan B. Anthony in the *library*. Another word for "verse" or "rhyme" is *poem*. Susan said: *"Failure is impossible."*

February 22

3rd   president: Thomas Jefferson
16th   president: Abraham Lincoln
25th   president: Theodore Roosevelt
27th   president: Woodrow Wilson
34th   president: John F. Kennedy
38th   president: Jimmy Carter.

March 12

The Girl Scout motto is "Be Prepared."
The slogan is "Do a good turn daily."

March 17

1. Blue and yellow
2. The Hulk
3. Emerald (The Blarney Stone)
4. Asparagus
5. Greenhouse, putting green, greenback, green thumb

April 7

bath
exercise
water
relax
diet
teeth

April 13

Thomas Jefferson

May 8

Switzerland

May 22

Sherlock Holmes

June 2

Jane
Dolley
Mary Todd
Eleanor

Jacqueline
Lady Bird
Betty
Rosalynn

Answers

June 28

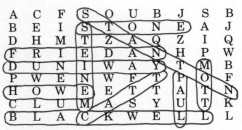

July 17

Across
2. gymnastics
4. Coubertin
5. tie
6. relay

Down
1. amateur
2. Greece
3. summer
4. continents

July 19

July 25

Amelia Earhart
I see a plane.
Open up!
Do you understand this rebus?

July 31

Evonne Goolagong
Billie Jean King
Bobby Riggs
Arthur Ashe
Bjorn Borg
Jimmy Connors

November 16

1. handbag
2. handshake
3. handsome (hand sum)
4. handout
5. handbook
6. handspring

November 17

1. time flies
2. on my (your) hands
3. timetable
4. the Times
5. marches on
6. timeless
7. a head of time
8. on time
9. behind time

November 30

Benjamin Franklin: Poor Richard (January 17)
Greta Gustaffson: Greta Garbo (September 18)
Ehrich Weiss: Harry Houdini (April 6)
Elizabeth Cochrane: Nellie Bly (November 14)
Don Marquis: a rchy the cockroach (July 29)
Frances Gumm: Judy Garland (June 10)
Charles Lutwidge Dodgson: Lewis Carroll (January 27)
Rosine Bernard: Sarah Bernhardt (October 22)
Carlo Lorenzini: Carlo Collodi (November 24)

December 7

Massachusetts
New Hampshire
Rhode Island
Connecticut
New York
New Jersey
Pennsylvania
Maryland
Virginia
North Carolina
South Carolina
Georgia

December 21

Across
2. boat
4. Massasoit
5. plus
7. eon
8. out
9. Alden
10. son

Down
1. Samoset
2. Bradford
3. Standish
4. Mullens
6. Squanto

December 29

Blue whale
U.S.S.R.
Sears Tower
Pacific
Jupiter
Lake Superior
Mount Everest

Things To Keep

Dates To Remember

Mardi Gras

1980—February 19
1981—March 3
1982—February 23
1983—February 15
1984—March 6
1985—February 19
1986—February 11
1987—March 3
1988—February 16
1989—February 7
1990—February 27

Passover

1980—April 1
1981—April 19
1982—April 8
1983—March 29
1984—April 17
1985—April 6
1986—April 24
1987—April 14
1988—April 2
1989—April 20
1990—April 10

Easter

1980—April 6
1981—April 19
1982—April 11
1983—April 3
1984—April 22
1985—April 7
1986—March 30
1987—April 19
1988—April 3
1989—March 26
1990—April 15

Rosh Hashanah

1980—September 11
1981—September 29
1982—September 18
1983—September 8
1984—September 27
1985—September 16
1986—October 4
1987—September 24
1988—September 12
1989—September 30
1990—September 20

Yom Kippur

1980—September 29
1981—October 8
1982—September 27
1983—September 17
1984—October 6
1985—September 25
1986—October 13
1987—October 3
1988—September 21
1989—October 9
1990—September 29

Chanukah

1980—December 3
1981—December 21
1982—December 11
1983—December 1
1984—December 19
1986—December 27
1987—December 16
1988—December 4
1989—December 23
1990—December 12

Mother's Day
Second Sunday in May

Memorial Day
Last Monday in May

Father's Day
Third Sunday in June

Friendship Day
First Sunday in August

Grandparents Day
Sunday after Labor Day

Native American Day
Fourth Friday in September

Labor Day
First Monday in September

Thanksgiving
Last Thursday in November